Ethics and Defence

ETHICS AND DEFENCE

Power and Responsibility in the Nuclear Age

Edited by
Howard Davis

Basil Blackwell

Copyright © Basil Blackwell Ltd 1986

First published 1986
First published in USA 1987

Basil Blackwell Ltd
108 Cowley Road, Oxford OX4 1JF, UK

Basil Blackwell Inc.
432 Park Avenue South, Suite 1503,
New York, NY 10016, USA

British Library Cataloguing in Publication Data

Ethics and defence: power and responsibility
in the nuclear age
1. Nuclear weapons—Religious aspects—
Christianity 2. Nuclear weapons—Great
Britain
I. Davis, Howard
261.8'73   BT736.2
ISBN 0-631-15174-5
ISBN 0-631-15175-3 Pbk

Library of Congress Cataloging in Publication Data

Ethics and defence.
Bibliography: p.
Includes index.
1. Nuclear warfare—Moral and ethical aspects.
I. Davis, Howard.
U263.E79 1986 172'.42 86-8057
ISBN 0-631-15174-5
ISBN 0-631-15175-3 (pbk.)

Typeset by DMB (Typesetting), Oxford
Printed in Great Britain by Page Bros (Norwich) Ltd

Contents

Preface

The 'nuclear debate' in Britain is an oddly stylized, limited and limiting form of communication. In reality it is a complex set of discourses which often refer to their own traditions more than to each other. This book is about the failure of dialogue and its military, political and social consequences. It responds critically to the posturings which pass for reasoned argument about defence and disarmament and seeks ways to promote an alternative kind of thinking which gives serious consideration to ethics instead of allowing them only as an afterthought or gloss on the 'realities' of international conflict. Although it is structured as a series of individual essays, it is the joint work of a study group convened by the Society, Religion and Technology (SRT) Project of the Church of Scotland. The group was formed in 1983 following requests from the Church of Scotland's General Assembly to promote study of the issues raised in current debates on defence and disarmament, including the discussion surrounding the Church of England Working Party's report, *The Church and the Bomb* (1982). The authors' aim is therefore to contribute further to the appraisal of defence policy – and nuclear deterrence in particular – from the perspective of Christian theology and ethics but engaging directly with contemporary social and political analyses.

At the beginning of 1983, when the Church of England General Synod was debating the report on *The Church and the Bomb* and when many other bodies were attempting by various means to engage the issues seriously, there was some danger that such a study group would duplicate existing efforts. Had not all the arguments been rehearsed *ad nauseam*? In fact it was admitted by some of those involved that the field of ethical debate was curiously restricted and that important tasks remained to be done. In the churches, the growing abhorrence of nuclear weapons has not removed the basic conceptual difficulties in defining the theological and ethical framework for addressing problems of defence and disarmament. This is not to say that greater clarity will automatically lead to greater influence in the public arena, for a further problem is that the agenda for public discussion tends to be set in ways which allow the minimum of scope for ethical argument and persuasion. What passes for ethical and theological analysis is often a more or less explicit attempt to legitimate existing policies after the event, or the basis for an attack on them which fails to engage the real issues. The result is that pragmatism generally prevails in matters of policy and ethical considerations are pushed to the margins of the decision-making process.

The common purpose of the contributions in this book is to try to give more prominence to these questions, not just by reasserting their importance but by showing that it is possible to express moral commitment in ways which give due weight to the historical origins, institutional dynamics and great complexity of our present global situation without falling into some of the mental traps which are set by ideological divisions, political tensions and power structures. In pursuing these themes, the SRT study group developed a style of working characterized by three elements in close combination. The first is concerned with the dimension of theology and ethics and the framework of assumptions about the conditions for peace, security and the conduct of war. The second is the process of bringing this language of theology and radical ethical questioning into the field of debate about ideology, politics and military strategy with their specialized assumptions and disciplines of thought. The third element is to show how criteria of accountability and responsibility may be brought into play in the activities of particular groups in society. This has been seriously neglected in the debate about morality and defence policy. An important aspect of the group's work in all of these areas has been to meet a wide variety of persons involved in the defence policy process, including some from eastern Europe and the Soviet Union, as well as the countries of the western Alliance.

Even a passing acquaintance with the defence debate shows that there are deep and difficult problems at all these levels. Traditionally, views of the morality of arms and armed conflict have been informed by Christian and secular teaching on the 'just war'. It has proved to be an imperfect but workable basis. Yet, at the very point at which some such vocabulary or framework is most needed, the conventional categories and definitions are found wanting. How can they be applied when military and political 'logic' leads to the possibility of mass annihilation? Similarly, the strategic paradigms which shaped the doctrines of nuclear deterrence have been rendered unworkable by developments in military technology. The nuclear arsenals are a fact of life in East–West relations; their meaning and purpose is anything but matter-of-fact. Then there are questions of a political nature which emerge from the opening up of areas of military and diplomatic expertise to public scrutiny. In the face of declining public confidence in international security arrangements, questions of power, responsibility and popular protest have assumed major proportions in a number of European countries.

The function of this book is not to attempt to solve all these problems. It does, however, recognize that a public forum has been opened up in recent years by the uncertainties of military strategy, by political strains within the western Alliance and by the movements of popular protest against nuclear weapons. Against this background it tries to respond to two particular pressures: the need within the churches to clarify and develop their understanding of the ethics of defence and disarmament, and the need to incorporate this into the wider domain of public policy. The authors perceive this task to be fundamental and necessary because what is at stake is survival, certainly, but survival with moral integrity. As the various contributions make clear, it is not an abstract, philosophical endeavour. The intellectual effort and the terms and categories of religious and ethical discourse must be capable of translation into types of human action at many levels, from the military commander to the private soldier, from the politician or professional expert to the ordinary voter.

The study group was ecumenical and multidisciplinary, made up of theologians, philosophers, social and political scientists and members of the legal and medical professions, and came from a variety of Christian traditions. They have tried to ensure that ethical questioning goes hand in hand with the analytical methods of social sciences and practical commitment to a just and peaceful solution to current conflicts. They are deeply concerned to overcome the polarities which are so pervasive in the 'defence debate' and have faced up to some of these in the extended group process of study and reflection which has brought together Protestant and Catholic traditions of ethical reasoning, a range of political convictions, and quite different styles of commitment to peace. This process is reflected in the structure and content of the book. It has involved some diminution of the difference and thus offers hope to those who are engaged in comparable discussions in other settings.

The book owes something of its character and contents to the Scottish context of church and public life from which background it comes. Scotland is the most heavily armed region of NATO and nuclear issues, both civil and military, have been hotly debated. On most issues of national importance the networks of contact between the churches in Scotland are close and relatively effective. The

degree of consensus among church statements on defence and disarmament, for example, is certainly greater than in other parts of
the UK. It amounts to a common mind on a number of crucial
issues, including moral condemnation of the threat to use as well as
the use of nuclear weapons, opposition to the Trident programme
and support for an immediate freeze. There is close cooperation between the churches and a wide variety of popular movements for
peace, and a sense of political as well as geographical distance from
Westminster which tends to sharpen the voice of protest. To the extent that the contributors are involved in these movements and the
political process, this book can be seen as an expression of the
widespread unease in Scotland concerning trends in defence policy
and the conduct of the 'defence debate' at the national level. It is a
response and a challenge to the many participants in this debate to
place the language of peace and security on a new, ethically more
secure, footing.

1

Introduction: Thinking the Unthinkable

Howard Davis

The paradox of defence in the nuclear age is that the greater the striving for power and security through nuclear weapons, the more elusive the goal of security becomes. The paradox of the nuclear weapons debate itself is that as discussion reaches new heights of sophistication, the harder it is to grasp the true meaning of peace and security. The existence of these paradoxes implies a basic problem of definition.

This problem also turns out to be the greatest moral challenge of our times. The unthinkable possibility of human self-destruction on a global scale poses a direct question to both Christian and humanist assumptions about the capacity of human beings to conduct their affairs in the light of reason. Such is the gravity of our situation that it cannot be left to 'experts' alone; an intelligent debate needs to be conducted with proper reference to origins, assumptions and values. For example, what difference should it make to the contemporary moral debate about nuclear deterrence to recognize that Britain's original motive for acquiring an independent retaliatory force had little to do with morality? What of the discussion of national pride (see Gowing, 1964)? It is a fundamental weakness of much current discussion that conflicting views fail to engage each other at the level of basic values. The frameworks of reference of strategy, diplomacy and defence economics, for example, are discontinuous at this level as well as at the technical level. This is not to say that moral questions are ignored, for a glance at the churches' involvement as well as contributions from philosophers and moralists inside and outside the defence establishment shows that much effort has been invested in developing theological and ethical approaches. However, there is still considerable confusion; several different languages, not one, are being spoken.

There is first the attempt to moralize about the possession and use of nuclear weapons. This has been a preoccupation of some

theologians and others who have sought to make a principled stand
for or against the policy of preparedness for nuclear retaliation.
However, this is not synonymous with the ethical debate. The
second cluster of issues, unlike the first, does not presuppose that all
decisions are made in the light of pure reason but that the complex
military, industrial and bureaucratic systems create their own problems of responsible conduct and accountability. Surprisingly for the
western democracies, these issues have been less fully explored.
Third, there is the language of national identity and solidarity,
permeated with values about the relative worth of national cultures
and traditions. Positive values of patriotism and loyalty become easily
entangled with negative views of the 'other' or the 'enemy'. In practice, the moral discourse includes all these voices and it has to be
acknowledged that Babel has affected the debate in the churches.
The aim of this book, which reflects a process of joint study within
the context of the churches' thinking, is to unravel some of these
strands and state as unambiguously as possible what can be constructed from the basic elements of Christian theology and the
ethical traditions without being irretrievably conditioned or diluted
by the prevailing ideologies of either West or East. This is an
ambitious aim and one which is open to the charge of arrogance (it is
presumptuous to try to arbitrate in terms of values when others stake
their careers, lives, and freedom itself in commitment to what they
believe to be right) or naiveté (because there is no source of insight
beyond the real world of politics and ideology). Our reply is that
there is no choice but to try. Where there is no dominant vision or
widely accepted framework of ethical values with which to shape
defence policy, and where the stakes are so high, the requirement for
a new language is both urgent and inescapable.

The contributions in this book try to assist the work of reconstruction in several ways. One is the task of reflecting critically on the
ethical tradition, in both its Christian and liberal humanist aspects,
which informs much of the current thinking about morality and
defence. The fact that there is a tradition shaped by the doctrine of
'just war' does not prevent confusion or contradiction, nor does it
mean that it can be applied automatically in the present context.
These problems have to be clarified, including the relationship between theology and ethics. Another question which has to be asked is
how far the explanations and justifications for defence policy offered
by those in positions of responsibility actually square with the traditions of ethical argument. This needs to be put to political as well as
military leaders. A further problem has to do with the political process which, as presently constituted, is unduly secretive and
unresponsive to legitimate but non-Establishment voices of doubt

and dissent. These are matters for detailed concrete analysis which call for an understanding and interpretation of the political, military, economic and cultural means by which power is exercised in contemporary society, supported by all the appropriate data and methods of social scientific analysis.

Many of the contributions in this book are critical of present power structures but the object of the critique is not power as such. In fact, one of the dominant themes is that power is an essential aspect of human action and that the neglect of a positive ethical approach to power in human affairs accounts for some of the difficulties we now face. In contrast to a number of influential social and political theories, our approach to power and power structures tries to avoid reductionism and determinism. The structures of moral action are defined by other aspects of being, which include justice and love as well as power. There is reason to believe that they can be articulated in even the most unpromising of situations. These are relationships which give us courage to say that a sense of proportion, a degree of sanity and safety *can* be restored to a world gripped by madness.

The new defence agenda

There has been a general decline in recent years in confidence and in the degree of consensus about defence issues. This has occurred in parallel with other major changes in British society including the ending of the two-party monopoly of the political process, the economic recession and the emergence or rebirth of a number of broadly-based popular protest movements. It would therefore be a mistake to set the defence agenda too narrowly when it is bound up with these wider changes. There are also some particular circumstances which have contributed to the realignment and restatement of positions in an altogether more complex variety than existed previously.

The first of these is the doubt and uncertainty which have been expressed over a number of years in government and military circles, often at a very senior level, about the implications of new weapons technologies, NATO's overreliance on nuclear weapons, the strategic doctrine of 'flexible response', the relative cost of nuclear and conventional forces and lack of progress in arms control. While these concerns have not yet been articulated in terms of an alternative defence policy, they do regularly lead to calls for a reassessment of goals. The second circumstance is the present stage in the development and deployment of nuclear weapons. The practical question of whether and how to replace the ageing UK Polaris deterrent force, the NATO decision to deploy Cruise and Pershing II missiles and, not least, the US President's Strategic Defense Initiative (SDI) have all been occasions for questioning the point and purpose of nuclear strategy. Third, there has been a sea-change in public opinion. What has occurred is a decline of confidence in present security arrangements and an increased willingness to see *both* superpowers, not just the USSR, as threats to peace and stability. While there is still substantial majority support for NATO and nuclear weapons, support for particular weapons like Cruise and Trident has diminished steadily in spite of the Government's strenuous efforts to bolster confidence in its policies. Finally, there has been the renaissance of the Campaign for Nuclear Disarmament (CND) and a wide range of other specialist groups in a new movement for peace and disarmament. Compared with earlier manifestations of protest – especially CND in its first phase of activity from 1958 to 1965 – this is a large, well-organized and fast-growing movement which has succeeded in putting its policies for unilateral disarmament firmly on the public agenda.

The immediate stimulus and focus for much of the recent public debate was the decision of NATO on 12 December 1979 to prepare to install an intermediate-range nuclear force (INF) of 572 missiles from the end of 1983 and simultaneously to negotiate arms control with the Soviet Union. This became known as the dual-track decision. Following the change in emphasis in NATO strategic doctrine from 'mutual assured destruction' to 'flexible response' which was approved in 1967, theatre and intermediate-range nuclear weapons in Europe began to assume increasing military and political importance. The new strategy required a level of weaponry between conventional weapons and intercontinental ballistic missiles (ICBMs) if it were to be plausible in military terms. Because battlefield nuclear weapons – including artillery and aircraft capable of delivering nuclear bombs – were considered too vulnerable, the military requirement was defined in terms of low-flying, accurate, intermediate-range missiles which would avoid detection by enemy radar. This military thinking happened to coincide with a major political problem in the alliance, namely European doubts about how far the US could be trusted to use its strategic forces on Europe's behalf in the event of war in Europe. The deployment of intermediate-range missiles was seen as one way of cementing the relationship. There was, then, a symbolic aspect to the 'Euromissiles' decision. The missiles (464 ground-launched Cruise missiles and 108 Pershing IIs), under American ownership and control, deployed in several European countries and linked to arms control negotiations, were intended more as a political sign of NATO solidarity than a response to a military threat from the Warsaw Pact.[1] The military considerations were less than compelling. The notion that the missiles are a necessary counter to the Soviet SS-20 missile (a different kind of weapon of much longer range, with three independently targetable warheads) is at best only partially true, though a convenient way of selling the INF modernization programme to domestic public opinion. Even in military terms, the role of nuclear weapons is not to counter the adversary's system directly; it is to support deterrence.

Of course, 'modernization' – a euphemism for new systems and strategies – is a feature of both NATO and the Warsaw Pact and it tends to have a momentum of its own making in the political economy of each side. The danger is that the logic of weapons development and deployment will seriously distort the political objectives of defence. In the conduct of the nuclear debate the overly narrow focus on individual weapons systems, questions of hardware, flight time, accuracy and so on has tended to divert attention away from the basic tenets of deterrence strategy. In military and political circles, in fact, these tenets – or at least the view that there is no workable alternative – have survived remarkably unscathed. Discussion and disagreement have not provoked a crisis at this level and neither have the arguments and campaigns for a freeze or pledge of 'no first use'. This is because deterrence and its moral justification are typically expressed in highly abstract terms which do not require reference to actual systems.

The important divide in the nuclear debate is therefore between those who accept the spirit and logic of deterrence, with the implied adversary relationship between the Soviet Union and the West, and those who are persuaded that such a view can only lead to disaster in the long term. The former tend to be in established positions of power, the latter tend not to be. Although public opinion in most of the European countries is heavily in favour of NATO, there is considerable popular resistance to the number of nuclear weapons on European soil and the possibility of their use implied in NATO strategy. This resistance has been increasing steadily in recent years. Those who support the logic of deterrence see this movement of opinion (and not just the organized 'peace movement') as a failure of nerve or crisis of will in large sections of European society and a lack of determination to face up to the choice between peace and freedom guaranteed by deterrence and totalitarian enslavement. These 'pacifist' doubts are interpreted as a positive threat because they encourage the adversary to think that populations will be submissive. This characterization of the public response in western

Europe is inaccurate because it mistakes a crisis of confidence for a crisis of will and critique for selfish concern. For their part, western European governments have not been forced or persuaded to bend before the pressures of public opinion but they have had to pay a political price. The INF deployment sowed division and served to mobilize and educate an opposition movement which is larger, better informed and better organized than anything hitherto.

CND was formed in 1958 in what has been described as a 'great moral and emotive spasm' (Taylor and Pritchard, 1980, p. 131). Its main object of protest at that time was the testing of nuclear weapons. When the Partial Test Ban Treaty was signed in 1963 and the Labour Government reneged on its unilateralist election promises, much of its momentum as a movement was lost or later diverted to other ends. What gave new impetus to CND in the late 1970s was the INF deployment decision, combined with the British government's commitment to Trident and other factors including the widespread unease about the Government's civil defence plans. (The hopelessly inadequate guidelines issued by the Home Office in 1980 met with much deserved criticism.) The membership of national CND grew from only 3,000 in 1979 to around 110,000 by the end of 1984. Similar movements developed in other European countries. The Labour Party affirmed its commitment to unilateral nuclear disarmament in its 1982 election manifesto as have many trade unions and the Trades Union Congress.

The contemporary movement, which includes many other groups with aims related to CND and working in close association with it, grew around a single issue, the Euromissile crisis. However, the objective of preventing deployment has not been achieved, so will the movement of the 1980s suffer the same fate as the movement of the 1960s? It seems unlikely. There is a more elaborate campaigning strategy, a more robust organization and a closer association with other institutions, including the trade unions, political parties, the churches and some professional bodies. These give the campaign a degree of permanence which does not depend on success in one particular area. There is also another criterion of 'success' which is probably more important in the long term. That is the raising of public consciousness of the wider issues associated with nuclear defence and disarmament. The contribution of the protest movements to the wider defence debate has therefore been significant, though not as yet decisive in the reshaping of policy.

The movement's contribution is more complex than many of those who reject 'unilateralism' would suppose. The moral objections to nuclear weapons naturally continue to play an important part. Many activists relate to the religious or non-religious pacifist traditions while others identify more closely with libertarian, socialist or feminist ideals. Both, however, are inclined towards a moral radicalism which is sharply critical of the assumptions behind current defence policies and deterrence in particular. But today's movement amounts to far more than a moral crusade. Much closer attention is being paid to the implications of current strategic doctrines, new technology, arms control negotiations, public opinion and many other issues. As a result, the protest against nuclear weapons is being taken further into the territory of those who have responsibility for defence policy. The protest is capable of being expressed in their language and is that much harder to ignore, especially when the special interest sections of the movement – such as Scientists Against Nuclear Arms (SANA) and the Medical Campaign Against Nuclear Weapons (MCANW) – bring their professional expertise to bear on the issues in a critical way. A further aspect of today's protest which sets it apart from the earlier phase is the attention being given to the question of other options. The opposition to Trident, for example, is supported by work on arms industry conversion and the development of other employment strategies in areas like Dumbarton. Another example is the serious attempt by 'doubters' in the military together with 'dissenters' in the protest movements to explore the options for an alternative type of non-nuclear defence (see the report of the Alternative Defence Commission, 1983). In academic research centres, the social and economic implications of current defence strategies (for example, the cost of the UK Trident programme) are being studied and the results being made available for public discussion. Taken altogether, these activities provide the protest movements with substantial resources for argument and persuasion to reinforce the basic moral motivation.

The future of protest is uncertain. According to one view, peace movements of the past and present have been discontinuous and fragmented because of their single-issue orientation, sectarian traditions and narrow social base. Their pattern is one of ebb and flow which never achieves more than a marginal effect on society and defence policy. This view finds some support from the present situation where it could be said that CND and other groups have managed to avoid fragmentation only by giving priority to campaigns against INF deployment and Trident, and skirting round more contentious long-term issues like the future of NATO or the question of conventional arms. Another view is that the issues are so compelling, and the motivation to seek a less threatening future so strong, that there is hope of achieving a new synthesis which will turn the movements of protest from being 'No!' movements to 'Yes!' movements capable of provoking a political transformation. What it will require is a long-term vision and an appropriate strategy for bringing it about, but neither is yet clearly worked out.

The protesters of course do not have a monopoly on moral arguments. A new dimension was added to the debate on 23 March 1983, when President Reagan launched his SDI, popularly known as 'Stars Wars'. He set out a vision of the future which promised hope:

> The human spirit must be capable of rising above dealing with other nations and human beings by threatening their existence . . . We must embark on a programme to counter the awesome Soviet missile threat with measures that are defensive . . . I call upon the scientific community who gave us nuclear weapons to turn their great talents to the cause of mankind and world peace; to give us the means of rendering these nuclear weapons impotent and obsolete.

The fantastic technological fix which Reagan offered is vastly expensive, of dubious practicality, leads to insoluble strategic problems and is a serious threat to arms control. Nevertheless, 80 per cent of Americans are said to support it and its moral appeal was sufficient to take the wind out of the sails of the US 'freeze' movement. SDI's reception in Europe has been anything but enthusiastic but it promises to release resources for research and development on such a scale that the European partners in the Alliance will not be able to afford being left out. Its full effect on the nuclear debate remains to be seen but it appears to have driven even deeper the wedge between the US and the European countries in NATO in terms of their perception of defence problems and global security.

In Britain, where the movement for a nuclear freeze has gained ground very slowly, there is on the present horizon no single issue like INF deployment to unite the movements in a single campaign. There are several fronts and more than one strategy. Whatever priorities the movement decides on, however, the years since 1980 have seen a fundamental change in the overall context within which defence issues are discussed, if not in policy. It has been transformed from a situation in which governments could form their own policies against a background of widespread public ignorance, indifference and apathy, to one in which much less confident political and military decision-making has to contend with a still divided but better-informed and concerned public. The churches could not and have not stood by. Their own debates have been a microcosm of the society-wide debate but with an important difference of emphasis. They have struggled in the light of Scripture, their understanding of the Christian traditions and their own political responsibilities to articulate a morality for the nuclear age; to what effect can be judged in the pages which follow.

Churches and the nuclear weapons debate

Some Christian churches have always regarded it as a sin to build nuclear weapons because they renounce all forms of war. Without seeking to underplay the significance of this pacifist witness it is necessary to devote most of the present discussion of the churches' contribution to the nuclear debate to those positions which are not pacifist but which accept that violence may be justified in some circumstances. The mainstream denominations without exception have addressed the issue of defence in general and deterrence in particular, and have in recent years been moving towards views which, to a greater or lesser degree, question the spirit and logic of deterrence. There remain significant divisions among them about what the ethical problems are, what they should be saying, by what authority and to whom. The process can appear strangely parochial and derivative in its tendency to follow secular modes of argument in the name of 'Christian realism'. At other times it is other-worldly to the point of ignoring the practical and professional problems of those who are responsible for defence and disarmament.

The most visible sign of the churches' involvement has been the stream of reports, statements and resolutions from synods and assemblies. While these have been very numerous in recent years, they are not without precedent. Until a relatively short time ago, the British churches were adopting stances similar to those they had taken in the years after 1945 when Britain acquired its own nuclear deterrent force. As far as their official statements and policies record, they were aligned with government: they supported NATO, the independent deterrent and the broad rationale of nuclear strategy as a means to deter war. Concerns were expressed about weapons testing and the possibility of first use implied in NATO strategy, for example, but the belief that 'we now have to live with the bomb' tended to prevail. Meanwhile, the strand of Christian pacifism remained alive and well but within the larger denominations it was regarded as an issue of individual conscience and a personal calling; a kind of withdrawal from public responsibility.

In the past decade, the churches have been influenced by the same external factors (modernization of strategic and intermediate-range nuclear forces, the new 'cold war', the revival of popular protest and so on) which have stimulated the defence debate in other circles. There have also been significant internal factors which give the churches' contribution a special quality. There is, first, the issue of how far the churches should engage with the political process other than through the activities of individual adherents. The problem is not new, but the understanding of the Church's relationship to secular society which prevailed during the years of the post-war social democratic consensus, now sharply challenged by the New Right, has had to be restated or redefined during the Falklands War, the coal strike, urban riots and other recent national experiences.[2] Second, the churches have been experiencing the effects of declining numbers, financial crisis and widespread popular disbelief or apathy. These consequences of secularization have both reminded the churches of their minority position in social and political terms and forced them to reflect in new ways on the fundamentals of their faith. As a result, new styles of thought and action are being developed alongside more traditional forms of activity. Where the answers to current social and political problems are sought within a distinctively Christian theological and ethical framework the churches' response will be more 'sectarian' than it has been hitherto, but this does not automatically imply a distancing from the political sphere. On the contrary, it can bring a fresh commitment to justice and peace. To understand how the churches' stance on defence issues is being worked out at an institutional level it is necessary to consider some examples.

In 1979, the General Synod of the Church of England requested its Board for Social Responsibility to study how 'the theological debate relating to discipleship in this field might be more effectively and purposefully conducted'. A Working Party was established under the chairmanship of John Austin Baker, Bishop of Salisbury, and its report *The Church and the Bomb* was already a best-seller by the time of the General Synod of February 1983 at which it was to be debated. The content of the report and its reception in the Church of England make a revealing case study. The structure of the report was unlike that of some official church documents which begin with a theological statement and proceed by more or less deductive steps to questions of policy and action. Instead, it began with a survey of the technological, strategic and political dimensions of the nuclear weapons issue. The report therefore allowed the world to set the agenda to the extent that the problem for the Church was defined as a common one for all citizens. It stressed that Christian ethics has no timeless moral conclusions in regard to nuclear weapons and that adequate moral judgements must take careful account of the facts of the issue. Before proceeding to the theological understanding of the problem, the report examined the common ethical tradition as expressed in teaching on the just war and in international law. The final part is an examination of the possible options in the light of the preceding sections and a set of recommendations. These were un-compromising in that the UK should renounce its strategic nuclear deterrent, cancel Trident, abandon its smaller nuclear weapons and remove US facilities which bring nuclear weapons, including Cruise missiles, to British soil.

It is small wonder that these recommendations provoked strong reactions in all quarters, for they provided a powerfully-argued alternative to the official view that the deterrent is a necessary evil in a world which is irreconcilably divided between East and West. The outcome of the debate in the General Synod was a defeat for the recommendations of the Working Party's report but support for a pledge of 'no first use' of nuclear weapons. The result was widely perceived to be a triumph for multilateralism and official policy; 'The Church backs the Bomb', said the *Daily Mirror*. In fact, it gave no more than qualified support and the no-first-use pledge would cause not a few difficulties for NATO governments and the military if they were to take it seriously. But they have not done so. The result can therefore be understood in terms of a holding operation which failed to provide a lasting or satisfying response to the General Synod's original request for guidance concerning Christian discipleship in a nuclear age.

The subsequent exchange of moral arguments cannot be describ-ed here in any detail. It has often taken the abstract and curiously restricted form of a discussion about the pure theory of deterrence and its moral legitimacy or illegitimacy, not the ethics which might be applicable to the actual political and military realities of nuclear confrontation. Thus the debate has produced diametrically opposed answers to such questions as whether nuclear deterrence is wrong in itself or wrong in its consequences, and whether the use of nuclear weapons in certain circumstances can be justified in terms of just war doctrines (cf. Bridger, 1983; Gill, 1984; Gladwin, 1985). Regardless of whether the answers to these questions are 'yes' or 'no', the effect of this debate is to give at least some moral legitimacy to the *status quo*. Others have emphasized the moral virtue of prudence (*prudentia,* the application of right means to good ends) in the conduct of state and military affairs. It is an essential quality in complex situations where the consequences of action are not entirely bad, good or even predictable, but it is often made to hang on the very slender thread of such clichés as 'nuclear weapons cannot be disinvented', 'nuclear weapons have kept the peace for 40 years' or 'the Soviet Union is an evil empire'. Prudence then becomes pragmatism. The churches' debate has unfortunately tended to mir-ror some of the unfruitful distinctions – between unilateralism and

multilateralism, realism and idealism, ethics of conviction and ethics
of responsibility – which have sterilized much of the discussion
elsewhere. The chairman of the Church of England Working Party
has subsequently drawn attention to the need for a more coherent
theology of power and a strategy to avoid being drawn into the over-
simplification of the unilateralist–multilateralist controversy, something which *The Church and the Bomb* tried but failed to do (Gladwin,
1985, pp. 141–3).

Another major contribution to the churches' debate is the US
Catholic Bishops' pastoral letter, 'The Challenge of Peace: God's
Promise and Our Response.' (1983). Although an American document, it has probably influenced Roman Catholic thinking in many
countries, including Britain, more than statements from those countries' own Bishops. Like the Anglican report it attempts to assess the
present circumstances, develop theological principles and make
moral applications, but it stops short of making specific policy
recommendations. It has been widely acclaimed within the churches
and beyond for its thorough research, careful argumentation and
breadth of concern. One feature of the document which
distinguishes it from the Anglican report is the detailed attention it
gives to its own authority. There is a full exposition of the Catholic
social teaching on war and peace but, the report says, the treatment
of concrete questions concerning the arms race or weapons systems
is not intended to carry the same moral authority. The 'pastoral'
function is, in the first instance, to enlighten the Catholic conscience, not to change government policies. It moves from a statement of theological vision of peace, through a discussion of the social
and political obstacles, to identify the contribution which a 'community of faith' should make and the personal tasks which this may
involve. The feature of the letter which made it controversial to
many, including the US adminstration, was its 'strictly conditioned
moral acceptance of deterrence' and the attempt to spell out criteria
for a moral assessment. These led to direct criticism of many aspects
of the US defence posture.

The influence of this document has a great deal to do with its
authoritative presentation of a theological ethic. It cannot be accused
of falling into an unreflective, ideological mode of argument nor of
restricting its range of moral concerns. However, there is a revealing
phrase which highlights a problem of method in all official church
statements. In referring to the relationship between the theological
and ethical aspects of the argument the letter reads, 'In the light of
the framework of Catholic teaching on the nature of peace, the
avoidance of war and the state's right to legitimate defence, we can
now spell out certain moral principles within the Catholic tradition

which provide guidance for public policy and individual choice.' The phrase 'in the light of' hints at the impossibility of straight-forward linear reasoning from specific theological premises to policy conclusions and allows room for differences, say, between Christian pacifism and positions based on just war principles. How does the letter convey such a powerful sense of consistency and authority when theology does not provide the 'warrant' for ethical principles? The answer is perhaps to be found in the extent to which it depends on an understanding of the Church as a community of moral discourse situated within a wider community or moral discourse. Few Protestant Church statements have had such a strong 'ecclesial' dimension to them and most lack the emphasis on the human family and the responsibilities of educators, parents, young people, scientists and many others as well as public officials and military leaders. To the extent that it facilitates the articulation of the Christian community with the wider community of publics, the pastoral letter may be one of the more enduring contributions to the churches' debate on defence and nuclear weapons.

A third example of an official church statement is that of the Assembly of the World Council of Churches (WCC) which took place in Vancouver in 1983. It has become an important point of reference in the churches' debate. The WCC is a worldwide confederation of Protestant, Anglican and Orthodox churches which is able to make pronouncements in its own right, its authority being 'only the weight which they carry by their own truth and wisdom', not necessarily with the unanimous approval of all the member churches (WCC Constitution, Rule X in *Uppsala Report,* 1968, p.480). The Assembly is therefore an important mechanism for expressing an ecumenical consensus. After several decades of uncertainty, the mood has changed emphatically against the spirit and logic of deterrence. In the report of a public hearing on nuclear weapons and disarmament organized by the WCC in Amsterdam in 1981, the use of nuclear weapons for fighting wars was unequivocally condemned although there was considerable discussion of the arguments surrounding the possession of and threat to use them. In the event, the report stated, 'We believe that [the strategy of nuclear deterrence and the weapons on which it depends] are evil, and that the possession of such weapons and the readiness to use them are wrong in the sight of God and should be treated as such by the churches' (Abrecht and Koshy, 1983, p. 29). This is what occurred at the Vancouver Assembly. The Statement on Peace and Justice, accepted by a large majority with only a few abstentions, reads, 'We believe that the time has come when the churches must unequivocally declare that the production and deployment as well as the use of nuclear weapons

are a crime against humanity and that such activities must be condemned on ethical and theological grounds' (WCC, 1983, p. 137). It
can be argued that this is the point towards which the majority of
Christian churches worldwide are moving on this issue and that
some in the UK are still relatively far behind. Established churches
in the old world are more insulated from the thinking of the
ecumenical movement than many others and it is likely that only a
minority of Christians in this country are aware of the above
declaration. But this does not detract from the growing ecumenical
consensus between East and West, North and South, not only in
condemnation of nuclear deterrence but in the positive Christian
understanding of peace.

A comprehensive analysis of recent church statements carried out
by Friedhelm Solms and Marc Reuver (1985) shows that, while important differences of method continue to exist, the convergence is
substantial, even between Protestant and Roman Catholic
statements which arise out of very different organizational structures. The conclusion which they draw has interesting implications
for political strategy as well as the life of the churches. They say:

> It has become conclusive that there is room for consensus and the formation
> of a common cause, even between the adherents of the two main sub-
> traditions of Christian ethical thought – pacifism and just war doctrine – as
> they address the challenge of Christian conscience posed by the dilemma of
> nuclear deterrence. In the nuclear age, both pacifists and advocates of the
> just war doctrine are under a common obligation despite their diverging
> theologies . . . Facing the threat of annihilation, both sides are compelled to
> elaborate common practical objectives, to advocate a way to the defence of
> justice and human rights which excludes the use of nuclear weapons and
> drastically forces the reduction and ultimate elimination of all weapons of
> mass destruction. (p. 65)

If this is correct, the priority task for the churches which have found
this consensus is to translate the theological-ethical rejection of
nuclear weapons into a political strategy which will make them
superfluous and bring into being a more just international order.

Such a strategy will not come from statements and resolutions
alone but through other kinds of activity including dialogue with
responsible authorities, education and mobilization of members for
specific ends. Although less visible than the output of published
documents, there are many direct and indirect channels of communication between church representatives and members of the
government and armed forces. This generally informal contact involves a relatively small number of people but allows for more open
communication of views than is possible in official statements, at
least on the churches' side.[3] The effect of these encounters is not easy

to assess, but they are usually welcomed on both sides as a way of smoothing out some of the misunderstandings which arise when Church and State part company on important policy questions. It would be foolish to believe, however, that this 'dialogue' at present is much more than a polite exchange of views. For the churches, the process so far has fallen far short of the 'Socratic' dialogue which some hope to experience. Their opposite numbers from the political and military spheres are most likely to see it as an exercise in public relations which need not involve any concessions to the churches' anxieties.

To the extent that the churches are involved in adult and youth education in a systematic way they play another kind of role in the nuclear debate. One of the functions of the study guides, reports and other resources which have been produced is to help congregations and individuals face up to the internal conflicts which arise when divisive issues are debated at synods and assemblies. But Christian education of this kind (like peace studies in schools and colleges), relatively independent of the mass media and official propaganda, contributes in turn to the formation of a more knowledgeable and politically more aware public. If there is a new public gaining experience in the theological-ethical evaluation of policy decisions this will perhaps prove to be one of the more significant contributions made by the churches to the political process in the longer term.

Finally, the churches' involvement in defence and disarmament issues extends in some cases to campaigning. In Scotland, for example, the churches have lent official support to the nuclear freeze campaign by providing the opportunity for members to endorse the aims in a sign-in. This cautious step towards a broadly-based campaign is a new departure and reflects the deep concern felt in the churches about the Government's lack of response to the very widespread doubt and dissent concerning its defence policy. This dimension of activity brings the churches into close contact and cooperation with other agencies. In fact, as the churches have been drawn further into the defence debate they have become increasingly (but only partially) identified with the wider movement of protest, internationally as well as nationally. They have the opportunity to play a unique role at the international level because of their supra-national character.

While the dangers of moralizing are all too evident from the churches' debate, any assessment has to take account of its multifaceted character, involving a variety of styles, arguments, activities and audiences. It would be doing less than justice to this diversity to judge the progress of the debate solely in terms of formal Church-State relationships. The undercurrents may be far more significant. With the decline of consensus politics and the tendency

for attitudes on the great issues to follow party political lines, the role
of public opinion – and the churches as opinion formers – has
become increasingly important. The churches, having entered this
particular arena of public policy and having been awakened to its
moral challenge, must now respond to the public expectation that
they will have something further and positive to say by way of moral
guidance.

Constructing a new agenda

The defence debate in recent years has progressively opened up
large areas of policy to closer public scrutiny. New political styles
have evolved in step with the arguments, raising new questions
about defence policy and the democratic process. However, by being
closely tied to particular developments in weaponry, strategy, East–
West relations and NATO politics, the debate has often suffered
from a lack of proportion and persepective. Theological, ethical,
social and political themes have not always been well integrated.
One of the primary aims of this book is therefore to bring the various
dimensions of 'security' into a close relationship with one another. It
attempts to counter those tendencies which polarize opinion and
marginalize dissent.

Much ground needs to be cleared first of all at the level of basic
concepts in theology and ethics. The first contribution in Part I,
'Defining the Problem', is on the tasks of theology. People may
expect either too much of theology or too little. Some expect it to
provide a blueprint for the Kingdom of Heaven on earth while
others look for nothing more than a religious gloss on public affairs.
Others argue that there is no distinctive Christian contribution to be
made at all. Duncan Forrester considers these views, then puts the
case for a theology which challenges and disturbs by questioning the
terms of discussion but also by reminding the entire Christian community of its calling. He identifies a number of distinct, though
related, tasks. The first, which has yet to be accepted as an obligation by all the churches in Britain, is 'confessional'. Some aspects of
war and defence policy need to be renounced by the churches
because they are in direct contradiction to Christian faith. They include nuclear war-fighting strategies and the indefinite commitment
to nuclear deterrence. The Christian conscience cannot accommodate them. It does allow room for pacifism, nuclear pacifism and
perhaps a strictly conditioned and temporary acceptance of existing
deterrent forces. Forrester notes with regret that some theologians do
not accept this, are not saying 'no' to the spirit and logic of deter-

rence, and continue to legitimate the institutionalized madness of the *status quo* in the name of realism and responsibility. Theology's second task is counterideological in the sense that it addresses critical questions to authority in the light of fundamental values. It presupposes that theology can and will engage directly with public issues by making its own and others' values explicit, a critical and 'demystifying' activity. Third, there is the need to articulate and, where necessary, renew these values, the Christian vision of peace. The fourth task, the 'prophetic', is what many people would identify as the Church's voice on issues of war and peace, raised in its public statements, declarations and elsewhere. Prophecy should speak of responsibility before God as well as the people, a theme which is taken up in other sections of the book. All these tasks have a practical, social dimension which extends well beyond the realm of the professional theologian. But Forrester's message is that theological concepts are *necessary*, not just an interesting intellectual exercise, for a rounded and adequate treatment of defence issues.

Theology is not synonymous with ethics. It has been one of the serious weaknesses of the churches' involvement in the nuclear debate that the connections between theological understanding and the criteria for making practical policy choices have been unclear. To assume that the Bible or theology will provide such criteria ready-made is misleading and may alienate others who are engaged in the same search for solutions but who do not necessarily share the same Christian assumptions. Chapters 3, 4 and 5 confront these difficult questions of how the quest for truth may be combined with analytical judgement and the practice of virtue in situations of great complexity where decision-making is highly rationalized and bureaucratized. There is, for example, urgent need for conceptual clarification of what an 'ethical' or 'moral' problem is. In chapter 3, Columba Ryan shows what is involved in descriptions of human action or proposed action (such as that which is implied by deterrence) and illustrates the disarray of moral argument. The practical relevance of the work of clarification is the demonstration that practical affairs cannot be conducted without reference to principles or ideals and that pragmatism, emotivism or other approaches which neglect or deny this amount to a shirking of responsibility.

The two chapters by Ian Thompson contribute in a systematic way to the reconstruction of the ethical debate. Defining the problem squarely in terms of the western intellectual tradition and the need to transcend both absolutist and relativist positions, he argues for a 'trans–moral' ethics. What lies behind this concept is the project of establishing rational grounds for the kind of constructive critique and dialogue between different ideologies which is so obviously lacking in the nuclear weapons debate. In chapter 4, Thompson examines the ethical tradition with a critical eye and puts forward his alternative construction. In chapter 5, he considers the understandings of freedom, determinism, rationality and evil which inform the various approaches and shows how they have direct relevance to the ways in which we interpret institutional behaviour and the exercise of power. The chapter, and the first part of the book, ends with a powerful plea for a positive ethic of power which is open to the test of ultimate values and authenticity at the level of personal conduct. Taken together, the chapters in this section amount to a strong indictment of the nuclear weapons debate in its present form and point to significant new ways forward.

Part II takes up a number of aspects of current defence policy for closer examination. One of the most common clichés in the nuclear debate is the assertion that 'nuclear weapons cannot be disinvented' and the simplification that the threat of mutual annihilation must remain a permanent feature of defence policy. Tony Carty goes behind the phrase to ask how nuclear weapons came to be deployed in the first place. His historical account, supported by much detailed evidence, shows how the strategic bombing campaign against Germany in the Second World War was a precursor of present nuclear strategies and how remote were any ethical considerations from the process of decision-making. All too often, the evolution of nuclear strategy has been described as though its own terms of reference were self-evidently logical and intelligible. Here it is revealed as a self-perpetuating irrational development, without a clearly-defined object. The so-called 'moral dilemma' posed by nuclear weapons is thus seen as a quite recent creation of human beings, the consequence of wrong actions; not a given unavoidable fact. Steps towards an alternative policy will require the moral honesty to face up to our collective guilt for the past and our responsibility for the future.

In the following chapter on the illegality of nuclear weapons, Carty carries his historical-juridical analysis into the domain of current international law. Although there is a consensus among lawyers that the use of nuclear weapons is illegal and that their possession is of almost equally doubtful legality, the nuclear powers continue to justify their possession in terms of their deterrence function. This gives rise to a legal paradox. On the one hand there is an assumption of legality (or at least legitimacy) for whatever serves to safeguard peace and that, in the opinion of many, includes deterrence. On the other, there is general agreement that no nuclear conflict could be made to conform to the traditional laws of war. The paradox, Carty argues, is a logical one which arises only because of the failure to see deterrence for what it really is. The professional legal establishment has been slow to recognize that nuclear weapons and strategy are in a direct line of descent from the ideology of total war developed in the 1930s and 1940s. The paradox diverts attention away from the legal and moral nihilism, the 'numbing absence' at the centre of nuclear strategy and decision-making. Nevertheless, Carty urges that the instruments of international law like the First Additional Protocol of 1977 to the Geneva Conventions be taken very seriously, provided they are brought to bear on actual policies and strategies, not just hypothetical examples.

David Holloway considers the prospects for change in current policies in the light of criteria drawn from the US Bishops' pastoral letter. The problem which he and they address is how the 'no' to nuclear war can be translated into the personal and public choices which would make for an international system more in keeping with the values and vision of the Kingdom of God. He reviews NATO and Soviet doctrines of deterrence and shows how closely developments in strategic thinking have been tied to political relationships between Europe and the USA and western and eastern Europe. He then makes clear the discrepancy between the American Bishops' criteria for assessing the moral acceptability of a deterrence policy and NATO's current policy. There follows an important warning: that the withdrawal of moral legitimacy must be accompanied by strategies which could lead to a sounder and more moral basis for peace. Holloway considers proposals for a no-first-use commitment by NATO, alternative defence policies, arms control and political measures, and comes to the conclusion that western Europe has considerable scope for devising its own policy and that it could make certain responsible unilateral moves without increasing the risk of war: a conclusion which governments and protest movements alike would do well to take seriously as the basis for a new political agenda.

One aspect of deterrence policy which causes profound unease is its logical dependence on a specific 'threat' from a known and hostile opponent. Howard Davis examines some contemporary manifestations of this 'demonizing' process in the light of theories of ideology and propaganda. The recent period is characterized by accelerated military build-up, interrupted negotiations, internal problems on both sides and intense propaganda campaigns which have renewed the images of the enemy which were current in the Cold War period of the 1940s and 1950s. Whereas in this earlier period deterrence through nuclear weapons was an underdeveloped military strategy with minor political significance, the highly dangerous feature of this new 'cold war' is that the political aspirations and intentions of the superpowers are likely to be deduced from weapons development, deployment and strategies, not from the traditional methods of diplomacy and observation of political behaviour.

The theme of the militarization of politics is developed further by John Eldridge in a chapter on the organization of power, the complex of military-bureaucratic-industrial institutions and the shaping of military decisions. He elaborates themes from the writings of C. Wright Mills who saw an increasing danger of war in the emergence of societies dominated by a power elite in which thinking, participating publics tend to be transformed into powerless masses. Like the other contributors, he identifies the inertial thrust of these developments as a target for action and social pressure for change as well as critical analysis.

The third section of the book brings the question of individual and collective responsibility into sharper focus. The nuclear weapons debate is not worthy of that description if it does not fairly represent the views of the wider public, or rather the numerous publics which constitute what we call 'public opinion'. Eldridge throws light on the role of the media in the debate and the dynamics involved in both western and eastern European societies. Journalists, like other 'professionals', have a particular and well-developed understanding of their responsibilites in relation to their work to each other, their employers, the state and the wider public. Recent events including the Falklands War, the banning of trade unions at Government Communications Headquarters and the Ponting affair have highlighted problems with these understandings. In a similar vein, Helen Zealley uses the example of the medical profession to show how the defence debate is impinging on professional commitment and traditional interpretations of responsibility, causing some members to re-examine their role.

Churches are no more exempt from these questions than any other section of society. As Bill Johnston shows in his chapter, they have to consider their own responsibilites as institutions and, in particular, the implications of adopting a dissenting voice. They have a measure of power, be it cultural or political. Short of renouncing it, an option they probably do not have, they can continue to address the powerful as they have done in the past, albeit more critically. But, in a challenging final chapter in this section, Elizabeth Templeton speaks of the Church exercising another kind of responsibility: to heed those without a voice. If they do not stand with the powerless, the fearful, those who seem to be excluded from the circles of debate, the churches do not speak with an authentic voice and fail to meet the demands which they would dare to make of others.

Part I
Defining the Problem

2

The Theological Task

Duncan Forrester

There is a responsibility laid upon theology to contribute to the debate about nuclear deterrence and it should be able to make a distinctive and useful input. But it is by no means obvious to everyone that such matters can or should be discussed in theological terms. Theology does not provide some free-floating, timeless and pure criteria for the assessment of defence policies; like all ways of thinking it is profoundly shaped by the various social and political contexts within which it operates. These are diverse, and each entails specific theological responsibilities so that there are in fact various complementary theological tasks rather than one, invariable task. Different theological emphases arise out of differing contexts, and theologians should be at pains to adapt their contributions to the various needs, responsibilities and situations of the audiences they address. There are, however, good grounds for saying that it is necessary to have recourse to theological concepts for a rounded and adequate treatment of defence issues. In this chapter the most important theological tasks in relation to the deterrence debate are distinguished, and some comments on the opportunities and risks involved in each are made. In addition, there is some brief discussion of how the theological task as a whole may be distinguished from, and related to, the ethical approach, and how both may be regarded as essential complements to the more technical discussions of defence and deterrence, which sometimes claim to be value-free and to operate more or less independently of the sort of fundamental considerations about God, human nature and society which may legitimately be called theological.

Theology is too important a matter to be left to the professional theologians, and in matters such as those which are the concern of this book an adequate fulfilment of the theological task calls for expertise and experience beyond that of the professional theologian. This chapter chiefly concerns the nature of the theological contribution and the varieties of the theological task rather than offering a sustained theological contribution of its own. Later chapters should be regarded as endeavours to fulfil, in a diversity of ways, the multifaceted theological responsibility.

Why theology?

What justification is there for believing that a theological contribution to the deterrence debate might be valid and useful? Three factors are particularly relevant in responding to this perfectly legitimate question: from the beginning of the nuclear age many responsible people have found it hard to explore the basic issues without recourse to theological language and religious symbols; any worthwhile theology in the Judaeo-Christian tradition, with its strong emphasis on God's activity in history, can only avoid this issue at the cost of massive impoverishment of its religious content; and the role of religion as a legitimator of political policy seems to have had a largely unexpected renaissance even in western secular societies, so that theology is expected and encouraged to take part in the discussion, and strenuous efforts are made to recruit theological support for one side or the other.

When the first atomic bomb was tested, Robert Oppenheimer declared that scientists had now 'known sin'. As he observed the test he found he could only explain his reactions in words borrowed from the *Bhagavad Gita*:

> If the radiance of a thousand suns
> were to burst into the sky,
> that would be like the radiance of the Mighty One.

And later, as he watched the mushroom cloud rise ominously above the Nevada desert, another line from the *Gita* came to mind: 'I am become Death, the shatterer of worlds.' Others present also found that only theological language and religious symbols were adequate to explore the implications of what was now beginning. General Farrell, for example, described the test explosion thus:

The whole country was lighted by a searing light with an intensity many times that of the midday sun . . . Thirty seconds after the explosion came first, the air blast pressing hard against the people and things, to be followed almost immediately by the strong, sustained awesome roar which warned of doomsday and made us feel that we puny things were blasphemous to dare tamper with the forces heretofore reserved to the Almighty. Words are inadequate tools for the job of acquainting those not present with the physical, mental and psychological effects. It had to be witnessed to be realized. (Jungk, 1960, pp. 183–4)

'This atomic bomb is the Second Coming in wrath,' commented Winston Churchill on hearing of the test (Garrison, 1980, p. 21). But if the impact of the test was dramatic, the dropping of the first atomic bomb on Hiroshima provided, in the words of the tailgunner of the Enola Gay, the plane which dropped the bomb, 'a peep into hell' (Garrison, 1980, p. 25). 'The bomb that fell on Hiroshima cut history in two like a knife . . . That cut is more abrupt, decisive and revolutionary than the cut made by the star over Bethlehem,' wrote Henry Wieman (Garrison, 1982, p. 68). And more recently Jerry Falwell and President Reagan, in some of his moods, interpret a coming nuclear destruction of the USSR in terms of Armageddon and other images drawn from the Book of Revelation. Their use of Scripture is simplistic and alarming, but they provide another example of how hard it is to interpret and respond to such horrendous possibilities without recourse to religious symbols.

Great issues, turning points of history, and encounters with radical evil, or authentic holiness, in history all call for religious symbols and theological language for their interpretation. More conventional tools seem quite inadequate for handling such portentous matters; here we are pressing across the limits of humanity's ability to comprehend and order the world into new and mysterious territory. The old maps often seem inadequate; people turn for guidance and illumination, sometimes in near desperation, to ancient symbolic systems, and long for the rebirth of religious images long dormant or forgotten. This straining for the recovery of old keys for the interpretation of what is radically new and threatening has its dangers, of course: the reference above to Jerry Falwell's and Ronald Reagan's recourse to the apocalyptic shows how certain religious symbols may be deployed to suggest that the use of nuclear weapons could be the best – and blessed – recourse in a final confrontation between absolute good and absolute evil. A turning to religious language and religious symbols may indicate the recognition that the issues are grave and unusual resources are needed to cope with them, but it does not guarantee that these matters will be handled wisely. Religious symbols may inflame rather than illumine, and religious rhetoric excite rather than clarify. But this is precisely the point at which a major theological responsibility comes into view: theologians are, or ought to be, people trained in the disciplined and critical investigation of religious symbolic structures and the careful and responsible use of religious language (skills much needed when people look to religion for guidance and illumination for the post-Hiroshima world).

The second point is that a living theology must have something to say on a burning issue such as this. A faith which stands within the prophetic tradition, which strives to 'discern the signs of the times', which believes that God acts in history, has to address itself to the question of the bomb. This is the test of the vitality and plausibility of a theology: that it grapples with the nuclear issue and strives to make some hopeful, helpful, and distinctive contribution to the debate. A theology which allows itself to become domesticated in the private realm, concerned with what E.R. Norman calls 'the ethereal qualities of immortality' (1979, p.2) and matters of personal morality to the exclusion of the public realm, has lost its integrity at least as much as a theology which has become radically politicized. In brief, those who believe that there *is* a theological task today must affirm that it has a bearing on the matters with which this book is concerned. They may disagree about what theology should say, or precisely what its contribution may be, but if they see no relation at all they are denying the relevance of theology and are cutting themselves off from a major strand in the Christian theological tradition.

In the third place, theology has now in Britain, the US and other western societies a more recognized and obvious political role. After a long period when the word theology denoted for many people impracticality and irrelevance, an unproductive luxury which is a distraction from the serious business of life, or a sugar coating in which some politicians like to case their policies but which others may safely ignore, politicians have developed a new interest in what theologians do and say. The theology which was believed to be redundant and capable of sustaining only a shadowy and innocuous existence in a few academic enclaves is now regularly denounced by government ministers and other politicians. As for the Church, it was widely assumed that numerical decline and the corrosion of secularization between them would ensure a steady decline in the Church's public influence and its identification as a club of like-minded people, almost exclusively concerned with the private and domestic spheres. But today the long check-list of areas of controversy between the churches and the Government, which can be found conveniently in the table of contents of a volume of essays by right-wing Christians (Anderson, 1984), indicates that we are in a new era in which many politicians believe that a major function of the Church is the legitimation of authority and of policy, that governments are entitled to look to the Church for support and solace, that the Church has a proper place 'at the centre of things'. And when the Church plays a different role from the one allocated to it, these same politicians are much disturbed.

The new political importance of theology and the churches is nowhere clearer than in relation to the peace issue. The publication of the Report of a Working Party of the Church of England's Board for Social Responsibility, *The Church and the Bomb* (1982), provoked a major campaign to ensure that the recommendations of the Report were not endorsed by the General Synod. Just before the crucial debate an article entitled 'Christians, Awake!' by Paul Johnson was published in *The Times* (Johnson, 1983). It occupied almost a full page, and was arranged around a cartoon by Peter Brookes, based on Holman Hunt's famous picture: Jesus Christ stands knocking at a door marked 'Pax', on his head a crown of thorns, and in his hand a lamp labelled 'Deterrence' containing the mushroom cloud of a nuclear explosion, presumably signifying the new light of the world in which our hope and trust may rest, the foundation of our peace. In Johnson's argument ethical, and more explicitly theological, considerations are interwoven with presuppositions about our society and the Soviet Union. The threat to our 'kind of moral society' is the USSR, which 'has a structural propensity to evil', which is 'a moral threat humanity has never contemplated before' quite commensurate with the threat of nuclear war, a country whose leaders 'we cannot suppose would scruple to use nuclear weapons, as well as any others, to put down opposition'. Somewhat surprisingly, Johnson suggests that crusades against the Soviet Union are not required of Christians in present circumstances; but containment is a clear moral obligation, and nuclear deterrence the necessary means. 'Hence,' Johnson concludes, 'by the dictates of prudence and justice, by arguments from necessity, and by the duty of choosing between unavoidable evils, there is little doubt that nuclear deterrence is not only a moral course but, in the present situation and state of knowledge, the *only* moral course.' It is thus 'obligatory' for Christians to subscribe to deterrence; this makes them 'morally secure', provided the deterrent is credible, minimal and regularly modernized while linked to a programme of civil defence. 'The true Christian course,' he concludes, 'is to support the deterrent policy.' The intended impact of the article is now clear: it is to persuade Christians, and particularly the members of the General Synod, that the whole weight of moral and theological argument tends not towards a reluctant, or questioning, or temporary acceptance of nuclear deterrence, but towards the Christian endorsement of the nuclear policies of Britain and of NATO without significant qualification. And furthermore, 'the structural propensity to evil' of the Soviet Union renders suspect any hope resting on arms control, disarmament, détente, or any other means of peacemaking; the present policies of deterrence are the *only* ways to contain the Soviet Union and thus maintain peace. The *sole* moral and Christian course is to threaten, and be clearly capable of delivering, a devasting nuclear strike.

This article, and the major campaign of which it was a part, were clear and public signs that the stance of the churches and what theologians say about nuclear deterrence are of political importance and a matter of major concern to 'the powers that be'. And, in addition, they showed at least some awareness that the agonizing choices and dilemmas of the nuclear debate are such that they cannot responsibly be discussed without reference to fundamental beliefs, values and attitudes: to religion and theology in fact.

The threefold setting of theology

Christian theology must be *Church* theology; but it also properly operates in the *court,* addressing the powerful and the decision-makers with challenge, support, solace and forgiveness; and it should see itself not as defending the interests of any religiously-defined fellowship or national group but as speaking on behalf of *humanity,* with a particular bias towards the weak and the poor.

A theologian does not enter the discussion as a free-floating expert, a specialist in speculation about divine things, but as a spokesperson for the household of faith, someone who represents a particular tradition and community of faith. This is not to deny that the theologian's attitude to the tradition may often be critical, and the relationship to the Church an uneasy one. But the theologian represents a catholic, world-wide fellowship which is the contemporary manifestation of a particular tradition, and which shares the responsibility for the doing of theology. Theology is a function of the whole Church; the theologian does not have a monopoly of theologizing and should be attentive, but not submissive, to the thinking of the whole Church. Theologians and Church leaders should remember that their statements and interventions are being monitored by churches and Christians throughout the world. They should welcome the opportunity to test their views on deterrence and peacemaking in the contemporary ecumenical arena lest they be sucked into some narrow nationalism or recruited as domestic chaplains of the powerful. During the Falklands War, for instance, the British churches were aware that their actions and statements were being watched by the *oikoumene,* and this powerfully inhibited any temptation to jingoism, for it was a standing reminder that the Church's primary and unconditional loyalty is to the Lord Jesus Christ and not to the nation and its purposes. The American Roman Catholic Bishops likewise found it necessary while composing their pastoral letter to maintain a regular dialogue with Rome and with other hierarchies struggling with the same issues. Some arguments about peace and deterrence, which seem quite convincing and theologically acceptable when considered within the confines of a particular nation or region, seem threadbare and implausible when exposed to a wider ecclesiastical forum such as the WCC.

However, theology is not simply the language-game of the Christian community, converse which makes no sense outside the Church, or an ideology dedicated to defending and advancing the interests of the ecclesiastical institution. It is concerned with the human, it strives to speak for humanity, and it sees the Church as a very partial and incomplete manifestation of the kind of universal community which is to be available for all. Statements of human and Christian solidarity, such as this by Richard Harries, are highly germane to the debate about deterrence:

When I think of people in Russia, ordinary people like myself, and I ask, 'Do I want to kill, or threaten to kill, such people?' the answer of course is, 'No.' When I remind myself that many of these people are Christians, for there is a higher proportion of avowed church members in Russia than there is in Britain, the answer is even more emphatically, 'No.' For these are people who not only laugh and make friends, as I do; many of them pray to the same Lord and receive the same sacraments. They are not only my fellow human beings but my brothers and sisters in Christ. (Harries, 1982, p. 87)

Harries unfortunately goes on to argue that such solidarity has no implications for relations between collectivities. In international relations, he says, citizens of different nations do not meet as brothers and sisters in Christ or as neighbours in the biblical sense; common humanity and common membership in the Body of Christ do not have a bearing on the relations between states. There is a dangerous half-truth here, which theologians who see their thought as properly rooted in the Church and in notions of common humanity will wish to resist: realism about politics as the cut-and-thrust of competing collective interests is to be tempered by commitment to that universal human community of which the Church is a sign and partial manifestation.

Good theology, then, is Church theology, or rather Kingdom theology, for it is orientated towards a fellowship far broader and more perfect than the Church. But it is also 'court theology' in the sense that is does not shirk addressing the powerful and attending to the dilemmas and problems which they face. A necessary awareness that the corridors of power are dangerous places does not in itself justify the theologian in deserting them to cultivate in detachment a supposedly 'pure' theology. Like any other system of ideas, theology can easily be sucked into becoming little more than an ideology justifying the ways of the powerful to themselves and to those without power, Christian on the surface, but in substance pure 'civil theology' with a thin coating of Christian rhetoric. Since the time of Constantine there have been court theologians in plenty, from Eusebius to the present. But good theology must live dangerously; indeed there is no other possibility before it. This means that the theologian should be close to the powerful and the experts, but not 'at home' among them, familiar with the corridors of power, but not at ease within them. For theology is both a speaking of truth to power and a voice for the weak and the powerless and the marginalized, for the victims, who have a special place in the Kingdom. Such a theology, addressed constructively to the decision-makers in a way that the weak and the powerless and the excluded may overhear, is both the most honest and the most authentic support that can be given them in their complex task and responsibility.

In matters of defence, deterrence and disarmament, as in many other areas of politics, the issues seem so complex and technical that ordinary citizens tend to withdraw and leave them to the experts who are presumed to know their way about, to understand the logic of the debate and the facts of the case, and to operate with a high degree of altruism and integrity. Theologians and others may enter the discussion only on condition of 'working within the terms and categories given them by politics itself': to make a useful contribution one must first accept the major presuppositions underlying the discussion, and then master a mass of highly technical detail. There is much validity in this argument. But sometimes those operating on the 'inside' find themselves lost in a maze, even caught in a web of absurdity and immorality, precisely because they have not questioned presuppositions and axioms. Presumably there were competent economists and chemists under Hitler who took part in highly technical discussions about the economics of transporting people to the extermination camps, and about the efficient operation of gas chambers. Certainly there were social scientists of repute in the US who wrote learned papers on what they called 'forced-draft urbanisation' during the Vietnam War which, when stripped of jargon, were really advice about ways of saturating the countryside with bombs so that the survivors would take refuge in the cities where they could be more easily controlled. Experts and the powerful are no more immune to sin, self-interest and distorted judgement than the rest of us. We have encountered experts in defence and deterrence who feel caught in a maze, who welcome theologians and others precisely in the hope that they will not accept the present terms and conditions of the debate, but will help to open it out. However, even decision-makers and experts who recognize the absurdity, danger and immorality of the situation cannot just cut and run. It would be less than honest for the theologian to disguise the fact that the situation *is* immoral and absurd; and less than responsible to refuse to support decision-makers in facing this absurdity and trying to move to a more secure, rational and peaceful world.

Indicative and imperative

Gordon Dunstan, in an article on 'Theological Method in the Deterrence Debate' argues that there is little direct theological contribution possible (Goodwin, 1982). The discussion should, he suggests, be conducted in secular terms, as a matter of prudential political ethics. The political realm must have a proper autonomy; its questions are such that there is no explicitly Christian answer to them, or Christian way of handling them. Any contribution that Christianity and Christian theology may have to offer will be indirect and limited. The play, he suggests, is not, and cannot be, Christian, but Christianity can provide an excellent school for actors and the backdrop for the action. Christianity (like Oxford 'Greats'!) sends people of character, integrity, and above all prudence, into the political arena; 'The Christian Gospel,' writes Dunstan, 'will be most effective in this political context in the character which it imprints upon Christian men [sic] carrying responsibility.' This is well said, and important. Yet one might hope that Christianity does more for decision-makers than train them in prudence and integrity; surely it offers them challenge, forgiveness, solace, and a disturbing vision; and there are other relevant Christian virtues which might contest the primacy accorded to prudence.

In the second place, Dunstan suggests, Christianity provides a kind of backdrop for the play. The backdrop is theological; the drama prudential ethics. Some backdrops highlight the action and aid the interpretation of its significance; others are so adaptable that any play may be performed before them. An alternative model for a similar relationship of theology to the deterrence debate (and to ethics in general) is that the theology provides a pious preface, or a holy postscript, to a secular discussion. Dunstan notes that Richard Harries's essay, 'The Morality of Nuclear Deterrence', 'begins with Christian orthodoxy, but argues his morality in the language of politics and military necessity' (Harries, 1982, p. 141), while Dunstan himself tends to conclude discussions of the limited usefulness of theology with remarks like, 'and there is the Everlasting Mercy for those who, in good faith, are driven to choose' (Goodwin, 1982, p. 50), and 'There remains a venture of faith, to inject into politics the power of what to philosophers is an Idea, and, to theologians, the quickening Word, full of grace and truth' (Harries, 1982, p. 144).

In a typically shrewd and judicious chapter on 'Nuclear Ethics' John Habgood endorses and elaborates Dunstan's position with great clarity:

The prime Christian contribution to social ethics is in the indicative rather than the imperative mood. In terms of the principles by which people should live and societies order themselves, Christians have little to say that could not be said by any reasonable person of goodwill. It is Christian belief about the kind of place the world is, about the depth of human sinfulness and the possibilities of divine grace, about judgement and hope, incarnation and salvation, God's concern for all and his care for each, about human freedom and divine purpose – it is beliefs such as these which make the difference, and provide the context within which the intractable realities of social and political life can be tackled with wisdom and integrity. (Habgood, 1983, p. 168)

This is well said, but I doubt whether Dunstan and Habgood provide us with an adequate account of the theological task. For one thing, statements like Habgood's quoted above are usually read in the light of a belief that there is a fundamental disjunction between fact and value; and no means of moving from an 'is' to an 'ought'. This assumption is peculiarly problematic for theology, which tends to recognize ethics and theology as distinct but interdependent subjects: dogma implies ethics, and ethics presupposes dogma. For example, it was the praxis and the ethics of Karl Barth's theological teachers in almost unanimously endorsing the Kaiser's cause in the First World War which first aroused his suspicion that something must be wrong with their *theology,* and gave him his lifelong conviction that ethics and dogmatics belong together.

This is not at all to deny the value of the kind of disciplined ethical reflection represented, for instance, by the theory of the just war. Just war theory is a way of thinking which has its roots in pre-Christian classical philosophy and Christian metaphysics. It is ethical rather than theological, and precisely because it does not presuppose any religious commitment or involve an explicit dogmatic element it often commends itself as peculiarly appropriate in a secular age. But for centuries just war thinking was conducted within the theological famework, and when it is detached from that framework it becomes liable to subtle but significant modification. The theological frame affirmed that war and violence call for repentance and need forgiveness, despite the fact that in a fallen world we must expect conflict to take place. Thus the Norman knights who triumphed at the Battle of Hastings in a cause that had been declared just by the Pope himself were still required to do penance for having shed human blood. Just war considerations were used to discourage recourse to violence (*ius ad bellum*) and to promote restraint in the conduct of war (*ius in bello*) within the general theological assumption that all participation in war is sinful. The greater the distance that developed between the theology of war and the ethics of the just war the easier it became to regard war as sometimes good, or even holy, rather than always inherently sinful. As just war theory was increasingly detached from classical Christian theology and grafted on to a modern, more optimistic view of human nature and the world, it could offer little effective resistance to the acceptance or glorification of war which springs from seeing the modern ideological war as a Manichean confrontation of absolute good and absolute evil. A theory once intended to express an abhorrence of war often became a means of justifying it.

I want to suggest that the indicative and the imperative are more integrally connected than Dunstan and Habgood seem willing to admit, and that the theological task is more extensive than they allow. My contention is that Christian theology provides more than 'the context within which the intractable realities of social and political life can be tackled with wisdom and integrity', but less than the kind of coherent intellectual framework which some people expect. Its contribution to the deterrence debate is likely to be fragmentary, disturbing and disconcerting, for reasons pointed by William Temple in 1939:

The world of today is one of which no Christian map can be made. It must be changed by Christ into something very unlike itself before a Christian map of it is possible. We used to believe in the sovereignty of the God of love a great deal too light-heartedly . . . There is a new task for the theologians today. We cannot come to the men of today, saying, 'You will find that all your experience fits together in a harmonious system if you will only look at it in the illumination of the Gospel.' . . . Our task with this world is not to explain it but to convert it. Its needs can be met, not by the discovery of its own immanent principle in signal manifestation through Jesus Christ, but only by the shattering impact upon its self-sufficiency and arrogance of the Son of God, crucified, risen and ascended, pouring forth that explosive and disruptive energy which is the Holy Ghost. (Ramsey, 1960, pp. 160–1)

Varied tasks and flexible responses

Christian theology at its heart is not so much a framework or a system of thought, logical, coherent, systematic, as a form of response to Jesus Christ. In one sense the theological task is always the same – to proclaim the Gospel – but the mode of fulfilment of the task is very variable. This is partly because theologians cannot rise above the relativities, compromises and ambiguities of history and take their stand on the olympian heights of absolute justice and truth, from where they may judge the deeds of peoples and nations. They, too, are sinners, they are involved in the relativities of worldly existence, they 'see through a glass darkly', they need to live by forgiveness. They have themselves to strive, and help others as well, to live responsibly and seek peace, justice and freedom in the context in which they find themselves; they have to learn to respond flexibly and lovingly to the demands and questions of their situation, aware always that the possibilities are limited and the best that can be expected falls far short of the perfect will of God. The task also varies in relation to the audience addressed: the theologian is called to 'become all things to everyone', not to please people, or dilute the Gospel, or look after his own interests, but that he 'might by all means save some' (I Corinthians 9.22). The one Gospel is expressed in different and specific ways to different people; it always addresses the whole person in the context of that person's responsibilities, vocation and skills as well as the person's fears and failures and need for forgiveness and encouragement.

The underlying consistency and complementarity in these various theological tasks can best be understood when we regard the various theological tasks as serious endeavours to respond to Jesus Christ, and Christian praxis as a way of participating in the activity of God within history. When theologians attempted to outline and discuss Christ's central role and activity as reconciler, mediator and peacemaker, they found it helpful to speak of his 'threefold office' as prophet, priest and king: three different modes of peacemaking, three different emphases, relating to three different contexts. These three were complementary rather than being in competition, they were perfectly consistent with one another, and in each Christ calls his followers to participate, but not necessarily simultaneously or putting the same emphasis on each office. The prophet is a mouthpiece for God; one who interprets God's will to the people; recalls them to the hope of final peace; proclaims the message of reconciliation. It is a role not to be entered upon lightly or too eagerly. Many of the Old Testament prophets were reluctant to accept their calling, with its dangers, opportunities and risks, particularly the risk of self-righteousness on the one hand or the denial of one's calling on the other. Jesus fulfils the prophetic office by showing what is in the heart of God. As priest, Christ is our peace; the priestly office is one of mediation, of bringing together the estranged and hostile, of opening communication and making community. The kingly office involves leadership and authority, and an understanding of what responsibility means. Jesus showed in his life and expressed in his teaching a sharp distinction between the kind of authority of the kings of the Gentiles, who delight in power for its own sake, who 'lord it over people', and the servant-authority of the disciples, who are willing to spend themselves and give themselves for the people for whom they are responsible. Power and authority are necessary for maintaining community, fellowship and peace, but the kingly role also involves pointing beyond the compromises and the relative peace possible in this sort of world to the Kingdom that is to come, and leading the people towards God's future.

We should not expect theology which sees itself as a response to Jesus Christ to be always the same; but there should be an underlying complementarity and consistency in the fulfilment of the theological task. No one theological task has a monopoly; neither separately nor together are they an adequate response to God's call and God's grace. But as modest and penitent attempts to be faithful in the particularities of a world in which multitudes fear a nuclear holocaust and others see nuclear deterrence as the only way to maintain a relative peace, the *confession,* the *demystifying,* the *visionary* and the *prophetic* tasks deserve further consideration as the major modes in which theological responsibility may be exercised.

The confessional task

When Luther in Worms proclaimed: 'Here I stand; I can do no other; so help me God,' he was proclaiming that, amid all the uncertainties of life, for him at that moment confession of the truth of the Gospel was inseparable from a specific course of action. He was taking a costly, risky stand, not so much something that he had coolly chosen to do as something that had been forced upon him. When in 1934 the representatives of the 'Confessing Church' in Germany, led by Barth and Niemoller, formulated and subscribed to the theological Declaration of Barmen they were, with immense courage, not only affirming the truth of the Gospel but declaring Nazism to be incompatible with the Christian faith, precisely because it was a new paganism which put the nation, the race and the Führer in the place which should be occupied by Christ alone. Many of the same Christians joined with others after the war in confessing, 'We are with our people in a great communion of suffering, but also a solidarity of guilt . . . We repent for not having more courageously confessed, more faithfully, prayed, more ardently loved.' In a different context, in 1968 the Joint Theological Commission of the South African Council of Churches and the South

African Catholic Bishops' Conference produced *A Message to the People of South Africa*. After a credal outline of the Gospel, the *Message* notes that Christians are called to witness to the Gospel in their particular circumstances of time and place. This means in the context of apartheid, which has become for many

a false faith, a novel Gospel which offers happiness and peace for the community and for the individual. It holds out to men a security built not upon Christ but on the theory of separation and the preservation of their racial identity. It presents separate development of our race-groups as a way for the people of South Africa to save themselves. Such a claim inevitably conflicts with the Christian Gospel, which offers salvation, both social and individual, through faith in Christ alone. (Gruchy and Villa-Vicencio, 1983, p.155)

It is impossible to witness to the truth of the Gospel without witnessing against false gospels; Christians must be helped to discriminate between the truth and falsehood; and certain social structures and patterns of behaviour are so radically incompatible with the Gospel that Christians must realize that here they cannot compromise with what is in fact idolatry. In the same tradition in more recent times the Lutheran World Federation, the World Alliance of Reformed Churches and the WCC have all declared apartheid to be sinful and those Christians who defend it theologically to be in a state of heresy.

　Underlying this kind of confessional political statement there is a belief that within the complexities there is a simple, yet hard and costly choice: do we put our ultimate trust in God or in something else? Is the Gospel true, or is truth to be found elsewhere? The problem is that the issues rarely appear as clear-cut as this, and even when the choice is in fact a simple one there are many who depict it as complex. It is true that in most situations the movement between fundamentals of Christian belief and political stances is a complicated and ambiguous matter. Hence there are many who see the Christian contribution as laying down 'Christian principles' of a high level of generality, but not engaging directly with policies. The problem here is often that the distinctively Christian elements are filtered out in the passage from faith to political choices, and we are left with purely prudential conclusions, or conclusions determined by some secular ideology. But there *is* a tension between faith and policy which must be affirmed and recognized rather than dissolved away if the faith is to be authentically confessed in politics, as was recognized by thinkers as diverse as Reinhold Niebuhr and Dietrich Bonhoeffer. As Niebuhr put it:

Those of us who regard the ethic of Jesus as finally and ultimately normative, but not as immediately applicable to the task of securing justice in a sinful world, are very foolish if we try to reduce the ethic so that it will cover and justify our prudential and relative standards and strategies. To do this is to reduce the ethic of love to a new legalism . . . It is dangerous and confusing to give these tentative and relative standards final and absolute religious sanction. (Niebuhr, 1940, p. 16)

And Bonhoeffer saw his faith as leading him into conspiracy against Hitler without making this activity 'good' or justified in any simple sense; he had to learn to live and act responsibly in dependence upon the divine grace and forgiveness.

Is the nuclear issue in its essence a simple one, in which honest and serious Christians should be at one in espousing a certain line of policy? The historic 'peace churches' and Christian pacifists in all churches continue to make this affirmation and believe that confession of Christian faith necessarily involves adopting a pacifist stand and witnessing against war and all forms of violence. No Christian can dismiss this position lightly: there is a great deal in the New Testament and the practice of the early Church to support it. And even those Christians who do not believe that their confession of the faith implies a pacifist or nuclear pacifist stance should be grateful that this unconditional witness against war is made, and respect those who make it. Non-pacifist Christians also have a confessional task; they may not isolate their faith from their attitudes to nuclear war and deterrence. Confession of the true God, as we saw in relation to Nazism and apartheid, involves the repudiation of false gospels and the rejection of idolatry. Idolatry in the Bible frequently refers not to the worship of a false god understood as such, but rather to putting one's fundamental trust in something other than God: fortifications, armaments, foreign alliances or human powers themselves. It is not that the Bible sees these things as unimportant; they are of great significance in their proper place and provided people recognize their limitations. But when a nation turns to these things for its ultimate security it is misunderstanding their true nature and absolutizing them in a way which is fundamentally idolatrous. In the context of a biblical view it should cause no surprise when a nation which seeks absolute security for itself through arms, nuclear or otherwise, ends up with less security than ever, for in such a case the search for a kind of security which is not available in this world but which we may only possess proleptically, in hope, has become 'a false faith, a novel gospel'. This is a point made clearly by Eisenhower when he said, 'No matter how much we send for arms, there is no safety in arms alone. Our security is the total product of our economic, intellectual, moral and military strengths . . . There is no way in which a country can satisfy the craving for absolute security – but it easily can bankrupt itself, morally and economically, in attempting to reach that illusory goal through arms alone' (Pursell, 1972).

Confession of the Christian faith is only compatible with nuclear deterrence if it is, in the words of the Pope, regarded 'certainly not as an end in itself but as a step on the way toward a progressive disarmament' (John Paul II, 1982, p. 3). Any Christian acceptance of deterrence must be hedged about with qualifications, which 'cut it down to size', and ensure that our attitude towards nuclear deterrence is not inappropriate and idolatrous.

These qualifications should guarantee that deterrence is minimal, that the claimed need for parity is not used as a cover for developing superiority, that there is a deep seriousness about arms control and disarmament, and that deterrence is regarded as only one among many complementary ways of seeking peace. All these qualifications must make Christians who give a provisional and limited assent to nuclear deterrence uneasy, and passionately determined to cut down to size, question its pretensions and demand of government and military alike a real seriousness about peacemaking.

The US Catholic Bishops have identified very clearly another implication of confessing the Christian faith today:

If nuclear deterrence exists only to prevent the *use* of nuclear weapons by others, then proposals to go beyond this to planning for prolonged periods of repeated nuclear strikes or counterstrikes, or 'prevailing' in nuclear war are not acceptable. They encourage notions that nuclear war can be engaged in with tolerable human and moral consequences. Rather, we must continually say no to the ideal of nuclear war. (US Catholic Bishops, 1983, p. 18)

It is accordingly deeply disturbing to find that a number of British Christians and theologians move beyond a provisional and limited acceptance of nuclear deterrence to suggesting that there may be a theological justification for nuclear war fighting in some circumstances:

It is therefore possible, in theory, to envisage a just use of nuclear weapons . . . My own judgement is that to use nuclear weapons other than on relatively isolated military targets would be morally worse than the evil of submitting to an alien power, but that to hold a conditional intention to use them is less evil than the alternatives. (Harries, 1982, pp. 98, 197)

While recognising the utterly appalling prospect of the use of nuclear weapons, I believe that their possession and use can be morally acceptable as a way of exercising our moral responsibility in a fallen world. (Leonard, in Martin and Mullen, 1983, p. 193)

It is in this situation where we face obliteration as a people, that I would think it permissible to launch a nuclear response, if that response had any hope of preventing our obliteration. (Ward, in Bridger, 1983, p. 59)

I do not think it morally acceptable to acquire and maintain capabilities if we are sure that their actual use would certainly and in all circumstances be immoral . . . In my view possession is not justifiable if we are sure no circumstances can be conceived in which actual use could be legitimate. (Quinlan, 1985, p. 26)

It is surely sad and ironic that, at a time when there is a near consensus among international lawyers that nuclear war-fighting would be illegal, and medical people and scientists are asserting ever more strongly that nuclear war-fighting would be suicidal and would have devastating implications for the globe for centuries, some theologians are suggesting that nuclear war-fighting may be legitimate on Christian grounds. The confessional task is continually to say NO to the idea of nuclear war; deterrence is only temporarily tolerable as long as it deters, sustaining a relative peace within which a more securely based peace may be sought.

The demystifying task

Theologians here operate like the little child in Hans Christian Andersen's story of the Emperor's new clothes. Shaking themselves free from ideological blinkers and social conditioning they say what they see. The child is not an 'expert', the 'tailors', and in a more prudent and responsible way the courtiers, are the experts, Nor is he a decision-maker; that is the role of the Emperor. King, courtiers and adults in the crowd are all bewildered by the contrived mystique of power arranged for their own advantage by the 'tailors'. The child stands with the weak, in *sancta simplicitas*; he tells the simple truth because he is not yet caught up in the web of social pressure to deny it; his word destroys the mystique of power, revealing the Emperor to be but a fallible human being like the rest of us. The idolatry of power cannot survive the truth-telling of the child.

It is perhaps good for theologians to be reminded that, although there is no return to innocence possible, only those who become as little children may enter the Kingdom of Heaven, for theologians and the Christian faith have been accused with not little justice by Marxists and other of *mystifying* politics, of declaring the established order to be God-given and sacred, of using mystification as an agency of social control. A wrong exercise of the visionary task is just this. But a major responsibility of the theologian is to ask questions, questions that sometimes appear to be naive at first, like the questions that Jesus asked. In a sense this is the Socratic role; the questions are deceptively simple; they show up ignorance masquerading as wisdom. The child in the story expresses the absurdity of the situation, the laughter he provokes cuts the Emperor, and the tailors and their collusive pretensions down to size. But the child does more than ask questions; he says quite simply what seems to be true to those who stand outside the circle of power, who are not experts, who are ignorant of the technical arguments but sometimes capable of seeing through the pretensions and mystifications of power, and whose hopes and fears are dominated by the bomb.

The theologian in fulfilling the demystifying task asks questions which expose the absurdity of our situation, so that a hard-headed realistic politician like Enoch Powell is not left on his own in declaring that the policy of nuclear deterrence is 'insane'. Questions must be asked about the meaning of 'defence' if it may involve genocide, including the genocide of one's own people, and about the kind of 'security' which may be secured through nuclear armament, together with its limits and its costs. We must enquire why balance and parity are important, why every new deployment by one side must be equalled or surpassed by the other when both sides already have many times more nuclear warheads than are required for effective deterrence. We must ask what other hidden motivations are at work here. We must investigate the image of 'the Enemy' so emotively portrayed in Paul Johnson's article, and found in some other theological contributors to the debate, and ask 'whether it has clothes on'. We must strive for a simple and childlike honesty, remembering, perhaps, that some of us supported a British deterrent because we believed it when we were told that this would give our country a seat at the table to negotiate for disarmament; but now we find that our country refuses to put our deterrent on the table, or our feet under it. We have to challenge *fatalism* by questioning statements like Richard Harries's: 'It is not possible for a major power to have even tolerable security without possessing nuclear weapons. Nuclear deterrence comes under the head of "absolute necessity"' (Harries, 1982, p. 106).

Too much thinking, even theological thinking, is mesmerized and inhibited by the bomb. It needs the childlike voice, speaking the simple truth, to demystify the complexities and technicalities.

The visionary task

Faith and theology are concerned with visions because they are concerned with hope, with goals, with long-term objectives, with the fundamental values which religion implants in a culture and a society over many centuries, with ideals and ends which need constant refreshment and renewal. Theology has a responsibility to sustain a

Christian social and political vision so that technical discussions and the pursuit of short-term objectives may be viewed *sub specie aeternitatis*. This is a vision which motivates and orientates; but is not itself policy, and is only reduced to a policy blueprint at the cost of its integrity. The vision is concerned with ultimates, and therefore relativizes many more immediate concerns. The Christian vision is eschatological and is expressed either in poetic and symbolic language, or as a kind of negative eschatology: the Kingdom is not this, not that. It is quite impossible to understand the Christian project, or the imperatives and policies it asserts, without grasping the outlines of the vision within which the project is set. If the sustaining of vision is a continuing responsibility for the Church, and the Christian vision is recognized as having inescapably political content, there still remain dangers. The vision may be treated as a pipe-dream, a way of escaping from engagement rather than an incentive to engage with contemporary political reality. It may be allowed to become private, vacuous and irrelevant; or the attempt may be made to declare the vision of immediate applicability as a political programme. Balance is required within the vision: justice, peace and freedom must embrace rather than conflict. Accordingly the proper stewardship of the Christian vision is no simple task, but a responsibility laid squarely on the shoulders of theologians.

Abelard, the great visionary theologian, sang:

> Truly Jerusalem name we that shore,
> 'Vision of peace, that brings joy evermore'
> Wish and fulfilment can severed be ne'er,
> Nor the thing prayed for come short of the prayer.

He thus pointed to the centrality of the vision of *shalom* in the Christian scheme of things.

Shalom is in biblical Hebrew a term for completeness, soundness, wellbeing; it indicates personal and corporate flourishing, health and prosperity, always rooted in harmony and concord. Individual *shalom* is inseparable from the corporate *shalom* of the fellowship. It is the normal and proper condition for individuals and societies, and is enjoyed most intimately in the family circle. *Shalom* is a gift of God, which will be bestowed most fully when the Prince of Peace inaugurates the messianic age. The suffering servant in Isaiah brings *shalom* to the nations (Isaiah 53.5). *Shalom* is inseparably linked to justice, faithfulness and truth in the psalmist's vision.

> Let me hear what God the Lord will speak,
> for he will speak peace to his people,
> to his saints, to those who turn to him in their hearts.
> Surely his salvation is at hand for those who fear him,

that glory may dwell in our land.
Steadfast love and faithfulness will meet;
righteousness and peace will kiss each other.
Faithfulness will spring up from the ground,
and righteousness will look down from the sky.
Yea, the Lord will give what is good,
and our land will yield its increase.
Righteousness will go before him,
and make his footsteps a way.

(Psalm 85.10–13, Revised Standard Version)

The vision embraces the whole creation; the cosmos is involved in the covenant of peace. But it is in the midst of wars and rumours of wars that Israel's longing for *shalom* is most intense; they turn to the God who 'will break bow and sword and weapon of war and sweep them off the earth, so that all living creatures may lie down without fear' (Hosea 2.18, New English Bible), then they look for the day when 'nation shall not lift up sword against nation nor ever again be trained for war' (Micah 4.3, New English Bible). However, this is a messianic hope; *shalom* is not understood as something which can be achieved, immediately and by human beings in this kind of world; it is the gift of the coming messiah.

The Lukan narrative of the nativity speaks of angels heralding the birth of Jesus with a song of *shalom* restored to earth. In Jesus, *shalom* has come; by him it is bestowed; the writer of the letter to the Ephesians writes, 'He is our peace' (Ephesians 2.14). His disciples are called to be messengers of peace, and people who actively promote peace in a disordered world as they proclaim the inauguration of the messianic age, the promised Kingdom. As my colleague, J. I. H. McDonald, puts it:

The necessary paradox was that the One who embodied and activated *shalom* in a disordered world also brought into play the sword of opposition and conflict (cf. Luke 2.34f.). Rejected by the city 'that did not know the things that pertained to its peace', the climax of his ministry was the disfiguration of the Cross; yet this disfiguration was for our *shalom* (Isaiah 53.5b) – 'the chastisement of our peace was upon him' (AV). The benediction of the disfigured One is, 'Peace be with you.' Though still rejected by the cosmos which does not recognise the extent of its bondage to the powers of alienation, something of the reality of Christ's *shalom* remains with all who discern in him the One who has broken down the iron curtain of hostility and made possible a new health, wholeness and fulfilment. And, since this *shalom* is the gift of God to his creation, if redefines 'God's people' as the faithful community that transcends the boundaries of nationhood and race. This new community, founded on 'the stone that the builders rejected', constitutes 'a chosen race, a royal priesthood, a holy nation, a people for his possession', enjoying anew the mercy of God. (McDonald, 1986)

Yet the Church which enjoys and witnesses to the *shalom* that is in Jesus Christ does so in a world that is 'subject to futility', that 'groans in travail', that is still disordered. Christians may not detach themselves from this world, but must not become prisoners of worldly realities either. And McDonald continues:

They share its suffering but not its bondage: and, in the perspective of faith, these sufferings are the birth-pangs of a new age, an age already conceived in the ministry, death and resurrection of Jesus and slowly but surely gestating in the cosmic womb. Hence, since the Church as the community of faith is sensitive to the 'signals of transcendence' it must relay its faith and hope to a world which has its own longings to transcend its bondage. It must relay the 'absolutes' that proceed from the fuller picture, but do it in such a way that is credible within the limitations of the 'relative' world which sees its travail as the sign of death rather than of new and eternal life. (McDonald, 1986)

My purpose at this point is simply to show how theology may present, delineate and commend the *shalom* of the Kingdom as a vision which provides the indispensable context and motivation for peacemaking and maintenance of peace amidst the complexities of a broken world to which the King has come, but in which the Kingdom is not yet fully realized. It is along these lines that a theology of peace should be developed.

The visionary task involves sustaining, refining, exploring and commending the vision of *shalom*, as something which provides orientation and hope, together with insight into the present situation and its possibilities under God. The Church is not simply a community of peacemakers who nurture the vision of *shalom*; it is itself called, in its sinfulness and inadequacy, to be an anticipatory manifestation of *shalom*, the sacrament of *shalom* whose existence confirms the validity of the vision.

The prophetic task

The prophetic task relates in a more specific way to policy; it is impossible for a responsible political theology to remain indefinitely at the level of principle or generality. If principles or generalizations have validity they must have implications for policy options which can sometimes be spelled out even if they are more contentious or potentially divisive than the affirmation of principles. Prophecy is concerned with the actualities of power. It looks at them in the light of the Gospel, and at its best is capable of uncovering the realities of the situation in the deepest sense. When George Bell, Bishop of Chichester, denounced the saturation bombing of German cities during the Second World War on moral and theological grounds, he was denounced as unrealistic, utopian and not worth listening to. He was accused of advocating a course of action which was quite contrary to the dictates of prudence and wise strategy, but years later distinguished military commentators argued that Bell and the tiny handful who publicly endorsed his views at the time had in fact been advocating the more prudent and realistic, as well as the more moral, line. This case, of course, does no more than suggest that prophecy is capable of reaching beyond the immediate counsels of prudential ethics. However, there is also the danger that prophecy which is not rooted in careful social analysis may not take proper account of the intricacies of the situation and the ambiguities which are faced by the decision-makers. John Habgood has argued that 'to be close to those in power is to have some first-hand knowledge of the complexity of the actual choices facing them. This has a devastating effect on prophetic certainties. And actually to share responsibility is even more devastating' (Habgood, 1983, p. 105). The point is well taken, but must not be pressed too far. Decision-makers and the powerful are not the only ones who need sympathy and understanding. Those whose lives are affected by decisions, especially small and voiceless groups, have an even more pressing right to be heard by the theologian, whose task is never to give encouragement to politicians engaged in absurd and immoral policies, but rather to proclaim that forgiveness is available for sinners.

Theology as prophecy points steadily towards individual responsibility. Political, economic, scientific and strategic decisions are made and implemented by men and women, and affect men and women. Neither the market with its 'invisible hand' nor the State should be revered as powers following their own principles and beyond human control. The prophet constantly reminds people that they bear responsibility not just before an electorate but before God for their actions and for their decisions. A significant element in the prophetic impact of the US Catholic Bishops' pastoral letter lay in its insistence that various categories of people should face up to the specific responsiblities involved in their roles or vocations in society. Accordingly it addresses very precise challenges to priests and pastors, to educators, to parents, to youth, to men and women in military service, to those in defence industries, to scientists, to people in the media, to public officials and to Christian citizens. Each group was asked to consider its responsibilities in a disconcertingly wide framework, *sub specie aeternitatis*. The specificity of these challenges, and the refusal to accept narrow and artificial limits to responsibility, contributed both to the impact of the pastoral letter and to the alarm it roused in the corridors of power, for the theological task offers disturbance and questioning as much as comfort and support to the powerful.

In Max Weber's terminology, the prophetic task is concerned with an 'ethic of responsibility', just as the visionary task deals in an 'ethic of ultimate ends' (Gerth and Mills, 1948, p. 127). The two complement each other. Prophecy understands the nature and the constraints of responsibility, and in large part it is addressed to whose who are, or ought to be, aware that their decisions and actions affect the lives and flourishing of many others. These are people whose task is to pursue and advance the legitimate interests of those for whom they are responsible, and part of the theological vocation is to endeavour to see that these interests are not construed in too narrow or short term a fashion, and to affirm that responsibility is ultimately to God rather than simply to an electorate.

Dealings with those whose choices and decisions affect the destiny of millions, and who usually recognize that their freedom is so circumscribed that they cannot often do more than choose between two imperfect solutions to a problem, should induce humility in those who fulfil the prophetic task. But it should not discourage them from engaging with matters of policy and confining themselves exclusively to statements of principle, although there is certainly a case that prophetic interventions must be few if they are to be telling. Had the US Catholic Bishops or the Anglican report on *The Church and the Bomb* confined themselves to enunciations of principles and middle axioms it is likely that they would have had little impact. It was when they moved, in a humble, realistic and well-informed way, from the realm of principles into that of policies that they became challenging and truly prophetic. In their differing ways these two reports suggest how the prophetic task may be responsibly fulfilled today in relation to nuclear deterrence.

3

Moral Theory
and the Nuclear Debate

Columba Ryan

Two things are striking about the debate on morality and defence policy: one is that it appears to be a Babel of voices, an 'interminable' exchange (MacIntyre, 1981, pp. 6–12) between deaf-mutes; the other is what little practical difference it makes to policies. Democratic governments may find the clamour of peace movements and churchmen an irritant, even a brake on how they present their policies; the policies are pursued all the same. This stalemate is likely to continue unless we recognize some of the procedural assumptions which affect the course of the discussion.

Some arguments for and against nuclear war and the policy of deterrence

Many of the arguments for and against war and deterrence, whilst relevant to the question of morality in ways we will discuss, do not bear *directly* on this question. Arguments about the likely outcome of a nuclear exchange, about the balance of forces, about the effectiveness of deterrence, reach conclusions which are not *of themselves* moral conclusions.[1] About a plan for burgling, I may ask whether it will work, is economical, runs too many risks to perpetrator and victim alike, requires resources in my power; but even if I can answer all these questions satisfactorily to make it a 'good' plan, I have not answered the question whether it is right to burgle.

In outline, the directly moral arguments in the nuclear debate include the following ideas.

1 To take innocent life in war, except as a second effect not intended, and only in proportion to the primary intended effect, is wrong; nuclear weapons are so indiscriminate that innocent life must be

taken out of all due proportion to the effect intended. Hypothetical examples of the just use of tactical nuclear weapons against an isolated military target simply do not reflect actual weapons systems, strategic doctrines, and targeting policies (Ruston, 1981, chapter 7; Church of England Working Party, 1982, chapter 5; US Catholic Bishops, 1983, paragraphs 80 ff., 142 ff.).

2 There are consequences so appalling ('mega-deaths', genetic damage, nuclear winter) that no possible end could justify them. (This is the moral implication of Chivian, 1982; Prins, 1983; and others.)

3 The Christian ethic of love and *shalom* is totally incompatible with the cruelty and denial of life involved in nuclear deterrence policies (Church of England Working Party, 1982, chapter 6; Schneider, in Murnion, 1983, pp. 96–101).

4 Deterrence policy, which puts us on a permanent war footing, so corrodes democratic structures by suppression of information, secret policy-making, and curtailment of personal freedoms as to be morally unacceptable (Prins, 1983, chapter 8).

5 Threats of unlimited destruction infect our whole society, especially the young, with an unacceptable distortion of values (Aldridge, 1983, p. 291).

6 Any credible policy of deterrence requires the training of large numbers of servicemen and others to entertain an effectual intention of indiscriminate destruction of life, regardless of moral niceties (Ruston, 1983, p. 61; Kenny, 1985, p. 53).

There is less appeal to high moral ground on the other side, but such appeal is made, if only in reply to moral attacks.

7 It is the duty of government to defend national frontiers and the values of freedom and this is only possible by nuclear deterrence (Harries, 1982, p. 105; Leonard and Harries, in Bridger, 1983, pp. 9, 84; Johnson, 1983).

8 In the real world we may have to accept a lesser evil to avoid a greater (Hockaday in Goodwin, 1982, p. 85; Leonard and Ward in Bridger, 1983, pp. 16, 53; Johnson, 1983).

9 Opposition to the settled, constitutionally warranted, policy amounts to treachery, naive or criminal, by undermining the strength and unity of purpose required to stand up against an unscrupulous enemy and his divisive propaganda (Chalfont in Martin and Mullen, 1983, p.13, and much criticism of CND on these lines).

10 Moral principles have to be combined with prudential considerations which are best left to the experts who alone can find their

way through the complexities of strategic planning and international negotiations (Quinlan in Bridger, 1983, p. 149).

Unquestioned assumptions

These arguments recur, one set pitted against the other, and no headway seems to be made because they turn on unquestioned assumptions. The assumptions fall, I suggest, into three categories. Behind the second set of arguments there is often an impatience with moral theory as irrelevant to practical politics, especially arguments (7), (9), and (10). Behind both sets, there is an assumption first, that the moral argument is clear and, second, that the moral criteria we use scarcely affect our conclusions, though in fact they render these conclusions 'incommensurate' in the sense argued by MacIntyre (1981, p. 8).

The assumption that moral theory is irrelevant to practical politics

It would be unjust not to feel some sympathy for those with responsibility who are impatient with armchair moral purists. No one should underrate the pressures of decision-making. It may also seem unfair to tax policy-makers with the assumption that moral theory is irrelevant when they do, after all, talk of duty, treachery, or the values of peace and freedom. Nevertheless, their arguments *set* the problem of defence in a way which precludes more fundamental moral questions.

We are told that we face a threat to our very survival, without regard to whether this threat is real or merely perceived, nor whether our 'defence' is perceived by the other side as a threat to their survival. As Howard Davis argues (below, chapter 9), acceptance of deterrence is set in terms of an opposition which must be expected to last indefinitely (and so 'met') rather than one which it is imperative to resolve. Given this setting, the need for military 'containment', it is assumed that the right policies are those which will work pragmatically. These are the current policies, they alone will bring security, hence the appeal to close ranks (argument 9), to carry out our duty of defence (argument 7), to accept lesser evils than the greatest catastrophe (argument 8), and to leave it to the experts (argument 10). The simple question of whether these policies are morally acceptable is set aside as inapplicable to the urgency of our political situation.[2]

Taken to its farthest conclusion, there is hardly any recipe more suited to the promotion of totalitarian and utterly immoral policies.

One could imagine an excellent case made out for the National Socialist policy of extermination of the Jewish people. You are invited to accept (no further questions asked) that the Jews are a mortal threat to our national wellbeing. The only way to defend our heritage is by their liquidation. Only financial experts can assess the magnitude of this threat, and members of the Party know how unavailing all attempts to resolve it otherwise have been. Experts in the transport of population groups know the proper techniques of management, others have studied the most humane and economical methods of extermination. National security requires top secrecy, lest the guilty race finds means of escape. Opposition to the policy must be at least suspect of treachery to the State. Given the initial setting of the problem, there is a hideous logic about everything that ensues.

The assumption throughout is that moral theory has nothing to say in political decision-making. Philosophy and theology are all very well in their place, but the practical man must get on with the business in hand, and with what works. The plea is as old as that encountered by Plato in his youth, that he should devote himself to practical affairs, not the pursuit of wisdom. Plato himself would have nothing to do with such a distinction. His ideal was that of the philospher king, the ruler trained in philosophy, judging in the light of the transcendent good. Whatever we may think of his solution, he exposed the pretence of the practical men that they themselves were taking no philosophical position; his men of affairs, Callicles and his friends, were taking in effect the position that might is right. There is indeed no line of action which does not embody some moral theory, or several confusedly mixed moral theories at once.

The assumption that the language of moral argument is clear

As soon as we engage in moral argument, however, we encounter language that has a specious clarity. Arguments on both sides of the debate are about actions, consequences, effects, circumstances and intentions. It is the common coinage of everyday moral discussion. 'It all depends on the consequences', 'on the circumstances', 'on your intentions'; we assume we know what we are talking about.

However, a little reflection will face us with all sorts of puzzles. War, or a policy of deterrence, are highly complex actions (or sets of actions) about which we ask deceptively simple questions concerning whether they are right or wrong. Yet even with the simplest actions puzzles arise. Where does an action end and its consequences begin? Consider the simple action of 'pulling a trigger', though even this might be broken down into 'flexing a finger' and 'exerting pressure'. I may be shooting someone, releasing a bomb-hatch, opening a catch on a tape-recorder. By itself, pulling a trigger seems innocuous enough, but what if I am doing so to murder someone? Even opening the tape-recorder could be the signal to an accomplice. In pulling the trigger, am I murdering, and if not then at what point does murder begin? Perhaps even earlier when I take aim or get into position?

We may say that the answer depends on the consequences of trigger-pulling, or the circumstances, or the intention. However, it is not clear what we mean by these phrases. Does the trigger-pulling remain itself innocent, whilst the consequences are evil, or the intention (but not the action) bad? Or is it that an otherwise innocent action is somehow rendered evil by the consequences (retrospectively!) or by the intention, whose influence on the action seems deeply mysterious? And what are to count as consequences? That a man was killed? But why not that the gun went off, and so a man was killed? Or that the gunpowder exploded, and so the gun went off, etc.? Where does an action end and the consequences begin? This may seem to be so much pettifogging, but unless we get clear about this language, our moral arguments head into confusion.

Action words.   The root of these puzzles lies in the way we speak of 'actions'. Moral judgements are about actions (and those who do them), but before ever we come to such judgements we must be clear what they are about. I shall try in this section to keep clear of the moral consideration as such.

When we use words like 'shooting', 'killing', 'building' and indeed any action words from the simplest, like 'scratching', to the most complex, like 'making war', we make a selection from observable events related to an agent and, from the need we have to refer often to that particular selection, we label those events with a single name or description. Events do not occur nor are they observed in isolation. They take their place in an historical continuum, and in space and within a world of subjects and objects themselves interrelated and having attributes. The selection of events is one we choose, and to that extent is arbitrary. It may suit our needs to select only a few events for the purpose of labelling with an action word, or for other needs a long stretch of events; 'scratching' is an example of the first, 'making war' of the second. Although our selection of events is arbitrary, their occurrence is not; they constitute the observable given.

Once we have chosen to label a set of events by an action word, that word may, and must, be used for any part (any single event) in the set of events. The reason for this is that, in using the chosen action word, we are no longer talking of any particular event in isolation but are naming it *in a context* with other events, antecedent and/or subsequent. A fanciful example, with invented words which have the advantage that they do not carry with them associations due to a common and confused usage, will illustrate this. We could imagine a society in which some craftsmen were concerned exclusively with laying foundations, others with building free-standing walls, others with building houses from the foundations upwards; and a very special guild of tradesmen building edificies complete with gas ovens for liquidating undesirables. These label their respective actions as 'spuffing' (laying foundations), 'spugging' (building free-standing walls), 'cragging' (building houses), and 'crovening' (erecting gas chembers). And for good measure, we will have a word for laying one brick beside another, 'bonging'.

We might be tempted to say that the 'croveners' in turn carried out the actions of 'bonging', 'spuffing', 'spugging' and 'cragging', but this would be incorrect. At every step they are 'crovening', and there is no point at which, having done with the earlier actions, they start in on 'crovening'. Every step taken in the context of events we have chosen to call 'crovening' must be said to be 'crovening'. Of course, had we chosen to use the word 'crovening' to label the installation of gas ovens in already built houses, that would be a different matter; then there would have been some 'cragging' done by themselves or others before they came to 'crovening'. But what we must not do when we use action words is to change their meaning in mid-stream; that will only land us in confusion. An action word names events not as taken in isolation, but as in a context of other events; and, according to the context in which we have named the event, so must it be called that action and no other. The unity of any given action depends on the context described. As the medievals said, *actus specificatur ab objecto,* which we may translate by saying that an action is what it is according to the context in which it is named.

To return now to the puzzles about 'trigger-pulling'. If we choose to name just the events of crooking a finger and applying pressure, then we may call them simply 'trigger-pulling'; but if we have chosen to speak of these same events in the context of others which make up 'shooting' then the trigger-pulling must itself be called 'shooting'; it is not simply 'trigger-pulling'. The action is specified by its object; the trigger-pulling is what it is according to the context in which we are speaking of it.

All too often in everyday use we oscillate, to our confusion, between one meaning of an action word and another. By 'bombing' we may refer simply to the action of dropping a bomb, and this could be to lighten our aircraft, to open up a quarry, or to destroy a city; but sometimes we refer, when we talk of 'bombing', to the whole stretch of events which includes dropping the bomb, destroying the city and everyone in it. Let us call this 'murder', using this word in a purely descriptive sense without importing into it any moral judgement. If we use 'bombing' in the second sense, equivalent to 'murder', then dropping the bomb is itself 'murder' and not just 'bombing' in the first sense. And if we are using 'bombing' in the second sense, it is confusing the issue to say, importing the first sense, 'I am only dropping a bomb, with unfortunate results.' We have to say, 'I am killing, or murdering.'

Fr Gerard Hughes, in a discussion of the morality of deterrence (Bridger, 1983, pp. 27–8), seems to me to illustrate the kind of confusion (with effects on his moral argument) which can arise in this connection. He writes:

Action-words pick out pieces of human behaviour as being of a certain type. Of course, we can do several *types* of things at once: we can make a contract, make someone happy and get married just by saying two words. Yet although in saying 'I do' a person might have performed all these actions, making a contract is not the same kind of action as making someone happy, nor is it the same *kind* of action as getting married . . . Very often what a person does is an *instance of several types* of action.[3] (my italics)

Now, to say that 'I do' is an *instance of several types or kinds* of action seems to me confusing. The only type or kind of which 'I do' is an instance is the set of 'I do' utterances. Taken by itself, 'I do' is simply the utterance of these words; taken in the context of other events, and depending on what events are selected for naming an action of which 'I do' is a part, it is either making a contract, or marrying, or making someone happy, but it is not all these things at once: it is one thing or another. If it sounds plausible to say that we can perform all these actions at once it is only because we seem to refer to one action by three different action words, but the definition of an action is determined by the context in which it is being referred to, and, since the contexts are different, it is not one action but three different actions.

Consequences.   Once we have understood how we use action words, the relation of consequences to actions falls more clearly into perspective. According to what selection of events we have chosen to label as a given action, so events will either be included in that action or they will fall outside it. If the action I am talking about is simply 'pulling a trigger' the events which follow or may follow – whether the gun going off, or a man falling dead – will be so many consequences of *that* action; but if the action I am speaking of is 'shooting' then the discharge of the gun is not a consequence of pulling the trigger; they are both involved in the action of 'shooting'. Consequences

of 'shooting' might be that a man fell dead, and I inherited a fortune. If the action I describe is 'murder' then the man's falling dead,
along with the trigger–pulling, are all murder; inheriting a fortune
would still be a consequence. What is important is that when we
speak of consequences we must be clear what we are referring to by
the use of any action word. This may seem obvious, but it needs saying. If I am using 'bombing' to mean simply the dropping of bombs,
the consequences may be the destruction of a military target and killing of citizens; but if by 'bombing' I mean dropping a bomb on a
populated military target, then these are not consequences but part of
the action of bombing; and I may not then change senses and say
bombing can be innocent enough because I could just be dropping
bombs, and what happens afterwards is none of my business.

Some consequences appear to be fortuitous, others inevitable.
That a child impetuously rushing out into the street should be killed
is a fortuitous consequence of my driving out. That innocent people
should be killed is the inevitable consequence of my dropping a
bomb on a city centre. And yet this is not absolutely inevitable; the
bomb might not explode, it might fall into marshy ground, the city
might have been evacuated. The consequence is probable, but not
inevitable. This being so, it seems better to distinguish between
those consequences which are reasonably foreseeable and those
which are not.

Proponents of the just war theory are in the habit of talking about
the *effects* of an action. There does not seem to me to be any important distinction between effects and consequences. I have written so
far as if any event subsequent to those events which may be named
as a given action could count as a consequence, but if we are to
speak of consequences there must be some causal link with the action.
If I go to bed and the sun rises next day, I could hardly call that a consequence of my going to bed, as I could the fact that I wake up
refreshed. Philosophers have been shy since the time of Hume of
talking about causes and effects but, whatever *analysis* we may give
of that relationship, it is one we cannot do without, as Hume himself
recognized. Perhaps it is simply that the formulation of the just war
theory antedates Hume. We could just as well talk of the principle of
double consequences, as of that of double effect.

The notion of 'circumstances'

One of the most troublesome expressions which occurs in moral
debate is 'that it depends on the circumstances' or 'in the circumstances' or 'in no circumstances'. It is troublesome because it can

mean any number of things. If people say they think a certain action is right 'given the circumstances' they may be referring to the consequences of the action, or to the balance of good versus bad consequences, or to the intention with which it is carried out or to some condition which, once fulfilled, will precipitate their action; the expression is so vague that it is best avoided. There is, however, one sense in which we may speak of the circumstances of an action which is at once more traditional and more exact. So far, in our analysis of action words, we have spoken of their being labels for a more or less extended *sequence* of events. But events, as we remarked earlier, take place not only in time, but in space and within a network of relationships. These are 'circumstances' immediately attendant on the events. We do indeed have special action words which incorporate such circumstances into a more comprehensively described action. I may kill my father in a sacred place and I can either say that the victim's being my father, or the sacred character of the place are circumstances of the killing, or are incorporated into the actions of 'parricide' and 'sacrilege'.

Intention.   One final strand in the tangle of words used in moral discussion needs to be considered. We so often speak of acting intentionally and intending certain consequences that we may not notice the difficulties. Anscombe has remarked:

From the seventeenth century till now what may be called Cartesian psychology has dominated the thought of philosophers and theologians. According to this psychology, an intention was an interior act of the mind which could be produced at will. Now, if intention is all important – as it is – in determining the goodness or badness of an action, then, on this theory of what intention is, a marvellous way offered itself of making any action lawful. You only had to 'direct your intention' in a suitable way. In practice this means making a little speech to yourself: 'What I mean to be doing is . . . ' (Anscombe, 1981, p. 58)

What this Cartesian theory of intention suggests is that whenever there is intentional action there are two things going on side by side: the overt action with its overt consequences, and a parallel interior action in which I am saying to myself, 'I am meaning to do this . . . I am intending those consequences.' A parallel to this theory of intention is one concerning meaning according to which when I speak significantly I am doing two things, talking, and (interiorly) meaning what I say. The trouble with both theories is that there is no way of explaining how the two parallel activities can be brought to bear on one another, to say nothing of the fact that the interior actions of thinking and meaning remain impenetrably private to the agent.

The truth is that neither meaning nor intending are actions going on 'in the head' of the agent. They are characteristics of the speech or the action in question. To act intentionally is to act in a certain way, just as to run fast is to run in a certain way (nobody would sup-. pose that besides the running there was something else going on which was speed). The characteristic of significant speech is that the words used are related syntactically, in a way that makes sense; the characteristic of intentional activity is that the events which make up the action are related as means to an end. The relating of one event to another (whether it be within the action or between the action and the consequences) is something about the way the action is performed, not something about a private mental process. Of course, to deny that intentional action is a matter of two processes, one of interior thought, the other of outward activity, is not to deny the possibility of 'mental acts'. But even with mental acts there must be something going on which has the characteristic of thoughtfulness, even though what is going on may not be outwardly observable. This is why it is perfectly possible to have intentions which are not carried into practice: the events within us are related as means to some end.[4] I may start by relating some events as means to another, but then relate it to some different event, or not relate it at all. These are all matters of how I am acting, not how I am on the one side acting and on the other making interior speeches to myself about my action. It is by reason of the means to end relationship that *intended* consequences have a kind of intimacy with any action we may consider.

This is a useful point at which to look back at some of the arguments used against nuclear war and deterrence. The 'just war' type of argument (1 and 6 above) takes for granted that we can say of some *actions* that they are right or wrong *in themselves,* that even actions good in themselves can be vitiated by evil *intended consequences,* and that in relation to *unintended but foreseeable consequences* we must take into account a 'balance' or 'proportion' between such consequences themselves, or such consequences and an intended consequence. The consideration of actions in themselves is abstract, to the extent that events do not occur in isolation but in a historical continuum and in a setting of place and relationships. To assess the morality of any action in the concrete it is therefore necessary to take into account not only the action itself but its intended and unintended foreseeable consequences (and circumstances). Unless an action is right in *all* these respects it is morally unacceptable.

For the utilitarians, however, there is no such thing as an action which is bad in itself, and they have little or nothing to say about any difference between intended and unintended consequences; for them an action is good or bad entirely according to what balance of good over bad consequences ensue. Arguments 2, 4 and 5 all focus on the consequences of nuclear war and deterrence, and are predominantly in a utilitarian mould. This is not to say that they do not bear weight with the proponents of 'just war' theory (since these are committed to consideration *inter alia* of consequences); but they will not be the only consideration, and, most importantly, no matter how greatly good consequences may outweight evil, they will not justify an action evil in itself, nor an intended evil consequence.

Of the remaining argument (3) about the incompatibility of love with cruelty, I will say no more than that it often appears in an emotivist form, where actions are not thought to be 'wrong in themselves' but are judged to be unacceptable in terms of the observer's preferences. But of the emotivist approach more will be said by Ian Thompson in the next chapter.

It is small wonder that the proponents of these various types of argument sometimes find themselves at cross-purposes.

Unspoken assumptions about moral theory

The concluding remarks of the previous section bring us face to face with the question of how different theories of morality affect the arguments used. We cannot assume that arguments which make sense against the background of one ethical theory will do so against another. One example must here suffice.

Broadly speaking, there are those for whom moral values are objective in some way or another. They are to be discovered, they are somehow in the nature of things. For the non-objectivist this is not so. As Mackie writes, 'Morality is not to be discovered but to be made' (1977). He 'invents' a moral system which will be valid in an 'institution': 'An institution will have rules or principles of action, or both, which participants will formulate fairly explicity, allow to guide their own actions, and infringements of which they will discourage and condemn.' The 'institution' may be as wide as mankind itself, its accepted rules arising from the needs of persons living together in their human predicament; but these rules are made by an updated social contract, and they may change with changing needs. There is of course something objective about this in that there are needs to be met according to the human predicament; but in the final resort the rules made to meet these needs are subjective and can be changed. For the moral objectivist it is 'the way things are' which dictates moral values; they cannot be changed, however much they may find different applications in different situations.

Perhaps such theory appears simply academic; but that the difference of ethical theory may have startling results is illustrated by one conclusion reached by Mackie. He says: 'Certain descriptions of actions (including "murder", "unjust judicial decisions" and "treachery") are such that actions that fall under these descriptions are *very nearly* out of the question . . . But *only nearly*; *regrettably such actions cannot be seen as completely out of the question*' (1977, p. 167, my italics). This is entirely honest, and consistent with his theory. Even more 'regrettably' it opens the floodgates to what may be permissible in any situation, and, for example, in war. Against the background of such an ethical theory it is difficult to see what conclusions could be reached which had anything in common with those of someone who, arguing against a different background, proposes a just war argument.

No one could expect to resolve, once and for all, the centuries-old controversies about ethical theory. But it may be useful to conclude this chapter by considering how it is that the just war argument, because of the presuppositions which it makes about moral theory, is at cross-purposes with other arguments in other traditions of thought, and how much parts of its argument, particularly its invoking a principle of proportionality between evils, or evil and good, operate quite differently when taken into other systems.

The just war argument developed in terms of an ethical theory which was teleological in character. It takes for granted that people in their actions fulfil or fail to fulfil their human nature; the good is whatever promotes this fulfilment, the evil whatever stands in its way. We must therefore have some idea of what it is to be human and the moral principles with which our actions should conform. But it may be worthwhile asking how we come by such principles, and whether in speaking of a conformity with principles we may not (as in the matter of intention) be subscribing to a Cartesian 'two world' theory, with principles in some abstract mental world, and actions in the everyday world in which we find ouselves. If that should be the case, we would relegate the moralist to making entirely general and abstract judgements, and would have to leave it to someone we might call a 'prudentialist' to decide whether a given action comes under this or that general principle. We would then say, as Fr Hughes says, that the moralist can speak of 'types of action' being right or wrong in themselves but we could not say that what a man has actually done is in itself right or wrong (Bridger, 1983, p. 28).

If this is so, the moralist becomes fairly irrelevant to the actual world in which we live. The alternative is to say, as I think Aristotle would say, for all his talk of principles, that our moral judgements bear upon contingent facts (*Nicomachean Ethics*, 1094, 1141-2).

Confronted with a given, and particular, action we say, 'This is right', or, 'This is wrong.' He recognizes in certain actions that they fulfil him as a human being, and in others that he is less than human. But this does not require that he first have an idea of what it is to be human with which to compare his action; rather he discovers his humanity by acting in certain ways, and his inhumanity by acting in other ways; much as when we take steps forward, we do not first have to think out a notion of 'forwardness' and then direct our steps accordingly, but in stepping forward we discover what it is to go forward.

At first sight this may seem to offer a kind of intuitionist ethic which claims to recognize in certain actions a quality of goodness (or humanity) and to put out of court any *argument* about what truly is good and human; whether, for example, it consists in pleasure or riches or a kind of practical wisdom. We would appear to have nothing to say against a man who *claimed,* for example, that in acting sadistically he discovered fulfilment as a human being. But the kind of answer we would give to such a man will itself show that our position is not simply intuitionist; we would invite him to consider when he acts sadistically whether this is compatible with his own continuing survival as the human being he knows himself to be, and we might point out to him that if others so acted he, as a human being, would be at risk. We could say that there was a contradiction between what he claims to be human action and what he knows himself as a human being to be. In short, our 'recognition' of humanity in certain actions and not in others is not simply a matter of intuition, but comes from a reasoned discussion of whether any particular action is compatible with or in contradiction of being human as we know ourselves already to be. Nor is it simply that the *consequences* of his action would threaten this humanity (as the second part of our reply to the sadist indicated) but that the very action itself puts his humanity at risk.

It is only when we have made judgements about particular actions (and I insist that moral judgement is in the first place about particular and contingent actions) that we can subsequently generalize on the basis of these judgements and formulate principles; only, for example, when we have judged this or that killing of innocent people (but not necessarily all killing) wrong that we can formulate a general principle that 'murder', meaning by this any killing of innocent people, is always wrong. We do not say murder is wrong, therefore this action is wrong, but rather, because this action is wrong, so any similar action is wrong.

If actions are wrong in themselves, no weighing-up of consequences, no balancing against 'a greater wrong', can make such actions morally acceptable. Here there can be no 'moral dilemmas'; we never *have* to choose between doing one of two actions evil *in themselves*: dilemmas appear when we consider the consequences of doing or not doing something. For the consequentialist, whose only criterion of the morality of an act is to be found in its consequences, these dilemmas are all-pervasive. For the teleologist, with the recognition of actions evil in themselves, there can be no choosing one or the other; both are out.

However, the teleologist must also take account of consequences; we are, after all, responsible not only for what we do but for the consequences of what we do. Yet here the distinction between intended consequences and those which, though foreseeable, are not intended, is cardinal. If a consequence is intended, and if intention is not simply a matter of making little speeches to oneself, but consists of the way we may be acting (relating an action as means to a consequence as end), the consequence is, by the intention, drawn into close association with the action, whether that action be the mental act of forming the intention or an outward action related as means to the consequence. This is why to intend evil is as immoral as to do evil. Here again there can be no choosing between two evils; for the just war theorist to hold nuclear weapons with the intention, in any circumstances, to use them is as much out as the using of them. The argument of a *Times* leader (19 October 1982) that the immorality of the intention to use nuclear weapons in extreme circumstances which we are sure will not arise is small by comparison with the certain benefits which accrue from a policy of deterrence, may make sense within a purely consequentialist ethic, but it cannot be permitted as an example of 'proportionality' invoked by just war theory. In actual nuclear planning the intention to fall back upon the most indiscriminate bombing if necessary, is built in; the intention is there, no matter how we may call it 'conditional', and no matter what we tell ourselves about the remoteness of the last resort. As such it must be ruled out on a just war theory. The only deterrence policy which might be acceptable is where there is *no intention* to use it. But deterrence which is simply bluff ceases to be credible.

We are left with those consequences which are not intended, but foreseeable. To the extent that they are foreseeable, we must be held responsible for them. But they are not linked by intention with our actions. Here at last, and here only, there enters 'proportionality'. Provided that our actions are good in themselves and provided that we intend no evil, we may have to accept that as a result of our actions such consequences happen. How this balance of the good with those evil consequences is struck must remain largely a matter of judgement; all we can say is that there are evils of such magnitude, and goods of such little importance, that everybody would recognize where the balance lay easily enough; but, as the contrast lessens, so is it more and more difficult to draw the line of demarcation.

In conclusion, a personal note may perhaps be allowed. On approaching the questions raised in this chapter, I found myself hesistant about the morality of a policy of nuclear deterrence although, like most Christians, I found no moral support for the actual use of nuclear weapons. But in the light of my conclusions I am now clear that no policy which includes any kind of intention to use these weapons can be morally acceptable. The decision between even a 'minimal' deterrent and surrender to an unscrupulous enemy determined to destroy our freedoms (to put it at its extreme) must be taken in terms of the consequences to which these two policies lead; we have to balance one set against the other. The risks of 'surrender' following political blackmail or even a direct attack for 'the enemy' remain static. But as time goes on, as nuclear weapons increase in force and number, as the arms race spirals upwards, and as negotiations stagnate, the consequences of a policy of deterrence grow ever more menacing, the risks ever greater. When the US Catholic Bishops accepted deterrence reluctantly (and, as I have suggested, on a basis which would make it very soon incredible), they gave notice that their acceptance could only be temporary, whilst alternative means of achieving peace were effectually explored. Perhaps the time is shorter than some imagine. We may have, in the name of morality, to take our courage in both hands. Christians at least have the advantage (as Duncan Forrester reminds us in the previous chapter) that their faith assures them that evil cannot in the long run prevail against the power of God, and the lesson of the Cross is that apparent surrender to the forces of evil becomes the moment of victory.

4

Questions of Method and Questions of Principle

Ian Thompson

The purpose of applying the tools of philosophical criticism to the issues of defence, deterrence and disarmament should be to elaborate rational methods of enquiry and criteria for distinguishing between truth and error, including the congruence or lack of congruence between theory and practice. This presupposes that rational debate about these matters is possible, permitted and is not being used by established interests to defend the *status quo*. It also requires that we recognize the different levels at which people may make appeal to moral arguments. For example, in any exchanges between the superpowers the arguments are complicated by fundamental ideological differences between 'capitalism' and 'communism', while within the Warsaw Pact or NATO alliance, questions of national sovereignty and autonomy play a part together with differences of state organization, party politics and pragmatic economic and military considerations. Within each country there are differences between the pro- and anti-nuclear factions, based on a wide range of religious, political, moral, economic and other partisan interests. Finally, at the personal level, individuals have to grapple with the question of their own moral standpoint on peace and justice, decisions about how to vote on defence policy and expenditure, whether to participate in military service or become conscientious objectors, where to work or where to invest their money. At each of these levels protagonists and antagonists appeal to moral and other arguments to justify their own actions and policies, or to criticize those of their opponents. There are clearly great obstacles to debating these issues in a reasonable manner in order to reach common understanding. Are we then faced with inevitable disagreement, irresolvable differences, a perennial Babel of confusion, or is there some possibility for rational negotiation to create structures which protect us from chaos and destruction?

Is a dialogue possible between different ideologies?

According to the political rhetoric of East–West diplomacy, the development, deployment and stockpiling of nuclear weapons (including the threat to use them if necessary) is justified for the western Alliance by the need to defend our liberal traditions and democratic institutions against ideological subversion by communism, or direct attack by the Soviet Union or Warsaw Pact countries, seeking to impose their repressive and authoritarian policies and totalitarian system of government on our societies. From this point of view it is sometimes said that we should be 'better dead than red!' Soviet ideology has a no less simplistic view of the capitalist threat. The assumptions underlying this rhetoric need to be questioned and challenged.

The fears behind the rhetoric need to be challenged too. This practical task, one for a kind of geo-political clinical psychology, is not unrelated to the theoretical question about the possibility of finding some rational basis for the critical examination of ideological differences. If we are to deal therapeutically with the pathology of political relationships contaminated by mutual fear, hostility and aggression, then we must have some faith that it is possible to reason together and negotiate on the basis of mutually agreed general principles. Philosophy cannot do all this on its own, any more than the creation of the United Nations Organisation (UNO) and the formulation of a Universal Declaration of Human Rights can guarantee world peace. However, both of them can make a contribution in clarifying the basis and framework of conditions within which peaceful negotiation can take place.

It is also pertinent to ask to what extent the labels applied by each side to the other and claims made for their own world views and social systems are accurate or justified. Are the 'liberal democracies' really liberal or democratic, and the communist states 'repressive' and 'totalitarian'? Alternatively, does 'socialism' or 'communism' achieve social justice in practice, and are 'capitalist' economies necessarily 'exploitative' and neglectful of the needs of the many for the profit of the few? The only way to answer these questions would appear to be if we could give a detailed and accurate description of the political and economic facts in each case, if we could make an impartial judgement about the consistency of theory and practice in each system, if we could stand outside the ideological assumptions of our own social system and reach some kind of independent viewpoint from which to judge different systems and ideologies. However, descriptions are not theory-neutral. The very way we select data for description and recognize their significance is informed by the theories and beliefs we already hold (though we may sometimes modify these in the light of new evidence). What are to count as 'facts' will be predetermined to some extent by the ideological presuppositions and previous historical experience which form our world view and provide the horizon within which we perceive things.

Philosophers of many different persuasions have believed that it was possible to provide an alternative independent and objective basis for the description and critique of ideologies and social systems. However, insofar as philosophers attempt to judge or criticize another ideology on the basis of their own self-styled neutral method, they are open to the allegation of unconscious bias or being captive to some other ideology. Marxist dialectic is supposed to provide the communist philosopher with 'objective' and 'scientific' tools for the critique of other ideologies; it leads to the argument that all variants of western philosophy since Kant are types of subjective idealism whose *raison d'être* is to provide directly or indirectly an apology for capitalism. Conversely, western analytic philosophers tend to represent the forms of logical and semantic analysis which they have developed in this century as ideologically neutral, and castigate Marxist philosophers as ideologists trapped in a closed system of scholastic defence of Marxist orthodoxy.

Is one driven inevitably by these arguments to a radical and sceptical relativism, or is there an alternative? In his somewhat pretentious-sounding 'Groundwork to the Metaphysic of Morals', Kant attempted to lay bare the constitutive and regulative principles of ethics (1949b). The result is interesting because, while it may appear empty and formal, it has universal application. He argued that the concept of person serves to define what we mean by a moral community and that respect for persons is the fundamental basis for the construction of a moral community and the rights of its members. However, without a principle of justice, a principle in terms of which we can universalize the demands of respect for persons, to secure if possible the rights of all persons, the first principle alone would not be sufficient. Furthermore, unless we recognize that not all persons are autonomous adults capable of defending their rights, that all people are at times highly vulnerable and in need of others to defend their rights, and unless we recognize a reciprocal duty to care, to do to others what we would have them do for us, the moral community cannot function so as to encourage the development and expression of the full human and rational potential of each person.

By logical argument Kant sought to demonstrate that an adequate ethical system requires at least three fundamental principles which qualify and reinforce each other, namely the principles of respect for persons, justice and beneficence (or duty to care). Kant's endeavours, while they may yield results that are purely formal, or may seem to end in a religion of pure reason, nevertheless have abiding value for philosophy for several different reasons: first, they represent a serious attempt to demonstrate the possibility of an answer to sceptical relativism in a form of analysis that lays bare the commonalities which underline ethical systems; second, he demonstrates his faith in reason by the example of his monumental efforts to bring order into an area of confusion and controversy; third, he points beyond mankind to a transcendent source of rational order and value in which faith alone can neutralize the destructive acid of scepticism and provide a methodological basis for the comparative study of ethical systems which avoids cynical relativism.

Vaihinger (1961) built on Kant's transcendental analysis a methodology which suggests a way by which we can sustain a faith in rational debate and enquiry about science and ethics without being forced to choose between absolutism and relativism. In effect, he suggests we can discipline ourselves to practise in relation to other ideological or belief systems what Coleridge called an imaginative 'suspension of disbelief'. This is only possible if our commitment to our own belief system is qualified by a recognition of its own limited and contingent nature with reference to the transcendent ground and source of truth and value.

From the standpoint of Christian theology or Christian ethics it is not possible to provide a genuinely independent critique of other belief systems or ideologies if we rest our case on a fundamentalist faith in the infallibility of Scripture or the Magisterium of the Church. Neither Scripture nor the teaching of the Church provides us with ready-made answers or a basis for unqualified endorsement or denunciation of capitalism or communism. The attitude of fundamentalists of all types, that they enjoy proprietorship of the truth, or that they enjoy a privileged God's-eye view in terms of which they may judge all other truths, has to be challenged on religious grounds: first of all as a type of crypto-idolatry (albeit in the name of Christ), and second as self-righteousness and intellectual arrogance.

What Christian ethics may learn from Kant – and Cusanus, as Tillich (1951, pp. 91 ff.) observed – is the wisdom of the *docta ignorantia* – the learned ignorance of those who recognize in the light of the genuinely transcendent the contingent and relative character of our empirical and rational structures of thought. In theological terms this means, if we believe that God is not just a fiction of our imagination but is really the ultimate ground of our being and source of all meaning in human life, if we believe that 'God was in

Christ reconciling the world to himself' (1 Corinthians 5.19), then the Cross really is a crucial criterion by which not only ideological and political systems must be judged, but also our formulations of Christian ethics and the structures of the Church. From this standpoint Christians do not claim to have privileged access to truth through possession of the Gospel, but claim rather that in faith they can have the courage to see all their beliefs and values brought under the judgement of the Cross.

By demonstrating the relativity and finitude, the partial and incomplete nature of all ideologies, Christian theology seeks to protect us from idolatry of all kinds with their associated forms of tyranny over people's minds and lives. By the same token it is possible for theology to draw attention to the fact that, while partial and limited in its view of things, each ideology may incorporate valid insights and emphasize complementary aspects of human experience, which we overlook at our peril. Christian ethics can thus serve a vital mediating role between contending ideologies, encouraging humility and tolerance, and perhaps creating the conditions for constructive dialogue and rational debate, where the fallibility of all theories and solutions will be recognized in the light of the transcendent Logos.

The dialectic which we require if we are to raise the debate above the level of mere rhetoric, propaganda and political demagoguery based on uncritical dogmatism or sceptical relativism resembles the dialectic proposed by Plato (Plato, 1960). This dialectic was based in the first place on a faith in a transcendent source of the good, the true and the beautiful. This faith made it possible for Socrates to adopt an attitude of agnosticism and critical detachment towards what we might call mankind's ideological and social constructs, creating the conditions for a rational examination of both. Christian ethics, rather than representing its own moral dogma as ultimate truth, should seek to transcend its own tendency towards self-righteous moralism in the name of a living truth which is genuinely transcendent and in a spirit of humility which recognizes that we do not have a monopoly of moral wisdom or insight into moral truth. Striving towards a 'trans-moral' Christian ethics (Tillich, 1963) should be our first task, and our first contribution to the nuclear debate.

Can we speak the truth in politics or government or pressure group activity?

If the first level at which the nuclear debate is conducted could be called the 'ideological', the second level of inter-governmental, national and local politics could be described as the 'political'. The difference here is that the 'political' debate tends to occur within the framework of accepted ideological positions and established state organization. Thus a majority of the public discussion of defence and disarmament takes place within the safe limits of established Party or sectarian dogma. Yet there is widespread cynicism about politics and politicians. It is almost a truism that you cannot trust what politicians say because they are preoccupied with the effect of what they say on the opposition or their own voters. The evasiveness of politicians when put under pressure by interviewers, the fact that politicians are seldom concerned with serious moral argument and their reluctance to accept criticism, reinforces the scepticism of the general public and undermines confidence in the rationality of the political process.

This pervasive mood of cynicism about political and moral debate and a rather pessimistic view of the efficacy of reason in dealing with human affairs lie behind the appeal of positivism as a philosophy and its prevailing influence on law, politics and morality since the First World War. The 'Boo–Hurrah' theory of value, which was popularized by positivist philosophy (Ayer, 1955) and more technically is described as the 'emotivist theory of value', appears to make eminent sense of mass behaviour: of the mass behaviour of people at a football match, where they alternately 'boo' or 'cheer' their opponents or heroes according to the run of play or resort to mindless violence if sufficiently provoked by alcohol or the opposition. The surge of patriotic feeling during and after the Falklands War illustrates the emotivist case that most people are ruled by emotions rather than reason, even in politics.

Before attempting a critique of emotivism we should consider how far attitudes found in the churches have encouraged the mood of irrationalism to which the 'Boo–Hurrah' theory appeals. Suspicion of human reason is deeply rooted in both the Protestant and Catholic traditions. The spiritual and moral dualism in Jansenist Catholicism and the fundamentalist Calvinist doctrine of total depravity, which represent deep undercurrents in popular Christian attitudes in Britain, hardly encourage faith in human reason or the rationality of the political process. Moral arguments on sex, marriage and politics in popular Christian ethics have been characterized more by their fundamentalist faith in the infallibility of Scripture or Papal pronouncements than appeal to reason (or even to Natural Law in the Catholic tradition). In practice, Christian attitudes have encouraged the view that moral beliefs relate to matters of faith, to intensely private feelings and convictions, and therefore belong to the private sphere.

This has reinforced the strand of subjectivism in ethics and politics. Emotivism marries very well with the view that moral beliefs and values belong entirely to the private sphere and are simply subjective or even arbitrary. If moral beliefs are simply expressions of subjective feelings and personal prejudice, then this leads to a dichotomy between the private and public spheres, and a divorce between morality and politics. This divorce is generally accepted in modern politics, and the 'pragmatism' or 'realism' claimed by politicians to justify their policies and actions is an attempt to rationalize the inchoate ethics of institutional and political life evacuated of traditional ethical principles. The view prevails that serious economic, military and political matters must either be left to 'the experts' or must be decided on 'realistic' and 'pragmatic' grounds by politicians in the light of the evidence.

This spirit of positivist philosophy engenders a style of politics concerned less with ultimate ends and the common good, and more with the pragmatic calculation of economic and military means to defend the *status quo*. It increasingly influences the law both in the civil and criminal spheres as well as internationally. There is a shift from reliance on an introspective psychology of intentions and motives (which are considered impalpable) to a behaviourist psychology of observable actions and events in determining guilt and punishment. Instead of belief that the common law rests on fundamental rational principles, natural law or inalienable human rights, all law is increasingly seen as statutory law, subject to the authority of sovereign parliaments or social contracts. International law, by the same token, is not seen to be based on universal moral and legal principles but rather to depend for its legitimacy on international conventions or agreements.

However, emotivism and positivism eventually collapse back into an arbitrariness and sceptical relativism which vitiate the very logic of those who use these arguments in an attempt to make sense of ethical and political debate. Unless they take for granted (as most do) the existing moral values and political consensus in society, or illicitly import ethical principles into the argument (by appeal to intuition or some concept of utility which masks other value assumptions), they cannot be a sufficient basis for ethics, law or politics. It is instructive to look more closely at the example of mass behaviour at a football match for, despite what the 'Boo–Hurrah' theory asserts, crowd behaviour is not simply arbitrary or irrational. Football hooliganism and drunkenness aside, crowd behaviour is reasonably predictable. The majority of football supporters have a deep love of the game, based on practical experience, knowledge of the rules and capabilities of players, and an appreciation of skill even in the opposition. The 'Boo–Hurrah' theory does not do justice even to football: to the skilled judgement and discrimination shown by a crowd in appreciation of a good competitive game, and frustration and disappointment at a bad game. The sense of outrage at some unfair decisions by the referee may well be expressed by supporters on both sides. All this points to the fact that, even in judgements about good or bad football, opinions are not just arbitrary or dictated by mass feeling, but rather that considerations of knowlege and skill, evidence and past experience inform arguments and give them at least a quasi-rational character. Supporters worldwide are capable of appreciating the brilliance of a Pelé, Cruyf or Keegan, and condemning the football violence at Brussels as incompatible with the spirit of the game. These judgements arise out of a complex universe of discourse in which knowledge and skills, facts and values, reasons and feelings play a part in rational judgement. Ethics and politics are not fundamentally dissimilar, but if the model of rationality required to understand football is complex it is certainly more so in these wider forms of human activity. Perhaps one of the chief weaknesses of rational theories applied to ethics and politics in the past has been that they have been too simplistic. 'Beware of the dreadful simplifiers,' warned Nietzsche (1955, Article 2, 24).

When philosophers, churchmen, or representatives of protest groups challenge politicians or military men to provide moral justification for the policy of nuclear deterrence, or challenge some of the well-worn clichés about the Soviet threat, a common response is the accusation that the peace movements are unwitting pawns in communist attempts to subvert western democracy and destabilize the NATO alliance. Alternatively they are dismissed as 'hopelessly naive and impractical', 'failing to grasp the complex military and political issues involved', or 'underrating the burden of responsibility carried by ministers and their military advisers in preventing war'. Some of this rhetoric is designed to smear the critics of NATO policy. However, part of the implied criticism may be justified.

In reality we may not have sufficient reliable or expert knowledge to make informed judgements, or to assess the wisdom of political decisions taken on our behalf without access to classified information. In practice we may be ignorant of crucial Cabinet decisions or consultations between governments. The complex interactions of intelligence-gathering, bureaucratic administration, political horse-trading, lobbying by the armaments manufacturing industries, pressure from the military establishment, investment from multinational companies and trade-offs with the superpowers or NATO allies, all in the context of domestic politics and national elections, mean that the models we seek to apply may indeed be so simplistic as to be either misleading or inappropriate. If these things are true then the protestations of politicians that they are not appreciated and understood are in part a response to the complexity of the political institutions within which they have to operate. There is some truth in the implicit criticism of philosophers and churchmen that they seek to apply the individualistic categories of personal morality to complex institutions and fail to understand the different rules and structures which govern them, or the difference between personal, professional and political responsibility. The reality of economic, military, and political power requires supra-personal categories for its interpretation and responsible deployment. Politicians and their moral critics may simply talk past one another to the extent that politicians are concerned with the pragmatics of power politics and moralists all too often with a narrow view of personal moral responsibility. This is not an argument for abandoning moral argument in the political sphere, but rather for developing an adequate political morality or ethics of power relations in institutional and political life.

If it is to be possible to speak the truth in politics, if we are to engage in a proper ethical examination of the nuclear debate, then we must find a way to restore public faith in the possibility of rational argument about politics and morals. The kind of rational dialectic which such ethical enquiry requires must first cut through the false rhetoric which bedevils any attempt at honest or critical examination of moral attitudes and moral assumptions. Next it must create the conditions of mutual trust, honesty and humility in which alone a constructive and cooperative search for truth can take place. Finally it must explore the actual dynamics of individual, social and political life and provide practical tests of the existential implications of policies.

Can ethics help us with personal moral dilemmas in the nuclear debate?

What do ethics or moral theory have to offer to those wrestling with real moral dilemmas; the individual facing military service, the civil servant handling sensitive information, the businessman attracted by profits in the armaments industry, or the housewife faced with the responsibility of protecting and caring for her children in the vicinity of a nuclear missile site?

Confronted with a real moral dilemma – that is, a real conflict of duties or conflicting moral demands of equal importance, *and* the necessity to make a decision – then there is little that an appeal to principles or moral theory can do to help, because, *ex hypothesi,* it is theoretical moral principles which are brought into conflict in the particular situation. We can only do one of two things: procrastinate and hope the dilemma will go away or resolve itself; or take direct action. Cutting the Gordian knot takes courage and a willingness to accept moral responsibility for a decision which may prove to be the wrong one. It can be creative and exemplary in that particular situation, but can never be generalized as a solution for everyone. Apart from the risk of wrong action, the benefit of courageous independent initiatives is that they may in some cases bring to light new knowledge or the possibility of new solutions which change the nature of the critical situation from dilemma to manageable problem.

It is very fashionable to talk of dilemmas in ethics and policies and it is easy to move from this to the demand for direct action. Armed with the sword of spirited conviction we launch forth to cut all the Gordian knots in sight. It becomes a touchstone of moral or political virility, of macho moral courage, that one is in the business of cutting through the 'dilemmas' of politics. But an attitude of moral arrogance, self-righteousness and naivety does little to resolve the complex problems of government in a modern state or find alternatives to the smug view that '[Nuclear weapons] cannot be disinvented; the only realistic course now available is to harness their existence to the service of peace in freedom, as NATO has done successfully for over thirty years' (Ministry of Defence, 1980). Even if everyone agreed that nuclear weapons were evil (and most people do), nevertheless any movement from the present situation to general or nuclear disarmament is enormously complex and difficult. The 'dilemmas' of politicians, paraphrased as the conflict of duties between their commitment to peace, and the responsibility to defend their country and allies, are real enough. While it would be wrong to make light of the 'dilemmas' of others, it is equally true that some may use the description of their problems as dilemmas as an excuse for inactivity.

In practice, few moral situations do present irresolvable moral dilemmas. They turn out on closer examination to be moral *problems*, not dilemmas: that is, situations where careful consideration of the evidence or analysis of the relative priority of different duties or principles does make a choice possible, however painful. Moral theory, of course, cannot be a substitute for practical moral experience. Personal commitment, motivation and ability to make difficult moral choices, authentic action, and willingness to accept personal responsibility for outcomes cannot be taught by courses in ethics, but are formed through experience. The value of moral theory or ethics is to counter irrationalism and capriciousness in individual behaviour and political life. It is fundamentally concerned with giving rational

coherence and intelligibility to our conduct and, by strengthening
our confidence in supra-personal rational criteria for debate about
moral and political action, creates the possibility for a common
universe of discourse and public negotiation about individual rights
and the common good, in terms of rational consensus about meanings
and values.

If we attempt a typology of popular moral positions the first point
to emphasize is that they occur within a context where the prevailing
atmosphere is anti-intellectual and sceptical and the agenda is set by
emotivism and for pragmatism. The result is that moral problems
are effectively reduced to practical problems and the value questions
set aside as imponderable or irrelevant. Nowhere is this more clearly
true than in thinking about nuclear deterrence and warfare. For
example, recollection of horrors of nuclear devastation caused 40
years ago by relatively small atomic bombs dropped on Hiroshima
and Nagasaki has strengthened the feeling of many that nuclear
weapons are an obscenity and insult to the human race, and that
nothing on earth could justify their use. From this point of view any
attempt to elaborate an ethics of nuclear war or even an ethics of
nuclear deterrence is *prima facie* absurd, strictly non-sense in human
terms, a kind of ethical self-contradiction in fact and in theory. This
is not the same as a simple moral condemnation of nuclear warfare.
It is the stronger claim that we cannot begin to talk meaningfully of
ethical categories applicable to nuclear warfare, for no conceivable
human values could justify the use of weapons which could obliterate
the human race and any past, present or future expression of human
values. From this standpoint, only tactical military considerations
can make sense of the production and deployment of nuclear
weapons, not moral arguments.

Another example is the way the just war doctrine has been used
pragmatically to construct an 'ethics of nuclear warfare', either
because people believe that limited nuclear war and limited survival
might be justified in extreme circumstances, or because they consider ethical principles are relevant to arguments about the means to
prevent nuclear war. What is interesting about this type of thinking
is that it tends to confuse prudential doctrine with principle, in the
name of 'practical realism'. The teaching about just war cannot
meaningfully be considered apart from the tradition of ethical and
legal principles to which it relates as an example of applied ethics or
prudential advice to those with political responsibility. It belongs to
the sphere of practical counsel and casuistry and cannot be elevated
into a statement of principle without confusing categories. It is this
kind of confusion which gives prudence a bad name. The virtue of
prudence, or practical wisdom, is not an end in itself but concerns

the necessary skill to apply general principles to choose the right means to achieve good ends (Aristotle, 1972). Prudence itself does not have the status of a principle and to confuse the two is to confuse means and ends. Without a principled basis, prudence becomes indistinguishable from cynical opportunism.

A typology of contemporary moral positions on nuclear defence

Given that there is something inherently odd or peculiar about attempts to elaborate an ethics of mass annihilation, it may be illuminating to consider the various positions in terms of a parallel with the solemn attempt in modern literature and existentialist philosophy to develop, for example, an 'ethics' of prostitution(!) or to discuss ethics from the standpoint of the 'outsider', whether that person be prostitute (Sartre, 1946), criminal (Genet, 1966; 1973) or resistance fighter (Sartre, 1946; Camus, 1954,; and Fanon, 1970). What these writers have in common is a disillusionment with or a contempt for traditional ethics, and in particular the analysis of moral theories. They are preoccupied instead with the meaning of personal commitment, motivation and ability to make practical moral choices, authenticity and integrity in moral action, and willingness to accept personal responsibility. These 'existential' aspects of moral life, which have in the past been the peculiar preserve of moral theology and the confessional, have in this secular and post-Christian era become the domain of existentialist philosophers and political radicals. The roles are strangely reversed. In the past it has been the role of Christian theology to challenge the formalism and empty rationalism of philosophical ethics – whether of the Classical or Enlightenment variety – and to attempt to fill out and give meaning to existential moral experience. Today Christian ethics finds itself challenged for its formalism or empty rationalism by passionately committed individuals and groups, and compelled to defend the rationality of ethics and universal validity of moral principles against the incipient irrationalism and anarchism of the quest for 'existential authenticity' or 'hard-headed political realism'.

In their quest for 'existential authenticity' and 'social realism' Sartre, Camus and Genet each explore the way certain individuals who live at the margins of society (and are commonly regarded as deviant, like the prostitute, criminal or resistance fighter) both provide by their unique life-styles a basis for the radical critique of bourgeois or conventional ethics, and serve as exemplars of individuals who are able to exist freely, and in their own terms authentically,

outside the constraints of ordinary society. The appeal of this
type of existentialist ethics is that it enables revolutionary or self-
styled 'radical' politicians to see themselves as standing above or
outside conventional morality, the arbiters of a higher, more authentic or realistic ethics.

Extrapolating from their analyses, we can distinguish four different moral postures, each with its own rationale: absolutism,
moral relativism, situation ethics and trans-moral ethics.

Absolutism

This is a position of outright condemnation (of prostitution or
nuclear war) as obscene, intrinsically evil and contrary to our
natural moral impulses and established moral principles. It has
become fashionable to decry absolutism and to contrast it
unfavourably with a utilitarian or pragmatic approach, which takes
account of the contingent demands of particular situations and complex practical problems. On the other hand the passionate and
unquestioning commitment of individuals and groups to absolute
moral principles (as in the case of radical pacifists) serves not only to
strengthen their resolve, but makes possible their uncompromising
courage and opposition to war, even in the face of torture. The
political impact of their witness cannot be underestimated and it is
undoubtedly more telling because it is not hedged about with prudent qualifications and practical compromises.

Whatever its strengths the absolutist position has several
weaknesses too. It creates a gap both logically and practically between moral theory and moral practice. The logical gap which cannot
be bridged satisfactorily is that between the unconditional demands
of the moral law and the contingent demands and conditions of
actual moral living with its risk, uncertainty and sometimes conflicting moral duties. If all moral principles are absolute then
discrimination between conflicting moral duties becomes impossible
and the distinction between grave and trivial moral evils without
meaning. In practice we have to exercise practical moral wisdom in
applying the demands of universal moral principles in particular
situations. The unconditional nature of moral principles as moral
principles means that they cannot be automatically applied to the
contingencies of every moral decision we face. We have to wrestle
with the practical questions of how we choose, in the light of our
principles, the right means to the right outcome, or the best means to
a good end. An absolutist ethics without the prudent consideration
of actual cases remains purely formal, as an ethics of prudence
without principles would degenerate into unscrupulous and

capricious opportunism. While uncompromising pacifism may have a signal value as a form of prophetic witness, its absolutism does not get us very far in dealing with how human conflicts are to be resolved or contained within reasonable limits.

Moral relativism

A radical approach based on moral relativism (namely, that the social mores of each group are valid only if understood as relative to the particular needs of each society and its norms) suggests that in order to understand prostitution or the issues of nuclear defence strategy it is necessary to consider these activities *sui generis*. We should not judge them by extrinsic moral principles, but should consider the inherent logic and values internal to these spheres of human activity. On this view each domain has its own 'ethics' – a set of norms and values proper to it – and must be understood in its own terms. We have from this point of view to start by recognizing prostitution and nuclear warfare as facts of life, accepting the inevitability of the tragic, and must seek to understand these forms of life for what they are.

Sartre, for example, in describing the milieu of the prostitute seeks to lay bare the network of both formal and informal rules which govern and give meaning to this sphere of human activity. The ethics of prostitution in these terms comprises not only the quasi-contractual relationship between prostitute and 'client', between pimp and prostitute as 'employer' and 'employee', and the 'codes of honour' among all involved in this subculture relative to one another, relative to the law, health authorities and the wider society, but also the complex ways in which the practice is justified by the participants with reference to conventional law and public morality.

A similar 'phenomenological' description might be attempted of the sphere of activity in which politicians and diplomats, arms manufacturers and military personnel are involved in complex negotiations about contracts, budgets, military manpower and material, arms control, foreign affairs and international relations. Although the complexity of this domain is of a different order of magnitude, it is the business of descriptive political science to explore it and to lay bare the rules and values which govern the different but overlapping 'language games' of politics, economics, military strategy, science and technology (Wittgenstein, 1958, I, 7 ff.).

Each of these subspheres has its own universe of discourse with its specialist jargon, professional values and etiquette, and skilled

experts. Each 'language game' or 'domain of activity' has its own constitutive and regulative principles. The Wittgensteinian metaphor of
the game is used here not to trivialize these often deadly serious activities, but to emphasize that these 'forms of life' are rule-governed
and each has its own norms and social mores. The positive challenge
of moral relativism with reference to the ethics of defence in the
nuclear age is that it impels us towards an accurate phenomenological description of the structures of power, rules and values which
govern communication and cooperation in complex institutions, and
determine the scope and limits of personal authority and responsibility of those working in the relevant spheres. It alerts us to the
dangers of assuming universal consensus or that common values are
applicable across all these different spheres of human activity, and
shows that the categories and forms of personal morality may not be
simply transferable to understanding the morality governing official
behaviour in complex institutions (Emmet, 1966; Downie, 1971).

We cannot simply apply our personalist ethics to professional, institutional and political life without an understanding of different
social roles and the nature and organization of power relations. An
ethics which prescinds from social analysis will not only fail to grasp
the relativities of different roles and their associated moral responsibilities, but will fail to make sense of institutional morality and the
nature of political power in both its positive and potentially destructive forms (Emmet, 1966). The very structures and forces which
make the state more powerful than the individual and capable of
conferring great benefits and protection also may provide the instruments for tyranny and oppression, the expression of institutionalized evil. In the case of nuclear defence the requirement is not
only a detailed knowledge of the history of the development of
policies which have justified the development and use of nuclear
weapons, but also a study of how past decisions and the institutionalized evil of systems based on a balance of terror have brought
us to our present impasse (see chapters 6 and 7 below).

Moral relativism should challenge us to an empirical study of the
rules and values which govern the different moral systems operating
in personal, professional, institutional and political life. By making
us aware of the complexities and relativities, the conflicting responsibilities and different priorities of different roles, it should make us
more tolerant, more able to face and accept the uncertainty and ambiguity of decision-making. However, if this encourages us to
become cynical, or to abrogate our moral responsibilities, then the
influence of moral relativism can only be destructive. If we jump
from an empirical study of the social mores of particular social
contexts to the conclusion that all moral values are relative (and

conclude, for example, that prostitution or threats of nuclear destruction are acceptable on their own terms), then we have compounded the moral confusion. Ethics must also be committed to the identification and study of the commonalities, the underlying principles which are 'presupposed by and necessary to ethics as such'.

Situation ethics

When Jean-Paul Sartre, a self-declared atheist, wrote 'La putain respectueuse' (1946), he was accused by an outraged establishment of not only sympathizing with the prostitute but of defiantly advocating a policy of immoralism. However, although part of his purpose was to give an unprejudiced picture of the prostitute's world, he was not so much concerned to create a new 'prostitute' morality as to use the dramatic analysis of 'the situation' to show up the deficiencies of a public morality based on conventional respectability bourgeois values and bad faith. While this and other similar plays were meant to shock, challenge and criticize conventional morality, their main purpose was to point out the inauthenticity of 'moral' behaviour based on the uncritical acceptance of externally imposed religious or moral laws, compared with the affirmation of one's own values in full personal freedom in the light of what is demanded by the situation.

Whether it is the prostitute or politician, criminal or resistance fighter who is the subject of analysis, the main burden of the existentialist message is the same; namely that traditional moral principles are based on the abstract analysis of human life and the quest for objective definitions in terms of essences when in reality, as Sartre insists, 'existence is prior to essence' (Sartre, 1956). An adequate framework for the moral life has to start with an existing subject in an actual situation, and explore inductively how values are discovered, affirmed and expressed by individuals acting on their own or freely interacting with other individuals in a given situation.

Sartre's ethics represents the two possible ways one might move in the attempt to derive appropriate values for living from an analysis of existential situations. The first involves the use of the outsider as an exemplar of a new kind of authentic moral action. The second drives Sartre towards Marxist sociology in an attempt to provide an alternative basis for the construction of values. The image of 'the outsider' who stands in lonely freedom outside the boundary of conventional morality, who must seek to act authentically in a situation without the security of given moral rules, who must freely choose personal values and act in good faith, is an image with considerable attractions for the romantic or for the politician who has to exercise awesome responsibility in lonely isolation. However, to the extent that such an individual sees himself or herself as exemplifying a higher kind of morality 'beyond good and evil' (Nietzsche, 1955), in terms of which conventional morality can be judged and found wanting, there is, as in the case of Nietzsche, the risk of delusions of grandeur and moral superiority of a dangerous kind. This 'higher morality' with its purported 'realism' and 'authenticity' can then easily become a new kind of absolutism with its own brand of intolerance and implicit totalitarian demands.

In contrast, the commonest stance of politicians who do not fall back on simple pragmatism in justifying their moral policies on deterrence, or arms control, is one which represents the more mundane imperative of situation ethics, namely, 'to act responsibly in the light of the demands of the situation'. What this can lead to Tony Carty demonstrates in his chapter on 'The Origins of the Doctrine of Deterrence' (Chapter 6, below). The situational analysis of the position of the Allies vis-à-vis Nazi Germany and the Axis Powers led to the abandonment of moral/legal conventions proscribing bombing of civilian targets and to advocacy of a policy of 'area bombardment'. This was justified on the basis that in a totalitarian state the distinction between civilian and military, between combatants and non-combatants, becomes meaningless. In a state organized for total war there are no innocents and, whether or not 'area bombardment' would succeed as a tactic (in creating panic and public pressure on enemy leaders to capitulate), the adoption of a strategy of 'total war' would be justified to meet such policies on the other side. The same thinking is now used to justify policies of nuclear deterrence. Situational analysis independent of, or thought to transcend, conventional moral and legal constraints, is the starting point for a terrifying 'logic' which runs from the justification of 'total war' against 'totalitarian tyrants' to the justification of recourse to nuclear weapons against 'the enemies of freedom and democracy', to preparations for uncontrollable nuclear war.

Trans-moral ethics: a constructive role for Christian ethics in the nuclear debate

It may seem paradoxical, in the light of arguments in the previous section, to conclude with a brief characterization of the critical and constructive role of Christian ethics in the nuclear debate as having the form of a type of 'trans-moral' ethics.

Starting with Jesus's attack, in the name of a gospel of truth and love, on the Pharisaic morality of self-righteousness and false guilt, Christian ethics has always been opposed in principle (if not in practice) to moralism, 'the morality of false guilt, the morality of taboos, of legalism, of sheer convention, of the domination of man from the outside, of spurious being' (Versfeld, 1972). To the extent that ordinary morality depends on human wisdom and social convention, and is moralistic in this sense, Christian ethics is necessarily 'trans-moral' in seeking to transcend conventional morality in the power of grace and a law of love. Grace and forgiveness alone make it possible to act with integrity and good faith; the inner law of love is not another set of rules and prescriptions but in the spirit of Augustine's 'love, and do as you like' creates the conditions for genuinely free and authentic moral action. The Christian faith goes beyond faith in an abstract principle and claims that the ultimate truth, transcendent principle, purpose and goal of history has been revealed in Jesus Christ, the divine word become flesh. In this it is necessarily 'trans-moral' both in principle and as a way of life. In a theological sense it is necessarily trans-moral in emphasizing the inability of human beings to achieve authentic moral living without the power of grace to transform people and society. However, it is also 'trans-moral' in several more formal senses which link it again to some of the deepest concerns of these other moral traditions.

Throughout this chapter we have argued that what is needed to deal adequately with the nuclear debate and the ethics of defence in all its aspects is a kind of moral dialectic which will enable us first to transcend the sterile polemic of conflicting ideologies; second, to cut through the rhetoric which bedevils any attempt at honest or critical discussion of moral attitudes and moral assumptions; and third, to address the personal moral dilemmas of individuals, not merely with a coherent framework of moral theory but with practical tests of the existential authenticity or moral action.

Christian ethics owes a great deal to reflection on the kind of moral dialectic developed by Plato in an attempt to deal with these three kinds of issues. Reflecting on the life and death of Socrates, his master, and through criticism of the sophists and politicians of his day, Plato developed a classical theory of ethics which still has some validity as a model for moral dialectic. Faced with the dogmatism of the experts and conflicting theories of the ideologues, Socrates professed a kind of agnosticism. His faith in the genuine transcendence of ultimate truth drove him to eschew and criticize an attitude which claimed proprietorship of the truth. His humility in the face of ultimate truth led him to practise a form of critical interrogation of the self-styled experts, designed to expose both the limitations of their knowledge and the inadequacy of their theories as well as their insincerity and deceit. The Socratic *elenchus* is not just a dispassionate analysis of ideas or refutation of arguments but; as

Kierkegaard appreciated, a passionate though indirect expression of
Socrates' commitment to truth (Kierkegaard, 1941a; Diem, 1959).
His desire was to convert people from falsehood and persuade them
to join him in a cooperative search for truth through an admission of
ignorance and humility based on recognition of error. The third and
final stage of this dialectic, the cooperative quest for the good, the
true and the beautiful, was not, as it is commonly represented,
merely an intellectual quest for union with that which is ultimate in
being and meaning, but the practical quest for virtue, authentic
moral life in harmony with truth, goodness and beauty as the essential forms of being itself, yet capable of being expressed in the real
world and political order.

Christian ethics has from the earliest time criticized Plato's moral
dialectic as placing too much confidence in human knowledge and
reason, and being too idealistic in failing to take seriously the reality
of sin in personal life and the structural forces of evil in society which
prevent people from leading the moral life they know they should
follow. As St Paul says in despair, 'The good that I would do I do
not, and the evil that I would not do, that I do!' (Romans 7.19).
However, while this criticism is important (and its implications
discussed more fully in the next chapter), the criticism is superficial
if it ignores the fact that Plato's teaching is set against the
background of the trial and death of Socrates at the hands of unjust
men, and Plato never promised anyone a rose garden, either in the
personal quest for virtue or in the struggle to overcome oligarchy
and tyranny and so establish a republic based on justice and truth.
Historically, the tendency in Christian ethics has all too often been
to take refuge, in the face of the moral and political evil in the world,
in an other-worldly puritanism and piety which is apolitical and
disengaged from the real world. Paradoxically it also leads to the
attempted enforcement on others of a narrow and bigoted moralism,
the irrational antithesis of an ethic of love and grace.

Nietzsche, the disillusioned son of a Lutheran pastor and victim of
syphilis, demands in the name of truth and morality a 'transvaluation of all values'. He challenges the anaemic and gutless love of
Christians and the hypocritical morality of the churches by a
glorification of erotic love and the Dionysian dimensions of human
life (Nietzsche, 1967). His recognition of the 'will-to-power' as the
dominant force in human life, individual and political, not only
demands a different kind of analysis of ethics and politics, but also
demands the transvaluation of all values in the light of a new kind of
ontology, based on a fundamental recognition of the importance of
power, and mankind's will-to-power in particular. Nietzsche
demands that ethics should transcend religious moralism and should

go 'beyond good and evil' as narrowly conceived by bourgeois society. This self-consciously post-Christian 'trans-moral ethics' attempts to provide the kind of analysis in terms of which it is possible to transcend ideological differences and the empty rhetoric of moralism towards a more realistic and practical ethics where inter-personal and political power relations are taken seriously. His analysis of power is more radical and ultimately more helpful (for all its romantic iconoclasm) than the radical individualism of the existentialists.

We have seen that there are dangerous totalitarian tendencies implicit in the various post-Christian forms of ethics which purport to transcend conventional morality, or to go 'beyond good and evil'. The claim to privileged access to truth, whether it be of the self-styled expert, or the 'higher morality' of the outsider, or the 'non-ideological' truth of Marxism, has led historically to a variety of forms of tyranny and political despotism in the past and fascist and communist police states in this century. So how can we have the temerity to suggest that Christian ethics can be 'trans-moral' and avoid these perversions of truth and justice, particularly when the history of the Church has not been without its expressions of religious tyranny? The paradox is that, while we believe the ultimate truth to have been revealed in Christ, we cannot as Christians claim *proprietorship* of the truth without reducing our Christ to an idol, without pretending that any finite and incomplete expression of Christian truth is identical with the Divine Word itself. If for this reason, as both Protestant and Catholic traditions can affirm, the Church is always *ecclesia semper reformanda,* then the same applies to Christian ethics. Christian ethics can seek always to be informed by and to embody in its practice the love and grace of God manifested in Jesus Christ, but it always stands under the judgement of the same Christ.

This theological perspective makes it possible in principle for the Christian to adopt a role which is both catholic and eirenic. It is catholic in recognizing and being able to affirm, each within its own terms, the validity of other belief and value systems, recognizing each ideology as the expression of mankind's painful quest for identity and meaning. It is able to emphasize what is positive and what may be learned from each ideology but, in the light of the Gospel and its transcendent source of truth and meaning, can point to the dangers which follow from elevating the relative and finite to ultimacy in human life and social organization. The Christian critique of ideologies is ultimately a critique of various forms of idolatry and the dehumanizing consequences which follow from unconditional and totalitarian claims being made for any ideology.

Conclusion

Attempting to assess not only the weaknesses but the strengths of other moral positions, as I have attempted to do here, will be an important part of the dialectic of a trans-moral Christian ethics, for this is not only a requirement of truthfulness but a prerequisite of any dialogue with representatives of other systems and ideologies.

Absolutism tends to foreclose the possibility of dialogue and, while the sincerity, courage and uncompromising stand of principled opposition may have value as a form of prophetic protest, it does not lead very far in negotiation nor does it give much help in the practical exercise of moral and political responsibility in complex situations, or where we face *prima facie* conflicts of duties. The prophetic protest needs to be qualified by the responsibilities of mediation and intercession (the priestly role) and the acceptance of a responsibility for others (the kingly role). Absolutism without prudence is empty and formal, just as casuistic prudence without principle is blind. The role of just war doctrines in providing some basis for international conventions and political responsibility for the protection of others must be recognized, but they need to be qualified by a respect for ultimate principles or their application can degenerate into mere pragmatism.

Ethical relativism provides a basis for tolerance, for the critique of dogmatism and empty rhetoric. However, without confidence in reason or transcendent values, it can easily engender despair of ethics as such, and lead to scepticism and subjectivism on the one hand or cynical 'positivism' or *realpolitik* on the other.

An incarnational Christianity can affirm much of what situation ethics says, for situation ethics emphasizes the need to be faithful to the demands of the actual situation, the need to evaluate principles, means and ends or consequences in the light of *real experience* rather than *a priori* preconceptions. It also stresses the need for sincerity, honesty and integrity in the authentic exercise of freedom and responsibility, not in slavish duty to externally opposed authority or obedience to superiors, but in fidelity to one's own humanity and others. The risk of wilful self-assertiveness and arbitrary and capricious affirmation of one's own personal will-to-power or will-to-self-fulfilment at the expense of others may result, however, from the denial of universal moral imperatives.

Ultimately, while the distortions of trans-moral ethics in the morality of the terrorist or fascist 'super-man', who sees himself and his cause as being 'beyond good and evil', cannot be accepted as legitimate (because of their self-contradictory existential consequences and inhuman political applications), nevertheless the challenge of the whole nuclear debate is to find a genuinely transcendent basis from which to develop a trans-moral critique of all systems and a foundation for a constructive dialogue about the nature and destiny of mankind.

Christian ethics, if it is to be adequate to its task, must comprise the following parts:

1 It must develop a philosophical and theological analysis of ideologies in terms of which it can perform both a critical and mediating role in the contemporary world, and in particular in the conflict of the superpowers.
2 It can learn much from classical and contemporary philosophy of the nature and forms of rhetoric used in moral and political debate, and must develop a moral dialectic which can cut through the rhetoric of popular moral and political debate, bringing 'trans-moral' consideration of transcendent values to bear on the moralisms of the day.
3 It must also develop an analysis of authentic moral action, an in-depth understanding of situations where moral responsibility is exercised in practice and an existential dialectic which makes possible the demonstration of consistency and contradictions between moral practice and the demands of a fully human life.
4 It must take the Incarnation seriously, which means among other things being willing to learn from secular sources the revelance of history, sociology and economics to an understanding of power relations and the development of an ethics which can do justice to the complexity of political life in the nuclear age.
5 Ultimately Christian ethics must develop a new anthropology and a new ontology if it is to escape from the pietistic and individualistic ethics of the past and is to develop a political ethics which will be taken seriously in the modern world.

In all this, Christian ethics can be principled *and* eclectic. It can be fundamentally committed to the possibility of a rational and objective system of moral principles, must defend the rationality of ethics, and demonstrate by example its commitment to rational negotiation about values but, in the light of faith in the Divine Word 'which enlightens every man that comes into the world' (John 1.9), it can in humility learn even from those we regard as hostile.

5

Liberal Values and Power Politics

Ian Thompson

The liberal model of democracy, based on the possibility of open rational debate about ethics and politics, presupposes a broad consensus about fundamental values if democracy is to work. Polarization of ideological standpoints, internal tensions created by racial or cultural pluralism or deep social class divisions, or major differences in educational standard or economic power, can all threaten genuine democratic government. Alternatively, societies with such deep divisions may adopt the outward forms and rhetorical expressions of liberal democracy while in fact remaining oligarchies, dominated either by traditional land barons, a wealthy ruling class or the military. The question central to this chapter, and this book, is whether the centralization and concentration of executive military and political power which is necessary to achieve control over manpower and economic resources, in preparation for possible nuclear war, is compatible with the maintenance of a free democratic society. It calls for careful study of both liberal humanism and institutions built on liberal values.

What do we mean by 'liberal values'?

In the context of our previous discussion of ideologies, as belief systems which serve to define the identity of mankind and forms of social organization in terms of certain fundamental human values, liberal humanism is also an ideology. It is not some neutral, rational and objective philosophy which embodies all that is essentially human, or which gives privileged insight into the human condition in terms of which all other ideologies can be judged and found wanting. Whatever its strengths and weaknesses, liberal humanism is the product of a particular history and culture with roots in both classical humanism and Judaeo-Christian religion. Its modern form has been shaped by the scientific and cultural developments associated with the Renaissance, Reformation and Enlightenment on the one hand and the socio-economic changes represented in the transition from feudal society to the bourgeois culture of Renaissance city states, and from emergent sovereign national states to the political economies created by the industrial revolution. Liberal humanism, as an ideology, embodies both a doctrine of mankind (anthropology) and a doctrine of the nature of society and culture (or sociology) in terms of which it seeks to derive its fundamental values. What it does not make explicit, however, is its doctrine of the nature of ultimate reality (or ontology) on which its anthropology and sociology rest, and herein lie some of the ambiguities and contradictions in the liberal tradition.

Broadly speaking, liberal humanism stands for a doctrine of mankind based on belief in human autonomy, that human beings are capable of responsible free action; belief in their essential rationality, that they are capable of intelligent solutions to their own problems; and belief in human rights grounded in an objective moral law, that mankind is subject to the imperatives implied in human nature as such. The sociological doctrine of liberal humanism finds its ideal form in capitalism, a civilization based upon faith in the self-sufficiency of the human and finite world and directed towards the establishment of human control over the world of nature and mind. These summary definitions need to be justified and their historical sources documented and explored. However, the main purpose of this chapter is to explore the strengths and weaknesses of its fundamental conceptions as providing a value-base for the ethics of defence and to consider the underlying reasons for the lack of confidence in liberal humanism as a basis for dealing with the moral and political issues surrounding nuclear weapons. We shall explore whether a Christian reinterpretation of the values of the liberal tradition can provide pointers towards a constructive political ethics, with a wider and more universal appeal than bourgeois liberalism.

Traditional doctrines of mankind and theories of knowledge were developed within the framework of assumptions about the nature of being and cosmos, provided either by Greek metaphysics or the Judaeo-Christian doctrine of creation. In the medieval doctrine of mankind, reason was analysed into two distinct but complementary parts: 'ratio' or that aspect of reason concerned with the calculation of means and consequences, and 'intellectus' or that faculty concerned with contemplation of being itself and reflection on the proper ends of human life (Pieper, 1952). The modern liberal doctrine of mankind rests, however, on a rationalistic conception of reason which grew out of Cartesian philosophy and Galilean science. It is a conception of reason which prescinds from ontology: it seeks to develop a theory of knowledge and values derived from reason itself rather than given structures of being or the essential nature of mankind. Similarly, its conception of society is rooted in a pragmatic doctrine of social contract, rather than an ontologically-based doctrine of natural law, and it is organized to serve broadly utilitarian ends (Maritain, 1964; 1974). The State exists to create the conditions in which people can exercise their rights as autonomous rational beings, by securing external peace and internal law and order. The State becomes distinguished from society as the concept of hierarchical order of being reflected in the natural orders of society but united in a sacramental community breaks down. It is replaced by the conception of society as an aggregate of rationally self-sufficient individuals, requiring some kind of supra-personal rational authority to ensure the operation of the social contract.

Kant has been said to stand in relation to the Protestant tradition in a position analogous to Aquinas in the Catholic tradition. If the latter summed up the philosophical and theological tradition of the Middle Ages, Kant summed up the philosophical and moral tradition of post-Reformation Enlightenment culture (Ritschl, 1900). We pointed out in the previous chapter that Kant provided a purely formal and abstract analysis of the constitutive and regulative principles of ethics as such. From this deductive analysis, which purports to derive these principles from the constitution of practical reason as such, we can derive the three universal principles of respect for persons, justice and beneficence. (US Department of Health, Education and Welfare, 1978; Beauchamp and Childress, 1979.) These moral principles are capable of being derived historically from other sources, as the duty to care (do as you would be done by) can be traced back to the Code of Hammurabi or the Old Testament, or the concept of justice to Greek philosophy or Roman law, or the concept of respect for persons to the Christian doctrine of the infinite value of each person in the sight of God. However, the distinctive feature of Kant's ethics is that he attempts to provide a purely logical or rational argument for the interdependence of the various categorical imperatives of ethics, which we have translated in this form. Whether these three principles can be derived logically from the nature of practical reason as such, or whether his analysis of practical reason happens to reflect intuitively the evolved consensus of liberal ethics in the eighteenth century, is open to debate. Kant, like Rousseau and the fathers of the American Constitution, saw himself as the spokesman for a new international order based on the rule of reason and the possibility of a universal bill of rights. His 'Essay on Perpetual Peace' (Kant, 1949a) and speculations about the possibility of world government are among the lineal ancestors of the institutions of the League of Nations and the UN. The UN Universal Declaration of Human Rights might well be taken as the supreme expression of the faith of the liberal tradition in the autonomy of mankind, and the efficacy of reason to create structures and institutions based on a recognition of universal human rights which will safeguard world peace. It, and the UN Organisation, stand as a monument to the liberal tradition and the possibility of human cooperation to achieve respect for personal rights, justice and peace.

Liberal humanism is a kind of step-child of successive marriages and divorces between medieval Catholicism and classical culture and Protestantism and post-Renaissance culture. Not surprisingly, both Catholic and Protestant traditions are deeply ambivalent towards liberalism. The former is suspicious of liberalism because of its historical links with anti-religious scepticism and anti-clericalism. At a deeper level, Catholic traditions of law and ethics based on the doctrine of natural law see these undermined by the nominalism of the liberal tradition. For instance, the abstract conception of the State does not provide an adequate context for the realization and expression of the living, organic, sacramental community with reciprocal rights and duties (Maritain, 1972). Protestant criticism of liberal humanism tends to focus on its rationalism, its unqualified belief in the self-sufficiency of finite human reason, its uncritical assumption of the essential goodness of mankind and consequently naive faith in human freedom and autonomy. For example, the Calvinist doctrines of total depravity, predestination and original sin challenge respectively the rationalist conception of pure reason by suggesting that reason itself is depraved, that human freedom is limited by divine predestination of individuals to salvation or damnation, and that original sin calls in question either the possibility of deriving adequate ethical values from reflection on mankind's essential nature or the possibility of the construction of a liberal utopia as a rational kingdom of ends.

Thus, while Christians would want to endorse the values and perhaps defend the institutions of liberal democracy, they would nevertheless be disinclined on theological and moral grounds to give either unqualified endorsement to the values of liberal humanism or unconditional commitment to defend our present institutions or way of life in western society. In fact a theological and ethical critique of liberal values and democratic institutions might well borrow insights, for example, from Marx in his critique of capitalist economy, or from other critics of the latent bellicism and imperialism of modern technical and industrial societies (Meszaros, 1970). In the nuclear debate, Christians often find themselves not siding unambiguously with either side, and certainly not believing that the West has a monopoly of moral righteousness or the East alone a record of exploitation and oppression.

The strengths and weaknesses of the liberal tradition

The strength and appeal of the liberal doctrine of mankind is based on its optimistic view of human nature and the belief that we can exercise our (God-given) freedom and intelligence to deal with moral and political problems in the light of reason and an understanding of the conditions that are necessary for human flourishing. However naive or realistic this optimism is in practice will depend on how effectively liberalism can deal both in theory and in economic and political practice with the countervailing forces of historical necessity, institutionalized power, and the limitations of human self-insight and the anti-rational forces in human life.

Much of what we associate with modern society has been both the practical expression of the values of secular liberal humanism and the result of applying scientific intelligence to the solution of human problems. Given the spectacular and incremental progress in science and technology in the past 300 years we have tended confidently to expect that the application of the same kind of scientific intelligence to the study of mankind, in psychology and anthropology, sociology and political science, would result in similar progress towards a more just and peaceful world. However, there have been more millions of people killed and more tens of millions dying of starvation, and proportionately more revolutions and wars in this than in any previous century. Does this mean there is something deficient in scientific intelligence or the liberal doctrine of mankind as an autonomous rational being?

Part of the problem may lie in the conception of reason underlying the modern quest for the liberal utopia. As remarked earlier, in the medieval doctrine of mankind, 'ratio' is subordinated to 'intellectus' in a conception of reason in which what Tillich has called 'technical' and 'ontological' reason (Tillich, 1951, I, p. 80 ff.) are seen as complementary to one another, and rooted in an awareness of the transcendent ground of meaning and value in what he calls the 'depth of reason'. In the liberal doctrine of mankind, 'ratio' or dominative critical reason which is concerned with calculating the means to satisfy human need (and greed) comes to take precedence over (or even to replace) 'intellectus', the reflective and contemplative intellect which is concerned with the common good and the ultimate ends of human life. The links between the liberal doctrine of reason and utilitarianism are not accidental. The rejection of a super-natural or metaphysical source of meaning and value in human life, in both rationalism and empiricism, and the attempt to find this either in the inherent structures of reason itself or the social contracts fabricated by the conventions of autonomous rational beings, leads inevitably from Descartes and Locke to the utilitarianism of Bentham and Mill.

Without an ontological basis for ethical values there is no way of clearly distinguishing between 'the common need' and 'the common good'. Just as Mill's utilitarianism has to presuppose some pre-existent social consensus about the proper ends of human life, and Kant has to appeal to the rational intuition of moral duties, both systems in practice depend upon, and are parasitic upon, a consensus rooted in the precepts of natural law in classical philosophy and Christian ethics. As long as this consensus lasts the investment of Christian culture provides a credit balance which can be drawn on, but when that is exhausted and the consensus is challenged or broken, in the clash with other cultures and secular ideologies, there is nothing left of liberal ethics but neo-intuitionist theories or naked utilitarianism. If the definition of the common good is not rooted in objective values derived from reflection on the given nature of mankind and the necessary conditions for us to realize our potential humanity and for human society to be humane, then in practice the definition of 'human rights' and 'the greatest happiness for the greatest number' becomes a calculus of utility where 'human needs' and the 'ends' sought are defined by those with the autonomy and power to determine the outcome of particular policies or actions (Pieper, 1952). The seductive attraction of this position, as Ayer pointed out (Ayer, 1955), is that it suggests that moral decisions resolve themselves into questions of fact to be decided by appropriate scientific experts, rather than facing the troublesome question of values and how we are to define the common good.

On the other hand, some of the weaknesses of the optimistic liberal doctrine of mankind may lie precisely in the view of humans as autonomous rational beings. The Christian tradition has always challenged idealistic rationalism on the basis of its failure to account adequately for the phenomenon of evil in mankind and human society or to do justice to actual power relations between people and in politics. Calvin and Luther, for example, were not simply giving expression to an anti-intellectual doctrine of faith based on super-natural grace alone, nor were they simply expressing their own hostility to rationalism (for both respected reason and science). Rather, they were concerned to emphasize the irrational forces that are at war in mankind and society, the destructive forces at work in the human personality and the body politic, which are inimical to a rational order of justice and peace, and which reason alone is impotent to exorcise or even to control (Tillich, 1968).

In practice, liberalism has recognized that pragmatic measures, like the division of powers between legislature, executive and judiciary, are necessary to prevent the powerful exploiting the weak. The liberal ideal is to transpose to the global level the same tripartite division of powers of government which has appeared to work in democratic societies to prevent the worst exesses or abuse of politicial power. The UN General Assembly, Security Council, International Court of Human Rights and the UN Peace-keeping Forces are supposed to represent at global level the legislature, executive and judicial powers of world government. It is currently fashionable to be cynical about UNO, to regard it as an expensive 'talking shop' without real authority or power. Part of this is no doubt due to the failure of UNO to prevent the numerous wars which have taken place since 1945, to control the political and military adventures of the superpowers or to control the spread of international terrorism. This in turn has no doubt been due to a lack of political will to make a system of global government work. Lack of financial resources and realistic executive and military power to perform its international peace-keeping role has undoubtedly made the liberal model virtually unworkable at international level. Nevertheless, the achievements of UNO have not been inconsiderable, even in the role of international policeman, negotiator, peace-keeper and watch-dog on human rights violations. The mechanism of Security Council diplomatic contact between the superpowers has arguably made at least as great a contribution to keeping the peace in the last 40 years as the much-vaunted nuclear deterrent.

However, it may be seriously questioned whether the liberal model can be made to work at international level. Some would see it as a pragmatic question to be solved by finding the right kinds of checks and balances in national and international politics, giving greater force and authority to international law, or ensuring that UNO has 'real teeth'. Others would see it more pessimistically as a question of ineradicable evil and depravity in mankind and human society. The reality of institutionalized greed and self–interest, institutionalized exploitation and violence does point up a major weakness in liberalism. Nevertheless, the pessimism of those who despair of the destructive forces in human society can be answered by a Christian faith which affirms and endorses liberal values with the appropriate qualifications based on a recognition that mankind is not self-sufficient, that reason alone is not enough, and that human rights need to be grounded in something more objective than either utility or subjective intuition.

One of the strengths of the liberal tradition is that it gives confidence in the possibility of inter-personal or trans-cultural moral consensus. In practice, although we may have difficulties sometimes in translating values across cultures, as we also have difficulty interpreting or translating from one language into another, nevertheless we do manage to express ourselves to one another and achieve some measure of mutual understanding. Inter-translatability of different languages is made possible because, beneath their surface differences, languages show common structural features of their 'deep grammar'. By analogy it might be argued, as both the natural law and liberal rationalist traditions argue, different systems of morality and social mores display on the surface the same bewildering variety of rules and taboos, but share certain common and universal features, which it is the particular task of philosophy to study and bring to light (US Department of Health, Education and Welfare, 1978, Beauchamp and Childress, 1979). The classical natural law tradition sees the ultimate common ground of meaning and value to be ontological, that is based on the given (or created) nature of being, and moral principles to express the necessary and sufficient conditions for us to achieve fulfilment of our being. The liberal rationalist tradition sees common human values and universal moral principles to be rooted in the inherent nature of reason and the requirements for people to lead fulfilled lives as rational beings. In both traditions the three-fold functions of philosophical dialectic are: to build moral consensus by eliciting awareness of these deeper commonalities; to articulate these common values and underlying principles; and to create the conditions which will sustain human understanding and cooperation.

As we have already observed, Kant provided a kind of formal and rational analysis in terms of which he sought to demonstrate that respect for persons, justice and beneficence are universal principles presupposed by and necessary to any coherent system of ethics. There is a growing consensus in comparative ethics that, while different societies may emphasize each of these three principles to different degrees, virtually all known systems of social morality incorporate respect for persons, justice and beneficence in some form or combination (Veatch, 1981). In fact the history of ethics illustrates that the principles complement and mutually presuppose one another, for to emphasize one to the exclusion of the others has often had disastrous consequences. In family life, in the tribe or in the traditional professions, where beneficence or the duty to care is recognized as the supreme duty of the responsible head, and respect and obedience the duty of those in subject positions, the whole system tends to be patronizing and dependency-creating at best and authoritarian at worst, unless qualified by the demands of justice and respect for persons. In democratic and libertarian societies where primary emphasis is given to personal rights and individual autonomy, in practice the weaker go to the wall and are patronized by philanthropic beneficence, unless adequate emphasis is given to the demands of social justice. Similarly many would see socialist societies, preoccupied with social justice and equality and the attempt to exercise beneficent control for the common good, as leading in practice to limitations being placed on the liberties of citizens and even the denial of fundamental human rights unless the system is balanced by proper respect for persons and their inherent human dignity.

Even granted that ideally a balanced system of ethics requires these three principles to be held in balance, there will be an unlimited number of different ways in which they can be combined and emphasized in different social systems and ideologies. We cannot simply say that one is right and another is wrong. For this reason, direct ethical criticism of other cultures and social systems tends to prejudge issues and miss the point of particular systems. For example, to maintain that Soviet communism in general shows no respect for individuals and their rights (because of its treatment of well-known dissidents) fails to understand how the organization of communist society *is* supposed to protect human rights and promote the wellbeing of its citizens. Similarly, to argue that capitalist societies are built on social injustice and exploitation of the working classes fails to recognize how democracies and free market economies are supposed to work to promote the common good, even though in practice they may be dominated by rich powerful minorities. Christ's words remain true of all ethical and social systems: 'By their fruits ye shall know them' (Matthew 7.16). While all societies fall short even of the ideals they set themselves, and some societies are palpably responsible for more suffering, persecution and oppression than others, it is also true that there is more concrete common ground between East and West, North and South than is apparent from the polarized nature of present political rhetoric.

If we examine the types of *moral* justification given by ministers of state within the western Alliance for the policy of nuclear deterrence, it is usually in terms of their duty to protect society from external threats (real or imagined) or possible internal subversion. For example, the Truman Doctrine: 'I believe that it must be the policy of the United States to support free peoples who are resisting attempted aggression by armed minorities or by outside pressures' (Clifford, 1984, p.28). Policy statements by UK governments have followed along similar lines: 'Our policy of nuclear deterrence, as members of NATO, has to show them (the whole Communist world), even before they embark on a military adventure, that whenever and however they might pitch their aggression against NATO, the Alliance will always have within its reach effective options for retaliation rather than accepting defeat' (Pym, 1980). The same rationale underlies the preamble to the North Atlantic Treaty: '[The parties to this Treaty] are determined to safeguard the freedom, common heritage and civilisation of their peoples, founded on the principles of democracy, individual liberty and the rule of law' (NATO, 1983).

Identical arguments are used by Soviet leaders such as Kruschev: 'War is not fatalistically inevitable. Today there are mighty social and political forces possessing formidable means (including nuclear weapons) to prevent the imperialists from unleashing war, and if they actually try to start it, to give a smashing rebuff to the aggressor and frustrate their adventurist plans' (Holloway, 1983). A Soviet policy document states: 'The duty of the Soviet Armed Forces is not to permit an enemy surprise attack on our country and, in the event of an attempt to accomplish one, not only to repel the attack successfully but also to deal the enemy counterblows, or even pre-emptive surprise blows, of terrible destructive force' (Holloway, 1983).

Leaving aside the element of rhetoric in these statements and the appeal to the right of self-defence, the underlying sense of moral self-justification for the military or political leader is one which rests on the duty to exercise paternalistic beneficence towards those committed to their care or who look to them for protection. Priority is given to beneficence, or the duty to care, over considerations of social justice or respect for human rights. Without being checked by proper regard for the principle of respect for persons the beneficent paternalism of the State can easily become authoritarian with consequent abrogation of fundamental human rights (a tendency for which communist societies can be criticized). However, subordination of demands of social justice to the demands of a policy of nuclear deterrence can mean that vital resources are squandered on arms which could be spent on economic and social development.

Part of the difficulty is that rational ethics in the 'liberal democracies' has fallen prey to the kind of positivism which effects a divorce between the private and public spheres, between ethics and politics. In practice liberal ethics in this century has been self-relegated to the exploration of individual morality at the expense of a proper understanding of social morality. Even the just war doctrine belongs to the domain of personal rather than social or institutional morality, and the concept of justice with which it operates is individualistic rather than political. The dynamics of moral responsibility in group or team activity, in institutional and political settings, each differ markedly from one another. The marriage of ethics and sociology is urgently necessary, and if the liberal tradition is to recover its cutting edge in the sphere of political ethics it has to recover some of the realism of its own historical tradition, in the writings of Locke and Mill for example.

However, there are inherent weaknesses in the liberal traditions of thinking about law and morality, to the extent that these are rooted in social contract theory and utilitarianism. Cowen (1961) has argued that the concept of human rights, and in particular international law or universal declarations of human rights, are insecure if based only in concepts of social contract and positive law rather than grounded in natural law. The dissolution of classical ontology in the nominalist theories of the Renaissance resulted in the modern concept of natural law since Grotius being based in the concept of social contract. All law becomes positive or statutory law and when this concept is married to that of the sovereignty of parliaments, or nation states, there is no higher court of appeal against unjust laws. If one cannot appeal to some higher or more fundamental law, when faced with discriminatory or oppressive legislation, then one has no moral defence against the power of the State. From the time of Sophocles in the fifth century BC, like Antigone people have appealed to divine or natural law to justify their resistance to tyranny. Like Cowen, Talmon (1952) argues that the liberal doctrine of justice and human rights with its conventionalist and utilitarian justification is no defence aginst totalitarian tendencies even in democratic society. Appeals to the Common Law or to the American Constitution can only be secure defences against the abuse of power by ruling parties so long as the judiciary remains independent enough to resist these pressures; but in principle sovereign parliaments are sovereign and can amend or even abrogate these constitutional safeguards. Hannah Arendt (1968) predicted long before the development of the modern white police state in South Africa that the combination of a liberal tradition in law and morality, with a Calvinist rejection of natural law and suspicion of rational ethics, made it the ideal candidate for totalitarian developments. The impotence of liberal doctrines of the rule of law to resist the rule of discriminatory and oppressive legislation by the apartheid regime should be both a sign and a warning.

What the liberal tradition in ethics requires if it is to be adequate to the task of analysing and informing modern politics, including nuclear politics, is an ontology of power which does justice to the actual dynamics of political processes but also provides a theoretical framework within which the concepts of love, power and justice can be understood in their ontological connections with one another (Tillich, 1954). Christian ethics must hold on to its own tradition of teaching about the transcendent basis or morality in divine and natural law, but it must also hold on to the positive confidence of the liberal tradition that human beings, through the exercise of both technical and contemplative reason, can define both the means and the ends to achieve a fully human life, and can exercise their (God-given) freedom to redirect the course of human history away from dependence on a 'balance of terror' to a more just and peaceful world. This will require Christians to be involved with and in the historical reality of institutional and political power relations at a practical and theoretical level, vigorously rejecting all forms of economic, social and technological determinism.

Freedom and determinism: is the arms race out of control?

Deterministic theories of history and the political process paralyse the public will to reform social structures and political institutions (Popper, 1957; 1977). They may in fact be actively propagated to undermine public confidence that things can be changed and thus may indirectly serve to reinforce the *status quo*. In the debate about nuclear weapons, deterministic arguments may be used to justify the continuation of the arms race ('The technology exists. If we do not develop the neutron bomb, then the Russians will'), or to rationalize despair that the arms race is out of control or uncontrollable ('Scientific progress and technological development has a life and momentum of its own, and the arms race is an inevitable consequence of this process').

Alternatively, anti-nuclear protesters often appeal to conspiracy theories which rely partly on the 'independent momentum' argument, but suggest that the arms race is controlled and manipulated by supra-individual and collective interests: for example, by multi-national armaments manufacturing companies, or by vested interests in the nexus of the military-industrial-scientific complex. Ironically, the politicians and representatives of the military-industrial sphere who use reductionist and deterministic arguments in the one context will rarely admit the inevitability of the process when challenged by critics, displaying their conviction (or delusion) that they do actually control the process.

The point of this analysis is not to suggest that the forces of social, economic or technological determinism do not exist, or that these forces do not severely limit our freedom and room for action, but rather to attack the totalitarian or authoritarian ideologies and political systems that can be built on deterministic arguments, and to attack the spirit of apathy and defeatism, or downright despair, which is engendered for those who believe that a particular deterministic myth and its eschatology must be correct, including Christian evangelical apocalyptism.

In principle, understanding the logic of historical processes, understanding the causes of war or the practical determinants of policies, should enhance rather than restrict the scope for freedom of choice, freedom to change policies and thus the course of history. In reality it may be more difficult, for the power to take such decisions is largely limited in practice to 'decision-makers' and we and they find it painfully difficult to face up to past defeats, past mistakes, past guilt, as we find it difficult to admit our vested interests, misplaced national pride, and satisfaction in believing we are right and our enemies wrong. However, eschewing the counsels of despair or cynical manipulation of others in the light of our determinist myths may be the beginning of both political wisdom and a new optimism that human resources can be mobilized for constructive change. If depression and/or delusions of grandeur are about our fears of losing control or being controlled, then these arguments may be important in addressing the issues in the nuclear debate, at the level of its individual and collective psycho-pathology. Tony Carty's historical analysis of the origins of nuclear strategy (chapter 6 below) demonstrates how thoroughly entangled modern debate and decision-making is with past decisions and perhaps unwillingness to admit guilt. Two different responses are possible to this evidence. The first is to predict the inevitable continuation of the same dialectic of denial and self-justification and to despair of progress in disarmament. The alternative is to face the history of guilt and self-righteous rationalization, recognizing how much this can block or frustrate progress in negotiations or reappraisal of moral positions, but to go forward in the faith that human beings and human history can be changed and redeemed. The latter response recognizes that, while people had *reasons* for acting as they did in the past, it does not follow that their reasons were the direct *causes* of things happening the way they did. Reasons and causes are not synonymous. Antecedent and consequent explanations of actions tend to have a different logic. The antecedent explanation in terms of *reasons* sees the events in terms of the self-determining actions of free individuals. The consequent analysis or explanation in terms of *causes* tends to see the events as determined, or to see the scope of choice as limited. The reasons given, along with many other factors at the time, may have been necessary conditions, and collectively they may have been sufficient for the bombing of Hamburg or Hiroshima, but we cannot say that either explanation alone is compelling in the sense that it is both necessary and sufficient to bring about that result. The process was not and is not inevitable. Dozens of minor decisions could have changed the course of history.

The more Christians emphasize the tragic power of sin and the structures of evil, or emphasize the omnipotence of God and the impotence of mankind (particularly the question of predestination to salvation or damnation), the more they will resort to eschatological 'solutions' or endorse historicist myths rather than commit themselves to political action in the present. But the confidence that Christ overcame 'the principalities and powers of darkness of this world' (Ephesians 1.22–3), abolished tragedy and liberated mankind from bondage should inspire in us a hope of the trans-historical redemption of human history, or the possibility of change and reform within history. Christians may be justifiably sceptical of the possibility of genuinely revolutionary change in human history, but should express that realism which leads to committed action to change the course of human history away from the threat of mutual destruction towards peace and reconciliation.

Rationality and evil: war prevention or peace promotion

Christian attitudes to power, like those of the liberal tradition, have been deeply ambivalent. It was Lord Acton, a leading Catholic of his day, who said, 'Power tends to corrupt, and absolute power corrupts absolutely. Great men are almost always bad men' (Acton, 1907). The attitude to political and economic power which is mirrored in the phrase 'all politics is dirty politics' is deeply rooted in Anglo-Saxon culture. Rationalistic liberalism is thus 'Pelagian' in seeing mankind as a sort of immaculate conception – characterized by essential freedom, rationality and intrinsic goodness – in terms of which politics is seen ideally as a rational process and a progressive movement towards a just and peaceful, if utopian, social order. Christian humanism has tended, since the Renaissance, to be predominantly 'Manichean' in seeing mankind as essentially split between that part which strives to realize essential freedom, rationality and goodness, and that which is in bondage to depravity and anti-rational forces within and without.

It is a truism that all politics is power politics but we undoubtedly need soundly based historical, psychological and sociological analyses of power in its positive and destructive manifestations if we are to make sense of power politics in a nuclear age. We have been slow to develop a political ethics in the 'liberal' , 'Christian' West that can either do justice to the positive exercise of power within the responsibilities of political life, or help us understand institutionalized evil and the destructive forces at work capable of creating and perpetuating violence and war. Christian moral theology can provide us with the basis for understanding, perhaps better than others, the nature of the demonic in mankind and society: that is, the sub-rational and trans-rational forces in mankind and society which are both the potential source of human creative energy and the source of destructive power. This needs to be complemented by a political theology (to which liberation theology may be an important early contribution for all its dependence on Marxist categories of analysis), which will be adequate to nuclear politics too. It is not enough either to provide just a clinical pathology of evil. As pathology needs to be complemented by an understanding of moral physiology, so a realistic Christian political ethics must not only provide a penetrating analysis of the pathological forms of diseased society and corrupt power, but must reaffirm its faith in the ultimate ascendance of the good and of the essential goodness of mankind and God's creation.

There is a particular logic and historical destiny (or necessity) which links western people's self-definition as 'rational animals' with the development of industrial and technical society. Power in modern politics is rooted in the knowledge-base of scientific and technical culture. In theory knowledge, like technics, is or should be neutral between all uses. In practice, and in contradiction to idealistic and liberal scientists, science and technology are captive to economic, political and economic interests, for as Francis Bacon said, 'Knowledge itself is power' (1950). Resources for scientific research do not come without strings attached but are controlled for the benefit of military, industrial or biomedical interests. Even pure research is not conducted 'disinterestedly' in the 'detached pursuit of truth'. Behind every quest for knowledge or improvement of technics lies a will-to-power. This may not be a crude will-to-dominate others, it may simply feed the self-esteem and feelings of superiority of the 'expert'. Nevertheless, the pursuit of knowledge is about the pursuit of power and the means of controlling people, things and processes (Nietzsche, 1909; 1955).

If knowledge is power, the converse is also true: that to be kept in a state of ignorance is to be kept in a state of impotence and dependence. For centuries doctors and medicine-men have known that the secret of their power lay in keeping their peculiar knowledge and expertise secret. For this reason many doctors are ambivalent in their attitude to health education. The focus on pathology leads in medicine to a focus on disease prevention rather than health promotion. The focus on the pathology of war means that all our energies and resources go into war prevention rather than peace promotion. The question is by what standards will we attempt to promote peace? Trying to define peace only in terms of war prevention is perverse. Clearly war prevention and peace promotion are complementary, as are disease prevention and health promotion, but it is crucially important where we place the emphasis.

To pursue the analogy with health services, the issue of whether the British National Health Service (NHS) is a national *health* service or a national *disease* service depends on priorities in the allocation of manpower, research expertise and resources. There is a perverse irony in the fact that 0.1 per cent of the £16.5 billion NHS budget is spent on direct health education and health promotion. Like the NHS budget, the defence budget of £18 billion is enormous but the balance between expenditure on military manpower and the technology of warfare, compared with peace-promotion and development, is roughly of the same proportions and order of magnitude, namely 1,000:1. When we talk about values – and ethics is fundamentally about values – then the real test is how we cash our statements of policy and commitment to peace in pounds and pence. It is easier to get resources for the treatment of disease or for the prevention of disease by immunization, prophylactic surgery, screening and rehabilitation of victims than it is to get resources for health education and health promotion. We are fascinated by pathology and the focus on pathology seems to get results. The effects of health education and health promotion are less palpable. If people do not get injured or suffer from diseases, you do not see them. There is increasing resistance by the medical establishment and Ministers of State for the Health and Social Services to community education and health promotion, as health education tends to make people challenge the authority of doctors, and community development initiatives often lead to demands for change in the structure of existing services. Similarly, we hear much about the need for resources and weaponry to prevent war, but we do not hear much about the case for resources for peace, for research on ways to promote and sustain peace, non-violence and cooperation. There is more political capital to be made from a Falklands campaign than from efforts to promote international peace and development.

However, if we are serious about promoting peace and preventing the conditions which breed violence, something can be done, if we have the will and the resources. At the level of individuals and communities it is possible to break the vicious circle of self-perpetuating violence and the cycle of deprivation. This has been shown time and again in exemplary projects and community development in both developed and underdeveloped countries. What applies at this level can be extrapolated to the international level. On the preventive side, more can be done to prevent the widening gap between North and South with the destabilizing consequences which that brings in its wake. We can make greater efforts to contain competition between the Big Powers – both in the economic and political spheres – to create the conditions for a de-escalation of the arms race and positive moves to disarmament. In terms of positive peace promotion, many more resources could be put into sustaining realistic international communication, scientific, technical and cultural exchange, and the building of confidence in our common humanity in shared cooperation for development, as well as disaster relief.

There may be nothing new in this but there is a risk of pessimism, and such a preoccupation with the pathology of the past and pains of the present that all our energy and resources will be channelled into treatment of symptoms rather than prevention of the causes of the malaise. The uneasy peace of 'cold war' is not real peace, and the increasing number and destructiveness of wars in the twentieth century makes the continued survival and flourishing of the human race look increasingly precarious. We have to celebrate and strengthen those peace-creating and peace-sustaining positive characteristics of love and understanding, cooperation for development, the will to survival and hope, which make for justice and peace. Peace and freedom are not simply given nor static; both need to be protected and nourished, strengthened and encouraged to develop by patient effort. Just as Rome was not built in a day nor the *Pax Romana* established without a whole culture, law and morality to support it, so the building of Augustine's *City of God* (1945) required strenuous effort on the part of mankind to cooperate with grace, to reorientate mankind's loves and the powers of the State to the rule of Christ, to make possible a real *Pax Christiana*.

Towards a positive political ethic: love, power and justice

In attempting to develop a positive political ethic we can hardly do better than go back to Christian origins and the doctrine of love which underlies Augustine's *City of God* (1945). For Augustine, love is not just an emotion but the very principle and power of mankind's being. 'Everything,' he says, 'comes forth by love, even evil.' Against the Greeks who define human nature in terms of rationality, Augustine argues that, if God is love and mankind made in the image of God, then the most definitive and essential characteristic of mankind is not intelligence but the capacity to love. In this doctrine of love as the very power of human being, we have a conception which relates love to justice and power in such a way that it can provide a starting-point from which to reconstruct a Christian political ethics.

Fundamental to Augustine's doctrine of love are the concepts of power and order. The finite, creaturely and dependent state of mankind makes us creatures of desire. Our *interests* in the world around us and in other people are rooted in our ontological state of *inter-esse,* as contingent beings. Our desires and loves are of manifold forms, ranging from biological needs for food and shelter and instincts for self-preservation and sexual reproduction, to the need for protective care and the desire for companionship, the striving for self-fulfilment and self-transcendence in the good, the true and the beautiful, and the love of God which inspires in us the possibility of self-sacrificial and redemptive love towards others. For Augustine there is a given hierarchical order in creation and the order of being in individual and political life should reflect this. For him the chief task of the moral life is 'to achieve the right order of priority amongst our loves'. While in Plato's ordering of loves, desire, friendship and care for others should be subordinated in that order to *eros* – the infinite longing for self-fulfilment through union with the good, the true and the beautiful – in Augustine's hierachy of loves, *agape* or *caritas* occupies the supreme place.

For Augustine, both psychologically and theologically it is axiomatic that we are only capable of loving if we have first been loved by someone else. We learn to love in response to the love we receive at the breast, or in response to the fatherly love of God revealed to us in the comforting mercy of Christ. This love too is fundamentally other-related rather than egocentric. Unlike Plato's ethics, in which all other loves are subordinated to the erotic striving for self-fulfilment and self-transcendence through union with the impersonal, trans-finite ground of being itself, Augustine's hierarchy of loves gives priority to personal love for God and our neighbour. The redemptive, self-sacrificial and forgiving love of God expressed to us in Jesus Christ is the basis for our capacity to accept, love and forgive ourselves. Without this *amor sui proprium,* a balanced and proper love of oneself, a capacity to affirm oneself and thus give and express love to others, our love of others and of God is distorted and may be expressed in many pathological forms.

We have learned a great deal in this century from depth psychology and psycho-pathology about the roots of violence and the will to self-destruction, about mental illness and the pathology of crime and domestic violence, in the pathology of loves. Emotional deprivation, physical and sexual abuse, traumatic loss and separation have often deeply tragic results in the derangement or stunting of personality, in the vicious circle of the abused child becoming the abusing parent, of the pathologically neglected child becoming the cold, ruthless psychopath. Psychological derangement and personality disorders have their roots in the derangement of love, the destructive disorder of lives and families where there is no priority given to the higher loves over the baser, where selfishness and greed, vindictiveness and hatred are not checked by redeeming love and forgiveness. These discoveries of the twentieth century are rediscoveries of the insights of Augustine and the great confessors, as Freud acknowledged. For Augustine evil is essentially the result and the expression of the derangement of mankind's loves.

For Augustine evil in itself is a state of privation, a state of non-being. In itself it has no power, no force. What evil does, however, is to parasitize on the good, to exploit the momentum of the positive impulses of mankind's loves, from the basest to the highest, and turn these to destructive use by the perversion of the will. *Love* (meaning all loves collectively) is by its very nature *centripetal,* that is tending to gravitate towards God, its creator and source. Mankind in a state of innocence or in a state of grace is so orientated, our will being focussed on God as love itself. All loves represent forces which work for the centring and integrating of personality, personal and social relationships. In the actual historical order, and in the sinful state of mankind, loves tend to be *centrifugal,* tend to become disordered and deranged and tend to destructure the structures of the personality and society, which love alone can build. The terrifying destructiveness of evil represents the power of love that has gone wrong and become deranged.

Love is then for Augustine the power of being, the integrative force in human personality and society, and justice is ultimately expressed in right order – the right order in the priority of mankind's loves, and the right order of society – ordered to the greater glory of God and for the wellbeing and happiness of all people. He says, 'If you wish to know what a man is, do not ask if he is good, but what he loves.' A good person and a just person will be someone whose self-affirmation is expressed in the love of God and the care of fellow human beings. 'Peace,' he says, 'is the tranquillity of right order.' By the same token a good and just society might be said to be likewise ordered by its loves to ensure the health and wellbeing of all, in the spirit of the World Health Organisation's definition of health as 'complete physical, mental and social wellbeing and not merely the absence of disease' (WHO, 1978). Cities, communities and states are not just built on economic, political and military power, but on love. 'Two loves have built two cities. The Earthly city on the love of self to the despite of God and the City of God on the love of God to the despite of self.'

In his elaborate study of the history of the earthly city (in particular the Roman Imperium) and the painful building of the City of God, Augustine emphasizes that the positive achievements of the earthly city are the creation of mankind's loves and desires, and the pathology of the declining and disintegrating Empire is the story of the derangement of its loves. Augustine's concept of love, the love which builds the City of God in the ruins of the earthly city, is not a sentimental affection or just an emotion, it is a concept which embraces the whole psychology and personality of mankind, the very *raison d'être* of our being, and the motive force of politics. The Church in Augustine's view is the focus of a new community within the corrupt social order of the earthly city. It represents not only the place of healing for those injured by evil but also a kind of counter-cultural force working for the transformation of the power structures, the order of social justice and peace, the reorientation of the loves of the earthly city Godwards. As such it represents the City of God in embryo, a viable community and exemplar of a society where justice and peace exemplify the order created by the *ordo* of love. This ontological doctrine of love unites love, power and justice in a form which makes it relevant to the analysis of institutions as much as personal psychology; and to the analysis of the driving forces of ambition, the will-to-power, desire for wealth, the pleasure in exercising authority, which are the stuff of social life and politics.

Arthur Conan Doyle's longer Sherlock Holmes stories (Conan Doyle, 1974) are brilliant if chilling illustrations in fiction of an essentially Augustinian view of how communities like the Mormons or Masons, which originally form around a common desire for brotherly love and mutual support, can very subtly and imperceptibly become perverted to criminal ends. The history and deeds of the Mafia exactly illustrate his thesis that the driving force which creates and sustains communities can become the pervese instrument of criminal violence and terror in the will-to-power of the 'Godfathers'. The secret *Broederbond* which was formed in South Africa to unite Afrikaners committed to resisting Milner's policy of compulsory Anglicization following the Boer War, and to defend the interests of an Afrikaner Calvinist and Christian nationalism, has become one of the most pernicious forces behind the white racist policy state in South Africa. Its connections with National Socialism in Germany remind us too how the idealism of Hitler's party and its adulation of him as a leader legitimated and made possible the near conquest of the whole of Europe and unimaginable atrocities against the Jews and other minorities.

A radical Christian doctrine of love provides us with the tools for a realistic political ethics, which can begin to interpret the positive psychology and sociology of institutions and politics, and the pathology of both as well. Group dynamics and the social construction of reality are ultimately about the nature of people's desires and needs, from the most basic to the most elevated and sublime. The pathology of Nazism or Stalinism is not just about the psychopathy of the individual personalities of Hitler or Stalin but also the psychopathology of their ideologies, political parties, secret services, armies and extermination camps. The pathology of the process which has led us from Hamburg and Dresden, Hiroshima and Nagasaki to the Cold War, the arms race and Star Wars is about anxiety and guilt neuroses, paranoia and delusions of grandeur which are also ultimately about the derangement of *our loves*.

The application of such a doctrine of love (uniting as it does the concepts of justice and power as integral to an adequate doctrine of being) is not merely of theoretical interest but of immense practical importance in individual psychotherapy and psychiatry, and also in the therapeutic approach to peace-making and the Christening of our political ideologies and institutions. Ideologies are simply conceptual tools for organizing the beliefs and values which are the expression of the things we love. As we have attempted to show, political power, institutionalized evil, terrorism, threats and counterthreats of mutually assured destruction do not make adequate sense in the rationalism of the liberal tradition. Instead, serious study of the logic of the passions and emotions may be the beginning of political wisdom. 'The heart has its reasons which are quite unknown to the head' (Pascal, 1966). As philosophical *eros* was the motive force of Plato's dialectic, so Christian love must govern the theory and practice of our own political ethics.

Part II
Aspects of Current Policy

6

The Origins of the Doctrine of Deterrence and the Legal Status of Nuclear Weapons

Tony Carty

Introduction

Surely nothing seems more firmly part of the international scene than the nuclear arms race. What possible value can there be in any discussion as to the legality of possession or threat to use nuclear weapons? The starting-point of any discussion of the issue has to be the declarations made by the UK and the US governments, upon signature of the First Additional Protocol to the Geneva Conventions on the Laws of War in 1977. The former insisted 'that the new rules introduced by the Protocol are not intended to have any effect on and do not regulate or prohibit the use of nuclear weapons'. The latter made a similar declaration, that the rules established by the Protocol are not intended to have any effect whatever on the employment of nuclear weapons, nor do they regulate or prohibit this employment.

The supreme importance of these declarations rests in the fact the First Additional Protocol is taken to have deprived the strategic air bombardment of Germany and Japan in the Second World War of the legal status of a precedent, whatever its legal validity may have been at the time (Meyrowitz, 1981, p. 4). It excludes any bombardment which has the object of terrorizing civilian populations and any blanket or area bombing which treats simply as one target what is a series of separate military targets in an urban conglomeration. The difficulty, as I hope to show, is that whether one views the matter in legal, moral or purely historical terms, there is no basis for distinguishing such aerial bombardment from the military and political rationale underlying the possession of nuclear weapons by

NATO countries or even by the Soviet Union, slightly different though they may be.

Strategic bombardment is a term not employed in the Additional Protocol. However, a number of uses of the word appear to show the irrelevance of the type of weapon used to carry it out. For instance Meyrowitz employs the expression to mean long-distance attacks, by plane, by long-range artillery or by ballistic missiles, where the land objects are beyond the zone of operations (p. 2). A fuller explanation of the concept is afforded by Powers. He distinguishes between strategy, as a broad theory of how to defeat the enemy, and the strategic bombing of the Second World War. He places the celebrated Presidential Directive (PD) 59 in a wider historical context:

The strategic bombing of World War II gave a new meaning to the term. Its targets were not military forces as such but the sources of an enemy's fundamental strength . . . Strategic war in its current sense retains the notion of striking at the sources of enemy strength, with the added meaning of striking from long range . . . Strategic war, then, is a kind of mighty hammering, across oceans and continents, at an enemy's whole capacity to wage war. The signal difference between conventional and strategic war is that in the latter one does not contemplate direct engagement of the enemy on the ground (except in peripheral theaters,) nor does one expect to occupy his territory at the close of hostilities. P.D.59, and the new S.I.O.P. [Strategic Integrated Operational Plan] it led to, put the 'war' back into strategic war. (Powers, 1982, p. 108)

This brings us back to the 1930s. At that time it was decided that aerial warfare as a weapon should be used against entire societies in order to bring the war to a speedy conclusion. The idea of total war, which this implied, was to break down the distinction between combatant and non-combatant, based on the traditional and outmoded idea that war should be a contest between the armed forces of the various participants. An attack at the heartland of the enemy became the main aim. This was to break down the industrial and other infrastructure supporting the war, and most of all to break the will of the enemy to fight. The doctrine of nuclear deterrence is an integral part of this development. Hence it is crucial to accept the contradiction in the US and UK declarations made on signing the 1977 First Protocol. The nuclear powers do not accept their applicability to the only form of strategic warfare which they are now likely to wage.

The effect of the doctrine of strategic warfare is to render the laws for the conduct of major wars obsolete. There is no real place for the traditional distinction between civilian and military objects, the latter alone being a legitimate goal for attack, when war is itself to be directed into the enemy heartland. International lawyers have not been willing to register the significance of this development. They have tended to play down the importance of the failure of the International War Tribunals of Nuremberg and Tokyo to censure the nature of air warfare. While there is a growing consensus that the type of warfare conducted during the Second World War is now illegal, it is precisely such ambiguity about recent history which leads to the circumstance that the only form which strategic warfare is likely to take in the future is effectively excluded from the scope of operation of the Protocol. The contradiction exists because present nuclear strategies are an institutionalization of Second World War methods of waging war. It is this history which makes it most likely that in the event of conflict breaking out nuclear strategies would be implemented.

So focusing attention on the question of 'the morality of nuclear deterrence' is a mystification of the real terms in which debate should be conducted. The argument that the threat to use the weapons is only conditional – upon the other side failing to observe the peace – is a historical accretion to a strategic policy which has not been regarded as fundamentally problematic by the military bureaucracies of the nuclear powers. Yet the doctrines of strategic warfare and the ideology of total war have a firm grip on the minds of governing elites. Therefore no declaration or decision as to legality or morality of the threat or use of nuclear weapons will be effective without the dismantling of generations of military doctrines and political ideologies. The void as to legal standards compels us to recognize the moral nihilism implicit in the present situation. International law is no more than a democratically arrived at consensus as to constraints which states may be reasonably expected to observe. The absence of such a consensus at present has to be squarely faced and understood.

The study which follows is divided into two parts. The first considers the origin of strategic warfare to the point where the area bombardment of Germany was completed. This is the crucial stage at which the minimum moral constraints contained in the traditional laws of war were put to one side and the two pillars of strategic warfare and total war were erected. The second part outlines how the use of nuclear weapons in 1945 was a mere continuation of practices already firmly entrenched and how immediate post-war strategy and policy were a continuation of a pattern of warfare which remained uncensured at Nuremberg. The moral and legal void has existed from this time.

Area bombardment and the origin of nuclear strategy

The preamble to the Declaration of St Petersburg (1868) states that the sole object of states waging war was to be the weakening of the military forces of the enemy. Even more important is the famous Marten's Clause, which forms part of the preamble to the 1907 Convention Respecting the Laws and Customs of War on Land. It provides:

Until a perfectly complete code of the laws of war has been issued, the high contracting Parties deem it expedient to declare that, in cases not included in the Regulations adopted by them, the inhabitants and the belligerents remain under the protection and the rule of the principles of the law of nations, as they result from the usages established among civilized peoples, from the laws of humanity, and the dictates of the public conscience.

In his history of the international law of armed conflict, Best draws attention to the fact that 'the degree of preciseness which Martens preferred – and always thought to be to the advantage of the weaker party – being, for political reasons, unobtainable, and to leave the matter wholly vague and general being, to his mind a confession of failure, his Declaration cannot have been, for him other than a second best' (Best, 1983, pp. 165–6). In other words, from the very beginning of the modern codification of the laws of war it can be seen that states which are not willing to bow to a specific prohibition of a military strategy or tactic would, nonetheless, accept a more general statement of a rule which itself was open to interpretation, by a process of logical deduction, possibly leading to the same result. The difficulties are the obvious ones that there is no compulsory supranational interpretation of international law, and that the law is supposed, ultimately, to rest upon the consent of states.

This difficulty was to arise immediately with respect to article 25 of the 1907 Convention just referred to. It provides that 'attack, or bombardment, by whatever means, of towns, villages, dwellings, or buildings which are undefended is prohibited.' Meyrowitz points out how the words 'by whatever means' were inserted in 1907 to encompass an interdiction of aerial attacks. Yet he admits that the question whether this wording, in a convention on land warfare, covered aerial bombardment as an autonomous strategy was regarded as controversial in the inter-war years. In his view, it did not touch the principle of the immunity of civilians, but rather the point whether, in an undefended locality, it was permitted to bombard military objectives (Meyrowitz, 1981, p. 5).

So it is hardly out of place to begin this part of the study by looking closely at the fate of the 1923 Hague Draft Rules on Aerial Warfare. Their terms exclude the pattern of the Second World War conflict as clearly as those of the First Protocol are incompatible with the use of nuclear weapons. Indeed it is possible to point to the general principles of the law of war already mentioned and say that the 'Rules' on aerial bombardment are a 'concrete' application of them. In fact the rules on aerial bombardment were regarded as legally binding. But why were the 'Rules' on aerial bombardment not ratified? In my view nothing could be more crucial than to trace exactly how the Rubicon was crossed with respect to strategic bombing.

After the First World War when the great powers took up the limitation of war, air warfare was at the top of the agenda. In the war, Britain, France and Germany had engaged in indiscriminate bombing of cities and the King of Spain had tried to bring the British and the German governments together on some limitation. The British Cabinet had agreed to consider the idea, while a statement in the Bavarian Parliment appeared to signify a German willingness to abandon air attacks on open towns if the Allies would do the same. Watt's account of the Cabinet's eventual decision is worth quoting at length:

The Cabinet considered this offer, fortified by a General Staff memorandum pointing out that with trench lines stretching from Switzerland to the sea, in some sense every German town was defended. They concluded that any limitation of bombing to the battlefield areas within the reach of the front line would add to the hazards suffered by the population of occupied northern France and of Belgium; whereas it was 'undesirable in the interests of future peace that the civilian population of Germany should be the one population among the belligerents to enjoy immunity'. (Watt, 1979, pp. 62–3)

A directive memorandum of a Cabinet committee in January 1918 had given as much weight to the attack upon civilian morale as to attacks on war industries. Heavy sustained bombing of large industrial centres was therefore particularly recommended as a 'method of attack by which every bomb dropped could be made to count' (Best, 1983, p. 271). This particular wording is especially interesting because it is relevant to the strategy of a nuclear power such as Britain or France which does not have a superabundance of nuclear weaponry.

The Hague Rules were drafted by a commission of jurists charged with the revision of the laws of war, following a directive of the 1922 Conference of Washington for the Limitation of Armaments. Meyrowitz points out that the members of the commission were not sitting in a personal capacity, but as delegates of their country, including an impressive number of military experts (Meyrowitz, 1981, p. 6). The key Article 24 (3) established that only military targets should be bombed, and then only if this could be achieved without the indiscriminate bombardment of civilians. Article 22 also prohibited aerial bombardment of a civilian population initiated with the clear objective of terrorizing them, or the damaging of private property without a military character or any injury of non-combatants. The UK Air Force Manual (1982) says that the 1923 Hague Draft Rules on Aerial Warfare are not legally binding since they were never ratified. They are, nonetheless, to be regarded as of persuasive authority. So what happened to them in the early 1940s?

A presentation of the history of the British bombing of Germany might popularly be expected to offer an account of a reprisal for the German bombing of British cities which eventually overreached itself and far surpassed anything which Germany had attempted. However, the verdict on events, particularly in terms of official and semi-official historical comment, has been that the bombardment was an application of the doctrine of strategic warfare, justified by the context of total war against an entire nation state dedicated to aggressive war. It would not be necessary to discount completely the role of the element of reprisal to maintain the thesis that the bombing was a central part of a war-waging strategy which was regarded as both militarily sound and morally or legally justifiable. Since such explicit discussion of policy followed rather than preceded the war, it is appropriate to begin with a detailed account of the official directives in terms of which the aerial war was conducted.

The strategic bombing campaign against Germany was not a reprisal in the technical sense of a response to the German blitz of Britain in 1940 and 1941. Strategic air bombing was what the RAF as an institution had planned to do since the 1930s. Planes were designed for this purpose, and once the political authority and the wherewithal, in terms of planes, became available this course was adopted (Best, 1983, pp. 272–8). Some commentators stress that Churchill lost no time in unleashing the bombers against the German civilian population: for instance Fuller points out that on the day after his assumption of the office of Prime Minister he ordered the bombing of the ancient university city of Freiburg im Breisgau (Fuller, 1972, p. 280).[1]

Best's interpretation of the place of the blitz of Britain in this context is that it was a German reprisal for previous British bombing of Berlin, a reprisal provoked in the hope that it would divert German energy away from more fruitful British military targets (Best, 1983, esp. p. 276). This is similar to the view accepted by Paskins and

Dockrill. The bare facts are a vast disproportion between a very small and accidental bombing of London, followed by an extensive bombing of Berlin, leading to a diversion of German activity at a vital stage in the Battle of Britain (Paskins and Dockrill, 1979, pp. 18–20).

The War Cabinet minutes throw some light on the issue without resolving it completely. They do indicate that there was an unwillingness to attack any targets located in or close to cities during the 'Twilight' or 'Phoney' War. Once the land battle commenced in the West attacks on oil refineries and marshalling yards were permitted. This was extended to aircraft factories (Cabinet War Minutes, 1940, 117, 119, 120, 122–3, 192). In the course of the late summer of 1940 the issue arose whether aircraft should be authorized to jettison bombs before returning. The Air Minister, Sinclair, said that bombers should adhere to the policy of aiming only at military targets. This was in response to a question raised by Churchill. However, Sinclair stressed that pilots were expected to make every effort not to bring back bombs, while they might still do so if they could find no military targets. Churchill said this could stand for the present (Cabinet War Minutes, 1940, 246).

It has to be remembered that at this stage of the war bomb aiming technology was very inaccurate, although it is not clear how far this was understood by the War Cabinet. In October 1940 Churchill stressed that whilst continuing to adhere to the rule that objectives should be military, at the same time the civilian populations in the civilian areas must be made to feel the weight of the war. He regarded this as a somewhat broader interpretation of present policy and not as a fundamental change. There was to be no public pronouncement on the subject (Cabinet War Minutes, 1940, 280).

The decisive change came in December 1940 in an extensive discussion of Operation Abigail. The Chief of Air Staff presented the argument that it was widely appreciated that German air policy had changed and that Britain must now prepare to retaliate in kind. Till now Britain had not concentrated upon the destruction of a town as such: 'the political question for decision by the War Cabinet was whether we were to concentrate as formidable a force of aircraft as we could command, with the object of causing the greatest possible havoc in a built up area.' If this political decision were to be taken, a military consideration was that the target should be a town of some industrial import, and the bombers should rely on fires, choosing a closely built-up town, where bomb craters in streets would impede fire fighters; 'since we aimed at affecting the enemy's morale, we should attempt to destroy the greater part of a particular town. The town chosen should not be too large.' Because of the movement of

considerable bomber resources from military targets such as oil installations to political targets, that is, civilian morale, the matter had
to be brought to the War Cabinet. The conclusion of the meeting
was to aim for one town 'which would be recognized as having a
predominantly industrial character, was suitably located and offered
a target vulnerable to concentrated air attack'. There was to be no
previous announcement that this attack was being carried out by
way of reprisal for German attacks on Coventry, Birmingham and
Bristol and no separate publicity was to be given to it afterwards
(Cabinet War Minutes, 1940, 305: Conclusions and Confidential
Annex).

There was no further extensive Cabinet discussion of targeting
policy throughout the war. The immediate sequel to this decision
was the bombing of Mannheim, where 14,000 incendiary bombs
were dropped. The Cabinet recorded that while there was to be no
formal declaration of official policy, so that people could believe that
civilians were not as such to be attacked, actions speak louder than
words. Information should become known on how German civilians
felt the weight of British attacks as well as the nature of the broad
principles of air policy (Cabinet War Minutes, 1940, 308; 1941,
308). In September 1942 Churchill brought to the attention of the
Cabinet memoranda by Harris and Trenchard on the extensiveness
of urban damage which could be done by bombing. The technique
avoids land battles of the 1914–18 variety, destroying instead the will
of the enemy to fight. As Trenchard puts it, 'in a single attack a third
of one of the most important areas of Germany was destroyed. The
Prime Minister has promised that forty other areas shall be dealt
with in the same way . . . Can anyone foretell the results of even
three months ruthless bombing of Germany on the Cologne scale?'
Churchill's comment to the Cabinet was that 'I do not adopt or endorse views which fall into the error of spoiling a good case by
overstatement'. Yet the two memoranda are written with force and
vigour and serve as a considerable answer to those who attack
the usefulness of our air policy (Cabinet Memoranda, 1942, 374,
399, 405).

In my view these Cabinet records show that the argument for
reprisals did no more than present a context in which to introduce a
policy of systematic bombing of German civilians with the object of
destroying their morale, and thereby, somehow or other, bringing
the war to a conclusion. The absence of any public declaration that a
policy of reprisals was to be pursued and the absence of any intention to observe a principle of proportionality both indicate that the
prime intentions were not to discourage German bombing policy or
to satisfy an aggrieved national population. It was simply felt that

the time was opportune to introduce a radically new form of warfare, strategic aerial bombardment against cities.

The key 'official' or juridical instruments of policy used by the air force itself are the Air Force Directives of 14 February 1942 and the Casablanca Directive of January 1943. They were decisive for the course of the war. The operative part of the former directive reads as follows:

4. In addition to the foregoing primary factor [the availability of a new bomb-aiming technology] a resumption of your offensive effort is considered desirable for the following reasons:

(i)   This is the time of the year to get the best effect from concentrated incendiary attacks.

(ii) It would enhearten and support the Russians if we were to resume our offensive on a heavy scale, while they were maintaining so effectively their own counter-offensive against the German armies.

(iii) The co-incidence of our own offensive with the Russian successes would further depress the enemy morale, which is known already to have been affected by the German armies' reverses on the Eastern front.

5. In accordance with these principles and conditions a review has been made of the directions given to you in the Air Ministry letter dated 9.7.41, and it has been decided that the primary object of your operations should now be focussed on the morale of the enemy civil population and in particular of the industrial workers. (Webster and Frankland, 1961, IV, p.144)

The Casablanca Directive was issued in the context of a determination to aim for the unconditional surrender of Germany and Japan. The Directive to British and US Bomber Commands in the UK had as its primary objective: 'the progressive destruction and dislocation of the German military, industrial and economic system, and the undermining of the morale of the German people to the point where their capacity for armed resistance is fatally weakened'. Webster and Frankland then note that the primary objectives, 'subject to the exigencies of weather and tactical feasibility' will be a number of military targets in order of descending priority, of which only the last was to be 'other targets in the enemy war industry'. They argue that it was the chief of British Bomber Command who interpreted the document as permitting a continuation of area bombing as a primary objective. He was able to interpret the 'subject to exigencies' clause to allow a concentration on the final 'other objectives' clause. In his letter to the Air Ministry of 6 March 1943, Sir Arthur Harris altered the first paragraph of the Casablanca Directive to read: 'the primary objective of Bomber Command will be the progressive destruction and dislocation of the German military, industrial and economic system aimed at undermining the morale of the German people to a point where their capacity for armed resistance is fatally weakened.' Webster and Frankland go on to point out that this misquotation did not engage the attention of the Air Ministry. It showed that Harris merely regarded the Directive as a reaffirmation of the Directive of February 1942. They conclude that it was, in any case, not an unreasonable misinterpretation, and that at the time area bombing was all that the RAF could technically do (Webster and Frankland, 1961, II, pp. 12–15).

Perhaps the most tangible and concrete way of grasping the meaning of these directives is to consider two examples of their application, to Hamburg and Dresden. They span the two technical stages of the 'area bombing' (the term for city-bombing) of Germany, the first up to the spring of 1944, and the second until the end of the war. In the first stage the technology did not exist for effective precision bombing, and there was not yet reason to believe that area bombing was ineffective in terms of its expected impact on civilian morale. However, in the second stage such technology did exist, and there were two years of 'experience' on the basis of which to judge that area bombing was having no visible results (Best, 1983, pp. 278–84).

Commenting on the February 1942 Directive, Middlebrook remarks that it never spelled out just what was expected to happen to the inhibitants of the German cities (Middlebrook, 1984, p. 259). Clearly no 'moral' issue arose. The choice between area and precision bombing was pragmatic, and not governed by 'abstract theories of right and wrong, nor by interpretations of international law' (Webster and Frankland, 1961, II, p. 22). The language of the particular directive for the bombing of Hamburg, Operation Order No. 173, 27 May 1943, has to be quoted at length, if one is to avoid generalities about what were the intentions of the attack:

The importance of Hamburg, the second largest city in Germany with a population of one and a half millions, is well known and needs no further emphasis. The total destruction of this city would achieve immeasurable results in reducing the industrial capacity of the enemy's war machine. This, together with the effect on German morale, which would be felt throughout the country, would play a very important part in shortening and in winning the war.
2. The 'Battle Of Hamburg' cannot be won in a single night. It is estimated that at least 10,000 tons of bombs will have to be dropped to complete the process of elimination. To achieve the maximum effect of air bombardment, this city should be subjected to sustained attack. (Middlebrook, 1984, p. 95)

It is arguable that a special responsibility for proceeding with the attack rested upon Harris because the 'Pointblank' Directive of 10 June 1943, while repeating the first paragraph of the Casablanca Directive, had called for a concentration on the sources of the German fighter aircraft industry (Webster and Frankland, 1961, IV, pp. 158–60). Nonetheless Harris proceeded with an operation which Bomber Command code named 'Operation Gomorrah'. The targets to be attacked in the city were all residential, with no substantial industrial establishments. 'No part of the attack was planned to fall south of the river where the U Boat yards and other major war industries were located' (Middlebrook, 1984, pp. 97–100). It is accepted that 44,600 civilians died in Hamburg, with an additional 800 servicemen. Middlebrook quotes reports that 15,802 of the dead were identified in the proportion of women, 50 per cent; men, 38 per cent; and children, 12 per cent. A high proportion of the male dead would have been beyond military age (p. 328). In addition, 56 per cent of the family dwelling units in the city were destroyed. Middlebrook comments:

The sad fact is that densely populated working areas like Hammerbrook, Billwarder Auschlag, Barmbek and Altona, which had shown little support for the Nazis, burned particularly well when hit by concentrations of incendiary bombs sometimes intended for other districts . . . The truth is that there never was a chance of any widespread, spontaneous rebellion against the authorities . . . If anything, the bombing was often counterproductive in terms of morale. The news of what had happened . . . certainly increased the will to fight to the end by the German forces. In Hamburg itself . . . they pulled together as they had never done before. (Middlebrook, 1984, pp. 330, 336)

The US Strategic Bombing Survey (USSBS) concluded, after the war, that the 'Battle' caused a loss of war production equivalent to the normal output of the entire city for 1.8 months of full production. Output returned to 80 per cent of normal in five months but full recovery was never achieved (1947, p. 332).

The 'Battle of Dresden' is a very well-known event. It is proposed to run briefly through its main features, and then to consider the 'official' explantion put together by Webster and Frankland. Best comments that two of the better-looking purposes first announced for the raid were not true. It was not an important industrial centre and the Russians had not asked for the city to be 'neutralized', although they had asked this of Leipzig and Berlin as transportation centres. It is well known that before the raid, and in time to call it off, RAF intelligence had learned that vital trains were going by a different route, rather than through Dresden. Indeed, comments Best, 'the seriousness with which it [the raid] had been thought out may be judged from the fact that the railway was working again, through the desert that was central Dresden, within three or four days' (Best, 1983, p. 365).

Webster and Frankland stress that the mass attacks on Dresden were not a fundamental change in bombing policy. Dresden 'was, indeed, the climax of the night air offensive. It was the crowning achievement in the long, arduous and relentless development of a principle of bombing which the Royal Air Force had initially adopted, as a retaliatory measure, in the attack on Mannheim of December 1940, and to which the greater part of Bomber Command effort had subsequently always been devoted' (Webster and Frankland, 1961, III, p. 109).

The 'case' is particularly interesting in that it affords a special elaboration of the notion of morale-breaking through the striking of a devastating blow at the 'enemy', in this case a city overflowing with refugees. The possibility was first broached, under the nomenclature 'Thunderclap', by the Joint Intelligence Committee which did not believe that devastation would lead to a breakdown of morale, but would be bound to create great confusion in communications and might demonstrate to the Russians a desire to help them. However, in the background lay the 'Portal Memorandum' of 1 August 1944 which had recommended a devastating blow against a preferably hitherto undamaged German city, with a view to causing immense devastation with catastrophic force, which might have in certain limited circumstances, along with other factors, the elusive effect of breaking German morale (1961, III, pp. 54–5).

In the face of hesitancy from the Air Ministry, Churchill asked what plans there were for 'basting the Germans in their retreat from Breslau'. He resolved a pragmatic argument about priorities, asserting that it might be more useful to hit oil plants, with an intervention which Webster and Frankland consider decisive. He asked whether Berlin and other large cities in east Germany might be considered especially attractive targets and, if so, whether they could be attacked at once (p. 103).

Perhaps of more interest is Webster and Frankland's treatment of Churchill's change of heart following the public outcry which the bombing provoked. They say that Germany was in virtual collapse by the end of March 1945, but that in February the situation was 'somewhat less promising and a great deal less clear'. The Prime Minister seemed to ignore this when, acting on the spur of the moment, he wrote the minute asking whether one should review a bombing of German cities 'simply for the sake of increasing the terror'. A concentration on military targets is more needed than 'mere acts of terror and wanton destruction, however impressive'.

Churchill was persuaded to change this 'least felicitous' minute (1961, IV, p. 112) for one which the official historians consider 'a somewhat more discreetly and fairly worded document', which was, as they put it, 'substantially acceptable to the Air Staff'. It reads:

> It seems to me that the moment has come when the question of the so-called 'area bombing' of German cities should be reviewed from the point of view of our own interests. If we come into control of an entirely ruined land, there will be a great shortage of accommodation for ourselves and our Allies: and we shall be unable to get housing materials out of Germany for our own needs because some temporary provision would have to be made for the Germans themselves. We must see to it that our attacks do not do more harm to ourselves in the long run than they do to the enemy's immediate war effort. Pray let me have your views. (1961, IV, p. 117)

Military necessity and legal nihilism

Historically the concept of strategic warfare is not separable from the ideology of total war. The crucial assumption of the theory of strategic bombing was that it could lead to the collapse of the will of the enemy to resist, a collapse of morale. It is well known that the chief 'philosopher' of this theory was the Italian General Douhet (Paskins and Dockrill, 1979, p. 7). Historians and moralists stress the fundamental point that fascination with the new military technology, implicit in aerial bombardment in Douhet's theories, was not matched in the 1930s by any systematic study of what such a breaking of morale was supposed to mean, or how it was actually to occur (Best, 1983, p. 272). Those who expected German morale to break never asked what was likely to be involved in a revolt against the Nazi adminstration, a failure of political imagination which was understandable in the military men who were the theorists of air power (Paskins and Dockrill, 1979, p. 45).

In my view this failure to specify war objectives follows directly from the abandonment of military targets. The language of strategic bombing never becomes any more precise than the expectation that unacceptable levels of injury are bound to make the enemy prefer surrender, given the assumption that anything is preferable to extermination. It was assumed that no one would want to fight a war to the point of extermination (Paskins and Dockrill, 1979, p. 6).

It is not simply Douhet's deliberate flouting of humanitarian standards which is significant, but also the fact that his goals are so vaguely set. He can only assume that they are still to be achieved, with more of the same means, so long as the enemy has not surrendered. In other words, it is not the exigency of military necessity in air warfare which leads to devastation bombing, but the absence of any clear indication of success in whatever bombing takes place which encourages the attacker to escalate. This is how I see the following passage:

War will always be inhuman, and the means which are needed in it cannot be classified as acceptable or not acceptable except according to their efficacy, potentiality, or hurtfulness to the enemy. The purpose of war is to harm the enemy as much as possible; and all means which contribute to this end will be employed, no matter what they are.

For these reasons 'bombing objectives should always be large'. The bombardment will be frightful, but the war will be quick, and thereby save lives, because the decisive blows will be directed against civilians, 'that element of the countries at war least able to sustain them' (Paskins and Dockrill, 1979, pp. 9–10).

The significance of the strategic bombing of Germany to the British war effort can hardly be exaggerated. It was the central feature of the conduct of the war against Germany. According to the USSBS, Britain devoted 40–50 per cent of its war production to its air forces. The rest was allocated to land and sea forces combined. Only 30 per cent of British and US bombs were dropped on military targets, 13 per cent on industrial, 24 per cent on urban, and 32 per cent on transport and synthetic oil plants. The RAF dropped half a million tons of bombs on 61 cities, primarily to destroy the morale of the industrial worker. As a result 300,000 were killed and 780,000 were injured. A population of 25 million and a labour force of 4.85 million workers were affected. The great majority of bombs were dropped after mid-1944, but the USSBS considers the effects difficult to distinguish from precision raidings except insofar as concerns intention (USSBS, 1945, pp. 71–4). Other figures of casualties seem to vary between 500,000 and 410,000.[2]

How is one to assess the effectiveness of strategic warfare from the German experience? The conclusion of the USSBS is quite clear. Bombing will affect civilian morale. It produced apathy and may have marginally affected the level of war production. However, in a totalitarian state there is very little the population can do by way of response. The Nazi Government, not itself the object of effective attack, was aware of the importance of after-raid relief and it was generally regarded as satisfactory. The bombing may have marginally speeded up the July 1944 plot, but its extensiveness was such as to disorganize opposition and preoccupy people in a struggle for survival. War production itself continued to increase until mid-1944, but terror held people in line. By January 1944, before most of the bombing had taken place, three-quarters of the German population thought the war lost, primarily because of major military defeats. Yet there was little choice of course open to them. The USSBS concludes that the power of a police state over its people cannot be underestimated (USSBS, 1945, pp. 95–108; 1947, pp. 15–20, 102–3). The attempt to break the morale of a population to wage war, undertaken as a political decision by the War Cabinet in December 1940, failed because given the political organization of the German state it could not mean anything militarily.

It being certain that hundreds of thousands of civilians were being killed, how could one accept little concrete or scientific assurance that area bombardment would 'save' lives by breaking civilian morale, thereby saving even more lives and ending the war? Howard provides, I believe, the correct avenue of approach in this study of the breakdown of the idea of limited war in favour of total war against Germany. He explains how Chamberlain insisted that a war was being fought against the German Government, rather than against the German people. However, by 1941 this attitude was shared by hardly anyone in Britain:

It became accepted as much on the Left as on the Right that this was a war specifically against Germany, against a philosophy which appeared to be distinctively German and one which inspired a depressingly high proportion of the German people. In November 1941 even Aneurin Bevan wrote that 'it was Prussian militarism, with all its terrible philosophy, that had to be got rid of from Europe for all time'; and the following September the President of the T.U.C. told his annual conference 'that until the German people, not alone their gangster rulers, have meted out to them what they have meted out to millions of their fellow creatures . . . the German people will again, if not prevented, make another attempt to enslave Europe. (Howard, 1981, pp. 108–10)

Middlebrook reveals how this general conception of the war is perfectly compatible with the deceit which he considers was practised on the British public. Indeed even aircrew were rarely told that bombing areas were residential as such, yet the popular saying was 'They have sown the wind; they will reap the whirlwind.' The armed forces shared the general public hatred of the Nazis, and the belief that they were engaged in a life-and-death struggle between nations. No one joined an institution, such as the RAF, in order deliberately to destroy German families. Middlebrook emphasizes that once someone joined the service, he took no decisions, but simply executed orders. Yet the average bomber crew saw themselves as a force of retribution against an inhuman philosophy. As for the general public, Middlebrook concludes that:

The general public, particularly in Britain, were happy to accept that their bombers were mainly engaged in destroying German industry and it must be said that the British people were not too much concerned if worker's housing was bombed at the same time. There was not an excess of sympathy to spare for German civilians at that time. The earlier, well-published bombings of Warsaw and Rotterdam, in particular, and of British cities were marvellous gifts to the British propaganda machine (Middlebrook, 1984, p. 245; see also 341–9)

Gallup poll figures for public support for reprisal raids against Germany do not show more than 50 per cent support. While Calder argues that as late as 1944 the overwhelming majority of the general public thought that bombing was of purely military targets (Calder, 1971, p. 556), Walzer comments that it might have been what they wanted to believe (Walzer, 1974, p. 97). The difficulty is simply how one could have kept actual bombing policy a closely guarded secret, in view of political exchanges such as the following, which Webster and Frankland cite to illustrate the moral basis of government policy. They note Churchill's repeated insistence that centres of population be attacked. The Foreign Secretary is then quoted as stressing the preferability of destroying smaller towns which are less well defended, as the psychological effects would be greater. These are determined not by the military or economic significance of the targets, but 'solely by the amount of destruction and dislocation caused'. Eden is stressing throughout the importance of the psychological impact of bombing. The final exchange should be the correspondence between an MP and the Air Minister in May 1942. The former writes that he was:

'all for the bombing of working class areas in German cities. I am Cromwellian – I believe in "slaying in the name of the Lord", because I do not believe you will ever bring home to the civil population of Germany the horrors of war until they have become tasted in this way.'

To this Sir Archibald Sinclair replied, on 26th May 1942, that he was 'delighted to find that you and I are in complete agreement about . . . bombing policy generally'. (Webster and Frankland, 1961, III, p. 115)

In other words there was not even an attempt to say that the bombing of cities was necessary in any strictly military sense. Writing in 1944, before the bombing of Japan had begun, Ford estimated that on any calculation of the civilian population contributing to a war effort, it could never come to more than one-third of the population. Taking figures from the US War Manpower Commission and various War Production Boards, he says that of a population of 135 million, it would be a very generous estimate which would place the number of those engaged in war work and essential activities (including mining, transportation, and even public offices) at more than 31 million (Ford, 1970, pp. 22–6). Clearly no question of military necessity in the traditional sense was involved. It is a matter of understanding the significance of the decision of state policy to kill as many German civilians as existing technology would permit.

Walzer considers the question of whether area bombing could have been justifiable in terms of the enormity of the Nazi regime. It was possible to suppose that civilization itself was at stake, in which case the question was should I wager this determinate crime against that immeasurable evil? Walzer quickly concludes that the worst destruction of German cities took place after the greatest danger had passed and so could not be defended by the extreme argument that any kind of resistance to overwhelming evil is permissible (Walzer, 1974, p. 101). Instead, the issue is the less apocalyptic one of whether the course adopted could be said to offer any reasonable guarantee that the war might be shortened and lives thereby saved. While Walzer agrees with Anscombe and others that the evidence does point towards a desire to punish the Germans as a people, or at least to hold them as hostages and pawns for the crimes of their leaders (pp. 95–6, 102), of more interest may be his particular reason for doubting any utilitarian justification for area bombing. While it may be possible, arguably, to justify killing a small number of people to save the lives of a large number, the sheer scale of the Second World War is remarkable:

To kill 278,966 civilians (the number is made up) in order to avoid the deaths of an unknown but probably larger number of civilians and soldiers is surely a bizarre, godlike, frightening, and horrendous act. This is not simply because no one can possibly know enough to justify murder on such a large scale (he would have to know everything), but also because the knowledge he claims to have and the evil he hopes to avoid are neither of them radical or extreme enough even to explain his action. He is guilty of a drastic attack on our civilization, and his only defense is that he hoped to save and may have saved some lives. (Walzer, 1974, p. 100)

There is only the slightest evidence that there were any reservations about policy in political circles at the time. Webster and Frankland note the problem of presentation of the practice of bombing of residential areas. For the Secretary of State for the Air it was a 'somewhat delicate and difficult' matter. The view that the Air Staff was responsible for what was 'perhaps, not inaccurately, described as "terror bombing"' has to be rejected. The policy was that of the Government, and indeed of the Allies, after the Casablanca meeting. The mistaken impression gained since the war was in part due to the fact that Sir Archibald Sinclair, for the Government, felt it advisable to conceal from the public that residential areas were themselves made a direct object of attack. The official historians explain that it 'was unfortunate to have to contend with such a widespread and deep-rooted ignorance of the operational problems involved'. So it was explained that damage to residential areas, however extensive, was nonetheless incidental: 'Only in this way, he explained to Sir Charles Portal in October 1943, could he satisfy the enquiries of the Archbishop of Canterbury, the Moderator of the Church of Scotland and other significant religious leaders, whose moral condemnation of the bomber offensive might, he observed, disturb the morale of Bomber Command' (Webster and Frankland, 1961, IV, p. 116; see also p. 114).

The Nuremberg Charter could have covered area bombardment in Article 6(b) which refers to the 'killing of hostages, plunder of public property, wanton destruction of cities, towns or villages, or devastation not justified by military necessity'. McDoughal and Feliciano comment that acceptance of terror bombing renders pointless any legal limits to the use of force. Indeed the best way to paralyse factory workers, one of the ostensible reasons for the bombing, would be to kill their wives, parents and children. Once such a logic is accepted why stop short of killing prisoners of war and the populations of occupied territories (McDoughal and Feliciano, 1961, pp. 656–8)?

Yet at Nuremberg the issue of the legality of area bombardment remained completely moot. The Tribunal did not evaluate evidence one way or the other (Schwarzenberger, 1968, pp. 151–3). The Tribunal might even have considered the fact that, according to the USSBS, only a third of Germans blamed the Allies for the bombing. Another third said such things were to be expected in war, of which three-fifths said that the bombing was to be expected because the Germans had done the same (USSBS, 1947, p. 20). However there seems to be a remarkable consensus in the literature that the conduct of strategic warfare made debate about questions of legality academic in the worst sense of the word.

It must be questionable whether strategic bombing was effective in any sense at all, and therefore could be said to serve a military objective. Blix, in a major review of the literature, notes the argument that the distinction between civilian and military objects was rendered obsolete by the conduct of area bombardment. He treats that history as somehow on the border of legality. Yet it is not his intention to discuss any proposed rule of law as already existing for the period of the war. Instead he believes that attention should be directed towards what might be regarded as binding for today. This he does without undertaking any examination of what is meant by the concept of military objectives in the context of total war. Most of all he does not take account of the legal significance of the fact that nuclear strategies are a continuation of the policy of area bombardment (Blix, 1978, pp. 38, 42, 58 and 59 *et seq.*). Such an approach will prove to be characteristic of the juridical perspective on the legality of nuclear weapons as it arises at the end of the 1950s and onwards. There will be a reiteration of the formal distinction between civilians and military and an obvious assertion that use of nuclear weapons is incompatible with this distinction. However, lawyers do not attempt to grapple with the concrete military implications of a concept of total war for the definition of civilian and military objectives. They do not face the question of how any civilians can be spared from an unbroken practice of targeting cities in the context of strategic warfare. This is because they are content to repeat standards found in diplomatic declarations without relating them to the actual way that nation states are organized to fight.

The A-bombing of Hiroshima and Nagasaki:
the absence of law

The question of whether it was necessary to drop A-bombs on Hiroshima and Nagasaki is very much more open than is sometimes appreciated. For instance, it is frequently presented as the contention of President Truman and Secretary of War Stimson that the losses and damage inflicted, in the atomic attacks which compelled the Japanese surrender, were proportionate to the losses that the military on both sides and Japanese society itself would have suffered had the atom bomb not been used (O'Brien, 1982, p. 85).

Yet the USSBS makes the remarkable claim that in the case of Japan the US was faced with a rational military enemy quite distinct from Nazi Germany. Far from being fanatical leaders determined to fight to the bitter end, the Japanese had resolved as early as the summer of 1944 that essential military advantages had been lost. In the opinion of the USSBS, the leadership was perfectly aware of the decisive implications of their air vulnerability. From this it drew vital conclusions about the place of attacks on civilian morale. The Japanese leadership's will to resist collapsed before that of the people as a whole, but the leaders were anxious not to move too far ahead of public opinion.

The US was aware in the spring of 1945 that Japan was seeking peace. However, it wanted a negotiated peace and the US was insisting on unconditional surrender. This is the context in which an all-out bombing campaign was launched. It was clear to the US, at the latest by 21 July, that Japan was searching for a way to surrender. The Japanese diplomatic codes had been broken, and the US knew in detail of the Japanese approaches to the Soviet Union. Indeed at this point Stimson had asked Truman to give a guarantee that the Emperor would not be made to abdicate. Instead he preferred to insist, in the Potsdam ultimatum, upon a repetition of the demand for unconditional surrender, threatening as an alternative the 'utter devastation of the Japanese homeland' (Bernstein and Matusow, 1966, pp. 25–9). The most that can be said against the desire of the Japanese to surrender was that the military had a list of items they wished to see negotiated. Feis points to a War Council Policy of 6 June 1945, which supposed that resistance to the expected invasion might be so hard as to lead the enemy to offer acceptable terms. Indeed he understood the Japanese terms at the time of Potsdam to have been: holding on to the traditional empire; no military occupation of Japan; a minimum army for national defence; and independence for the territories Japan continued to occupy. So the two sides were far apart. There was more at stake than the status of the Emperor (Feis, 1961, pp. 170–8).

Nonetheless it was not necessary to burn every city, destroy every factory and starve the people. It was enough to demonstrate that the US was capable of this. The destruction of the Japanese fleet and air force and the blockade of the country had already been decisive in confining Japan to its own second power resources. Indeed Japanese realization of this was the reason for the fall of Tojo in July 1944. From this time onwards peacemaking began and on 1 April 1945 a government was set up with specific mandate to end the war. The land armies were not defeated but they were isolated, and the generals hoped for no more than a negotiated peace. The more radical peace movers saw the bombing coming. It was the programme of strategic bombing which brought home to the population as a whole what the peace movers knew. Morale was lowered by demonstrating the disadvantages of total war directly. The atom-bombing merely accelerated the move within the War Cabinet away from a strategy of seeking a negotiated peace to one of virtual unconditional surrender; that is, the position of the Emperor was never conceded (USSBS, 1946a, pp. 10–13; Craven and Cate, 1953, pp. 735–56).

The USSBS clearly accepts that strategic bombing helped to end the war more quickly. However, it identifies the fact that the situation facing the US was not one of total war. The time lapse between military impotence and political acceptance of the inevitable might have been shorter had the political structure of Japan permitted a more rapid and decisive determination of national policies. Nonetheless the USSBS insists categorically that this only affected the time scale of surrender. Given the context of a total blockade, a holding action would have been quite sufficient. In its view a surrender would have been inevitable by 31 December, in all probability by 1 November, 'even if the atomic bombs had not been dropped, even if Russia had not entered the war, and even if no invasion had been planned or contemplated' (USSBS, 1946a).

So strategic bombing was intended to produce total victory, to beat the enemy in its entirety into complete submission. Within this wider framework it was hoped that a sufficiently intensive bombing would obviate any necessity for a land invasion of Japan. According to the USSBS, when the fire raids were initially undertaken they were largely seen as an easier way than precision bombing to get at war production which was dispersed in home industries. There was not the larger objective of securing a decision on surrender without invasion (USSBS, 1946b, p. 63). This must be the context in which to view the Tokyo fire raids of 8–10 March 1945. In these raids one million were rendered homeless, 83,793 people were killed and 40,918 were wounded. The bombing area included the heart of the residential district. The effect on Japanese moral was profound. A Home Office official is quoted as saying his colleagues could not report on the event 'because of horrifying conditions beyond imagination'. By June the six most important industrial cities were in ruins. They had been virtually undefended (Craven and Cate, 1953, pp. 615–58, and p. 756). This incendiary bombing of March to July 1945 seriously shook Japanese morale, leading one-half of the population to believe in defeat, although still ready to follow the Emperor (pp. 735–56).

The USSBS itself remarks that by April 1945 the threat to subsistence was enormous given the cut in imports, fishing and fertilizers. An attack on railways would have produced an almost immediate threat of starvation, given the exposed bottle-neck nature of the Japanese system, leading to rapid capitulation (USSBS, 1946b, p. 63).

However, the USSBS points out that it was then decided to launch incendiary attacks against urban areas of minor industrial importance to attack the social organization of the country and induce surrender without an invasion: 'Action which threatens the existence of large sections of the population and at the same time, through restricting communications, menaces the continuance of centralized and integrated social control, can exert powerful pressure towards termination of a war, even though invasion is not in the offing' (USSBS, 1946b, p. 63). Craven and Cate outline the terms under which the towns of lesser industrial importance were attacked. The choice of preferred targets was to be based on:

1 congestion and inflammability;
2 incidence of war industry;

3 incidence of transportation facilities;
4 size and population;
5 adaptability to radar bombing.

The authors conclude by quoting Prime Minister Suzuki as saying, 'It seemed to me unavoidable that in the long run Japan would be almost completely destroyed by air attack . . . the atomic bomb was just one additional reason for giving in . . . and gave us the opportune moment to open negotiations for peace' (Craven and Cate, 1953, pp. 615–58 and p. 756).

How was this bombing, the immediate precursor to the atom bombing itself, justified? Clearer evidence exists on the question of the latter, and inferences can be made given the official insistence that atom bombing raised no new moral issue. Truman and Stimson explained the bombing purely in terms of psychological warfare, the breaking of the will of the nation to resist, this time with nuclear weapons, and therefore in terms of what might properly be called nuclear deterrence. In Stimson's view there was no place for a distinction between combatant and non-combatant in any war: 'death is an inevitable part of every order a wartime leader gives . . . To discard or fail to use effectively any weapon that might spare them [the American soldiers transferred from Europe] further sacrifice would be irresponsibility so flagrant as to deserve condign punishment' (Stimson and McGeorge Bundy, 1948, pp. 631–3). Stimson explains that when the Potsdam ultimatum to the Japanese was rejected by the latter, the US was determined to show that it intended and meant 'the inevitable and complete destruction of the Japanese armed forces and just as inevitable the utter devastation of the Japanese homeland'. For such a purpose the atom bomb was eminently suitable. The test explosion of 16 July showed 'its use against the enemy might well be expected to produce exactly the kind of shock on the Japanese ruling oligarchy which we desired, strengthening the position of those who wished peace, and weakening that of the military party' (Bernstein and Matusow, 1966, p. 37).

Truman uses the familiar language of a holy war against a government which represents evil forces, of which the killing of another 100,000 civilians is a fitting punishment. It will clearly discourage the repetition of such behaviour in the future:

Having found the bomb we have used it. We have used it against those who attacked us without warning at Pearl Harbour, against those who have starved and beaten and executed American prisoners of war, against those who have abandoned all pretence of obeying international laws of war. We have used it in order to shorten the agony of war, in order to save the lives of thousands and thousands of young Americans. (Bernstein and Matusow, 1966, pp. 40–1)

In my view it has to be stressed that what was involved was not a military judgement about the proportion of lives which would be saved by avoiding an invasion. The evidence is that crushing the will to resist of an entire nation, taken as a corporate existence without fine distinctions, was considered an appropriate way to fight a total war. General Eisenhower told Stimson not to use the atom bomb because Japan was so nearly beaten (Feis, 1961, p. 178). The figure of a million American casualties is commonly given as the estimated cost of an American invasion. Yet the Joint Chiefs of Staff had, in fact, taken the view that casualty experience was so diverse that it was considered wrong to give an estimate, in numbers, of the cost of an invasion. They did stress their fear of the effect on the Japanese of an insistence upon an unconditional surrender (Bernstein and Matusow, 1966, p. 7).

In his defence of the atom bomb decision in the *Harper* magazine in February 1947, Stimson insists that Japan was far from accepting unconditional surrender. He adds that the two bombed cities were of some military and industrial significance. There is also no question but that he was deeply concerned about the prospect of expensive further loss of American lives. Stimson spoke with tense anxiety about the loss of the lives of more American soldiers, already exhausted by the war in Germany. He could conclude that 'it was the experience of what an atomic bombing will actually do to a community, plus the dread of many more, that was effective' (Bernstein and Matusow, 1966, pp. 31–2, 38–9).

Yet none of this must hide the essential point that it was not thought that any irreversible threshold was being crossed in the escalation to the use of atom bombs. Stimson himself writes that 'no effort was made, and none was seriously considered, to achieve surrender merely in order not to have to use the bomb' (Stimson and McGeorge Bundy, 1948, p. 629). Little thought was given to the possibility of making a concession to the Japanese on the status of the Emperor because no good reason was seen for not using the bomb. The decision was not influenced by moral and legal considerations (Feis, 1961, pp. 176–7, 179).

There was no question of an invasion before November and the Joint Chiefs of Staff expected only slight casualties before the assault. The Scientific Advisory Committee meeting on 16 June did not know this, and thought an imminent invasion the only alternative to use of the bomb. It gave no reasons for its view that there was no alternative to a military use of the bomb, except that demonstration bombs were in too short supply and, in any case, unreliable. Indeed another advisory committee, the Franck Committee, considered only the post-war political consequences, in terms of Soviet distrust, rather than moral or legal scruples, because of 'the necessarily a-moral climate in which wartime decisions have to be made'. In fact a Presidential Interim Committee had decided, as early as April 1945, that the atom bomb was to be used as quickly as possible on a dual target, a military installation or war plant surrounded by housing or other buildings which would be most susceptible to damage (Bernstein and Matusow, 1966, pp. 9–15).

At the time of the atomic bombing, Japan lodged a diplomatic protest, through the Swiss Government, that it had suffered 'a new offense against the civilization of mankind'. It referred to the principles set forth in the Annex to the Hague Convention respecting the Laws and Customs of War on Land, Articles 22 and 23(e), namely the causing of indiscriminate suffering and unnecessary pain (Falk, 1965, p. 765). Needless to say this point was not taken anywhere by the International Military Tribunal for the Far East.

The conclusions of the Tokyo Tribunal do include a heading for the 'Murder of Captured Airmen'. Japanese law had treated bombing a crime punishable with death, because attacks were upon ordinary people and objects of a non-military nature. US pilots were frequently tortured and otherwise maltreated, and their trials were very summary, if they took place at all. The only reference to the laws of air warfare is to a Japanese policy of indiscriminate bombing of Chinese cities in the 1930s. The Tribunal might well have mentioned that on 22 September 1937, the US made a protest to Japan about the bombing of Chinese cities, *inter alia,* in the following terms: 'This Government holds a view that any general bombing of an extensive area where there resides a large populace engaged in peaceful pursuits is unwarranted and contrary to principles of law and of humanity' (Brownlie, 1983, pp. 113–14).

Although neither the Nuremberg nor the Tokyo Tribunals made any comment on the legality of strategic warfare, the professional military view has remained that, to put it in deliberately vague terms, the actions taken were justifiable in one way or another. The Air Forces may have been engaged in morale 'busting' but the precedents of Rotterdam and other continental European cities existed. Besides, the targeting of industry, which is of fundamental importance to the conduct of war, is seen as permissible. If one adds communications such as rail and road connections the range of possible targets is very large, even discounting residential, cultural and commercial facilities.

Immediate post-war strategy: Cold War and total war

So it is hardly surprising that immediately after the Japanese surrender, military planning found a new focus. By October 1945, the
Pentagon had drawn up its 'first serious plan' which visualized a
limited air attack with atomic bombs on 20 Soviet cities. It contained
all the elements of every future plan: military forces, stockpiles,
bases and installations; economic and industrial centres; political
and administrative centres. A basic feature US strategic targeting
has been that none of these particular targeting elements has ever
been removed, with the possible exception of the civilian population
per se. This nuclear strategy was seen at the time as a continuation of
the strategic bombing of Germany and Japan: 'The principal objective of these plans was the destruction of critical war-supporting
industries in order to affect Soviet battlefield operations, the longer-
term ability of the Soviet economy to support combat, and the Soviet
will to continue the conflict' (Ball, 1983, pp. 3–4).

A plan adopted in late 1949, before the Soviet Union had
detonated an atomic bomb, served to govern US nuclear war planning until the late 1950s. It envisages the 'mix' of targets already
mentioned. It was intended, *inter alia*, to destroy main control centres and subcontrol centres: that is, the four largest cities and 18
others. Elimination of 75–80 per cent of the heavy industry of the
country would have the 'important by-product' of destruction of
political and administrative centres; 'in addition there would probably be an extreme psychological effect, which if exploited might induce early capitulation' (Ball, 1983, pp. 5–6).

This military strategy has, as always, to be accompanied by an
ideology of total war, now expressed in the language of the Cold
War. American love of freedom confronts the Soviet desire for world
domination. Complete American moral innocence excludes any
place for a recognition of mixed motives which might suggest
compromise or a process of negotiation. Whether one looks to
MacArthur, J. F. Dulles or Eisenhower, numerous expressions of
these beliefs can be found in the immediate post-war period
(Krakau, 1967, pp. 206–15). Just as area bombardment went well
beyond what a doctrine of reprisal might have justified, so the doctrine of massive retaliation against a totally wicked enemy goes far
beyond any concept of self-defence. It involves the complete physical
destruction of the enemy and an absolute change in the existing state
system, the same objective as that which the Casablanca system was
supposed to achieve (Krakau, 1967, pp. 216–18).

In Britain the question in 1945 was simply whether to produce the
atom bomb. The official historian, Gowing, records that the issue

was never really in doubt. The decision was not a response to an immediate military threat, but something fundamentalist, almost instinctive; that Britain must have so climactic a weapon to deter an enemy, that she had to acquire all new weapons as a Great Power, and in order to manifest a certain technical superiority. It was desired to avoid being bullied by the Americans, but the Government felt that the decision should be kept as secret as possible so as not to offend the Russians, who were not regarded at the time as the enemy. This was still seen to be Germany. In Gowing's view the bomb was firmly embedded in military research and development, but was related to strategy only in the vaguest way. No attempt was made to calculate how many were needed for the deterrent purposes they were supposed to serve (Gowing, 1964, pp. 184–8).

This is not to say there was any doubt about the types of targets which would be hit. For instance a Joint Chiefs of Staff memo of 1 January 1946 warned the Prime Minister that he must be prepared 'for aggressors who have widely dispersed industries and populations'. There was thus a need for hundreds rather than scores of bombs. It would take five years to prepare these, and so one could hardly wait to see what came of United Nations attempts to control nuclear weapons. In the summer of 1946 its Joint Technical Warfare Committee gave estimates of the number of bombs needed by the US, with and without British support, to devastate a large percentage of cities in Soviet Union, although this might not necessarily secure its collapse. Indeed, maintaining a measure of uncertainty was not undesirable. In any case the national effort necessary to deliver atom bombs would be very much less than that required to produce the same effect with normal bombs (Gowing, 1964, pp. 169–75).

The justification and rationale for the use of nuclear weapons had not changed up until the 1980s in the UK. The language of moral superiority takes over from any reference to protection of national self-interest in a context which can only be one of total war. A Ministry of Defence (MoD) paper puts it:

We need to convince Soviet leaders that . . . the British force could still inflict a blow so destructive that the penalty for aggression would have proved too high . . . There is no way of calculating exactly how much destruction in prospect would suffice to deter. [Since Britain is much smaller than the US] a much smaller penalty could therefore suffice to tilt his assessment against starting aggression that would risk incurring the penalty . . . [The Soviet Government might] be tempted to judge that if an opponent equipped himself with a force which had only a modest chance of inflicting intolerable damage there might be only a modest chance that he would have the resolve to use it at all. [The Government] concept of deterrence is concerned essentially with posing a potential threat to key aspects of Soviet state power. (MoD, 1980, p. 56)

In concrete terms the policy means that the type of targeting will depend upon the numbers of weapons available, and their capabilities (accuracy and penetration). As the exact targets remain secret, this allows the discussion of the legality of proposed attacks with nuclear weapons to remain at the level of vague generalities. They are clearly weapons of mass destruction and, as such, by definition incapable of distinguishing civilian and military targets. So it could be said that they are likely to cause indiscriminate suffering and unnecessary pain contrary to Article 23(e) of the 1907 Hague Convention on Land Warfare. Yet it is legitimate to balance military against civilian interest. As long as one is doing this much, actions with nuclear weapons could be said to have the object of weakening the military within the terms of the St Petersburg Declaration, therefore it is not possible to say that their use would necessarily always be illegal. Such a general approach, taking advantage of the ambiguity of the distinction between civilian and military targeting after the area bombardment of the Second World War, leaves out discussion of the more concrete question as to whether the most effective use of Britain's limited nuclear arsenal would be to attack centres of Soviet population such as Moscow and Leningrad. These are key aspects of Soviet state power. However, in the absence of precise knowledge of the targeting one appears to be left with the stark alternatives of accepting or opposing possession of the weapons.

In 1942 the possibility of an atom bomb became a serious issue for the Soviets. They knew of American, British and German work on the bomb. Although the war still hung in the balance, in Holloway's view, Stalin can hardly have thought that the bomb would affect the outcome of the war. It is speculation whether he prepared to confront a nuclear-armed German or Allied force. Progress on the bomb was well on the way by 1945, and yet the British and American ambassadors in Moscow record how the Soviets were acutely depressed by the bombing of Hiroshima and Nagasaki. It destroyed, at one blow, the belief that victory was going to guarantee them national security. An all-out effort to produce the bomb was to be made. Whether Allied cooperation might have led to nuclear arms control is a great historical might-have-been, but certainly the 'Soviet leaders regarded the use of the bomb in Japan as part of an effort to put pressure on them, as a demonstration that the United States was willing to use nuclear weapons' (Holloway, 1983, pp. 17–20). Apparently the shock of the Soviet atom-bomb testing helped to determine the American decision to produce a thermo-nuclear weapon despite official scientific advice that the extreme dangers to mankind in such a proposal outweighed the military advantage it afforded. Again the Soviets might possibly not have gone on to the thermo-nuclear stage of production (development began in 1947) if the Americans had postponed their own programme, in the sure knowledge that they could catch up: one more might-have-been (Holloway, 1983, pp. 24–6). However, of more interest to the argument here is the use to which Stalin proposed to put the weapons.

The policy first pursued by Stalin was to regard nuclear weapons as an important new form of massive firepower, analogous to other forms, such as artillery barrages and aviation bombardment. Policy continued to be to defeat the enemy by capturing the most important regions in the continental theatres of military operations, thereby compelling unconditional surrender. The new weapons would be especially useful for disruptive strikes against rear areas in theatres of military operations. This meant primarily air bases, mobilization areas, ports and military-industrial centres, such as munitions plants, oil refineries, shipyards and research installations. The Soviets discounted strategic bombing, noting that it neither broke German morale, not did it damage its war production. Japanese surrender was actually attributed to Soviet intervention in the war, and not to US strategic bombing and the use of the atom bomb. This does not appear to be a matter of Soviet military vanity, but rather of a completely different concept of military strategy:

Thus, from the Soviet military perspective, there was no evidence to support notions that the strategic bombing of cities with the purpose of inflicting punishment on the civilian population could have a substantial effect on the outcome of a war . . . [W]hile most Soviet military planners acknowledged that the bombing of enemy military-economic facilities might assist the overall war effort, the concept was relegated to a secondary role in the strategic offensive operation – in fact, the lowest in priority of all aviation missions . . . Since one of the primary goals of the strategic offensive was to capture enemy industrial-economic centres, the use of nuclear weapons against such facilities would have left little intact to seize and use for rebuilding Soviet industry . . . Western France and Britain would suffer more substantial nuclear strikes against their centres of military-industrial activity, ports and transport systems. However, even in the latter instances Soviet military planners were not contemplating massive strategic nuclear bombing of cities to kill populations, but rather to destroy military production capacity. (Meyer, 1984a, esp. pp. 10–11).

It is worth remarking, by way of conclusion to the immediate post-war strategies of the Great Powers, that the Soviets could be seen, at least in Holloway's view, to be maintaining large land forces in Eastern Europe as a counter to the American capacity to strike the Soviet homeland with atom bombs. The Soviets could not strike at the US, but they could deploy their army against western Europe in the event of war (Holloway, 1983, p. 27).

The foundations for total war waged with nuclear weapons, bringing with it the complete physical destruction of one's enemy, were firmly laid in 1945, for the US, and very shortly afterwards for the other nuclear powers. In fact they amount to nothing more or less than a continuation of the strategies used during the last war, resting on an identical political presupposition, the ideology of total war. The doctrines associated with nuclear deterrence come later and have not modified the essential strategic assumptions nor what the armed forces are actually organized to do. Questions of credibility of the deterrence, the morality of a conditional threat to carry out an act in itself admitted to be immoral, and even the issue of unilateral nuclear disarmament come along when there is already a commitment to a type of war in which the absolute destruction of one's opponent is regarded as the orthodox and normal form of combat.

Given this historical background, the debate about the morality of deterrence may well be no more than a desire on the part of some sections of the population among the Western allies to withdraw themselves from the consequences of policies which were designed originally for their enemies and not for themselves.

Any moral approach to the issue of nuclear strategies which does not take account of how they developed historically is in danger of taking the existing situation as a given, unavoidable fact. This view, while having the merit of stark realism, ignores other facts: that certain 'things' should never have occurred, and that certain policies have been perverse from the moment of their conception. It is not enough to say that now they have become institutionalized; one has to trace out and recognize exactly where responsibility for this institutionalization rests.

7

Legality and Nuclear Weapons: Doctrines of Nuclear War-fighting

Tony Carty

The most distinctive feature of nuclear arms language is the limited range of the debate, and the failure of such efforts as have been made to break out of what is a language of strategic warfare frozen since the 1940s. It is impossible to avoid becoming engrossed in the so-called technicalities of the nuclear arms debate unless one appreciates that it represents a militarization of thinking about international relations.

In the case of the US, both Wright Mills and Nisbet treat as decisive in recent history the institutionalization of a military perspective which took place there during the Second World War (Wright Mills, 1956, chapter 9; Nisbet, 1976, chapter 3). Wright Mills sees as the essential feature of a military cast of mind that it accepts a seemingly total and permanent war economy. Every nation is either friend or foe and all negotiation will be seen as appeasement (p. 206). Not merely diplomatic circles, in particular the State Department, but also publicly supported scientific circles (the very large part of which are so funded), have become involved in the militarization of public life. They have had to move into a vacuum of theoretical military studies, in which strategy and policy are virtually one, because of a preference for 'technique' over 'theory' (Wright Mills, 1956, pp. 218–19). Indeed this merging of professions is itself a natural reflection of the concept of total war. Wright Mills concludes by accepting the definition of military metaphysics as a case of the domination of means over ends, for the purpose of heightening the prestige of the military (1956, pp. 221–2).

In my view the perfect complement to this framework for a phenomenology of nuclear arms language is given by Nisbet. He asks himself why such sophisticated, graceful, brilliant men as Bundy,

Rostow, Schlesinger and McNamara pushed Kennedy into so much
military adventure. The reason is not an ingrained love of combat as
such, 'but one more instance of the fondness of intellectuals for
crisis,' their desire to be close to and to extend the seat of power, a
deep dislike of the economic (a mere businessman's regard for profits, wages and prices) and above all, an intoxication with power,
and of feeling free from ordinary constraints of caution, convention
and routine (1976, pp. 187–90). Hence the absence of a moral and
legal dimension is hardly surprising.

Holloway argues for the Soviet Union that its thinking, whether
military or otherwise, has been frozen (it is arguable how far) in the
period of the Second World War:

The legacy of 1941 is reflected in a more general way in the determination
of the Soviet leaders to build up the power of the state. They have not
wanted to be vulnerable to attack, or to expose any vulnerability to the
outside world. It is partially for this reason that they have regarded mutual
deterrence with suspicion, because it rests on the mutual vulnerability of
the United States and the Soviet Union to attack each other. Since the
1970s, however, they have made it clear that they recognize such
vulnerability as a fact of life, for the time being at least. They have dis-
avowed the pursuit of superiority, and have accepted parity as the proper
relationship with the United States and Nato. They have elaborated a deterrent and defensive rationale for Soviet strategic power. (Holloway, 1983,
p. 58)

The central fact has to be that nuclear firepower has made conventional firepower insignificant. Yet the basic goals of Soviet war
planning have not changed: the destruction of enemy military forces
in Europe, the occupation of European territory and the removal of
the US and Britain from the enemy war coalition (Meyer, 1984a,
pp. 17–18). It may be that there is no punishment dimension in a
Soviet targeting doctrine, yet the replacement of conventional by
massive nuclear firepower has not led to any change in Soviet
targeting policy. There is no intention to conduct unlimited
targeting if only because this is senseless. However, there seems to
be no inhibition to the extensive use of nuclear weapons in what is
called the disorganization of the enemy economy. The objective is
still clearly military and not deterrence against the civilian population, but what difference will it make? 'The objective is not to turn
large economic and industrial regions into a heap of ruins . . . but to
deliver strikes which will destroy combat means, paralyze enemy
military production, making it incapable of satisfying the priority
needs of the front and rear, and sharply reducing the enemy
capability to conduct strikes' (Meyer, 1984a, p. 32).

This political and military discussion appears to fly in the face of a consensus among international lawyers that terror-bombing of civilians or even very extensive attacks upon civilians, whether intentional or incidental, would be contrary to international law. There are aspects of legal discussions which could possibly be dismissed as 'technical'. However, the central point which they appear to make is that obliteration or saturation bombing is illegal, that this illegality has been confirmed by the First Additional Protocol to the Geneva Convention in 1977, and that although nuclear weapons are not named in this Protocol their effects are covered and prohibited by its clear and unambiguous language.

Yet there is a clear continuation of the superpowers' strategic thinking, which has not allowed itself to be modified by the very extensive deployment of nuclear weapons. A legal rule does not always have to be observed to be a legal rule. Law is a standard of conduct whose reason for being supposes even frequent deviation from its standard. However, when it happens that the subjects of a legal order are systematically and uniformly organized so as to violate the rules of a legal order, and the latter is ostensibly based upon a consensus of the legal subjects, one has to ask whether the rules really enjoy a legal character.

The apparently 'technical' question, whether two western nuclear powers, Britain and the US, can make declarations or reservations concerning their weapons which appear to run counter to the terms of the Protocol they have signed, is as good a framework as any for a pin-pointing of where the international community really stands on the issue of the legality of nuclear weapons. One has to ask whether the fate of the First Protocol is not to be compared to that of the Hague Draft Rules on Air Warfare.

The argument that use of nuclear weapons is illegal

There is no specific prohibition on the use of nuclear weapons. However, there is equally no dispute that they are governed by general rules of international law. This is consistent with the approach of British, West German and US manuals of the Laws of War. They each note that there is no specific prohibition of nuclear weapons, but that their use is governed by the general rules of the laws of war. So those who wish to support the argument of illegality feel that they need only argue that their use would be incompatible with the terms of the First Protocol of 1977 to the 1949 Geneva Coventions on the Laws of War.

Part IV of the Protocol virtually bans the whole concept of total war. Article 51 states that the civilian population as such shall not be the object of attack, and acts or threats of violence, the primary purpose of which is to spread terror among the civilian population, are prohibited. This would be appear to be a very precise condemnation of the form of the British deterrent which is a threat of obliteration against Soviet cities. There is no point in arguing that the motive of the threat is to discourage Soviet leaders. The intention of the threatened act itself is what counts morally and legally.

Great stress can be placed on the uncontrollable nature of nuclear weapons in considering the Protocol's provisions on the nature of indiscriminate attacks. In the words of a US Naval War College study, the efficiency which is relied upon as a factor in establishing the lawfulness of a weapon is military efficacy in the controlled destruction of lawful military objectives. (1966, p. 162). Nuclear weapons, as also biological and chemical weapons, may be uncontrollable. An International Commission of the Red Cross Draft Rule of 1956 understands that word to mean harmful effects which could spread 'to an unforeseen degree or escape, either in space or in time, from the control of those who employ them, thus endangering the civilian population' (Naval War College, 1966, p. 181). So Article 51 describes as indiscriminate any attack which employs a means of combat which cannot be directed at a specific military objective. The prohibition includes treating as a single military objective a number of clearly separated military objectives located in an urban area.

Prohibition of total war extends to protection of objects indispensable to the survival of the civilian population. Starvation as a method of warfare, including attacks upon agricultural areas and water installations, are prohibited by Article 54. This protection extends to the natural environment in the terms of Article 55. It may not be the subject of widespread, long-term and severe damage, particularly where this may prejudice the health or survival of the population. Indeed dams, dykes and nuclear electrical generating stations may not be made the object of attack even where they are military targets, 'if such attack may cause the release of dangerous forces and consequent severe losses among the civilian population', according to Article 56.

The central feature of the First Protocol is that it renders illegal the concept of total war, that is, a war which does not distinguish civilian and military objectives, and which, indeed, wages more war against women and children than against military objectives (Rauch, 1980, pp. 58–63, 77, 80–3). The language of the Protocol puts stress on the effects which weapons have and can be taken to exclude any use of force which cannot bring itself within its terms. Indeed the approach of the International Committee of the Red Cross (ICRC) itself, in introducing the Protocol to states for consideration, was to stress the technical distinction between conventions on the effects of weapons and conventions regulating the particularities of individual weapons. In this respect it drew no particular line between nuclear and other weapons, such as bacteriological or chemical weapons, supposed to be conventional but which are indiscriminate in their effect or which cause superfluous suffering. They all remain outside the scope of the Protocol. What the ICRC did not propose, and the Conference itself rejected proposals to the same effect, was any specific absolute prohibition on the use of nuclear weapons or, for that matter, weapons such as incendiary or fragmentation bombs.

In my view it is essential to try to arrive at a correct interpretation of the events surrounding the conclusion of the First Protocol to the 1949 Geneva Conventions on the Laws of War. These inevitably somewhat abstruse proceedings cannot be dismissed, as being of purely legal technical interest, by those who wish to recommend ethical standards of conduct to states. That would merely be to operate in a vacuum. In my view lawyers who oppose the legality of the use of nuclear weapons are perhaps too readily helped along in their reasoning by the apparent consistency with which basic rules of humanitarian law seem always to contain a distinction between civilian and combatant and, related to this, to reassert the doctrines of proportionality and the prohibition of indiscriminate use of force. To this extent the First Protocol may appear merely to state the obvious more precisely. So much may even be said to apply to the specific prohibition of terror attacks on civilians. Yet the question remains whether such a declaration can have the effect of undoing practices and policies developed over a period of at least 40 years in disregard of such principles.

One has to ask what the rules specifically relevant to strategic warfare are worth, given the position of the nuclear powers. As Meyrowitz points out, neither Britain nor the US has any intention of bombarding the Warsaw Pact countries except with nuclear weapons (Meyrowitz, 1979, p. 912). So one has to take very seriously their declarations excluding nuclear weapons from the scope of the Protocol. A highly 'technical' debate can be mounted concerning the exact legal significance of the declarations made by Britain and the US. It may be claimed that the declarations are of no legal significance, and that the clear terms of a convention could only be altered by a declaration if it amounted to a contextual agreement to which all the convention parties adhered. The two declarations could only have the status of particular reservations to the main convention. In international law reservations which are incompatible

with the main object and purpose of a treaty are *ipso facto* invalid.
The party making them fails thereby to become a party to the treaty.
So one might conclude that it is not possible for Britain and the US
to reserve to themselves the right to conduct strategic nuclear warfare, as this could not be squared with the terms of the Protocol, and
particularly of Article 51 (Rauch, 1980, pp. 74–7, 91–8).

It is nonetheless somewhat strange that the assembled international community did not bother to make any objection to the British
and American declarations. Of the 96 states participating no other
state took particular and direct exception to the declarations. This
might be said to show that the two powers were taken to have been
stating the obvious, that the Protocol did not affect the use of nuclear
weapons in any way. Indeed the attempts of some states, such as
India and China, to have nuclear weapons as such prohibited were
not approved by the Conference. It might suggest that official
opinion has no expectation that the rules of war will be allowed to
regulate the use of nuclear weapons. Indeed, should we not understand the absence of a reaction by so many states as fatalistic
resignation?[1]

In one view the British and American declarations are a recognition of two salient facts about the risk of future strategic warfare.
First, nuclear weapons are virtually unusable in the context of
classical warfare. Second, and related to this, their very quality as
massively indiscriminate weapons gives them a dual character as annihilatory weapons and as a means of political dissuasion. It is their
virtual uselessness in classical warfare which is the root of their
dissuasive power, and it is the latter which is taken to be their main
function. Strategic warfare always contained within itself a feature
which rendered classical warfare obsolete. This tendency has now
reached completion. It does not follow that the declarations, taken
together with the First Protocol, can be said to have legalized the use
of nuclear weapons. Their normal use would clearly violate the Protocol. Indeed Meyrowitz accepts that their use, as proposed in the
event of failure of deterrence, would be illegal. (It will be noted at
the conclusion of this section how remarkable it is that a lawyer as
technically sophisticated and rigorous as Meyrowitz can find no way
to outlaw the doctrine of deterrence and yet be relentless in excluding the legality of most forms of nuclear war-fighting which
would actually be employed as contrary to the traditional law of
war.) Yet this is a factual situation leading to a 'legal' paradox which
is now historically unavoidable. The argument may continue that
the Warsaw Pact has recognized this by joining the abstaining
voters in the periodic UN debates on the issue of the legality of the
use of nuclear weapons. Neither science, technology nor law can

render nuclear war impossible. Mankind must live with the bomb as a fact (Meyrowitz, 1979, pp. 913–29, 933–8, 942–61).

So one might ask whether the Protocol itself does not risk the same fate as the Hague Draft Rules on Area Bombardment. Thirty-three states are parties to the Protocol, compared to the 62 which originally signed it in 1977, and to the 156 states which are parties to the Geneva Conventions. Of those 33 states the most significant western countries are Sweden, followed by Denmark, Austria, Finland and Switzerland. Of 'socialist' states there are China, Vietnam, Cuba, Yugoslavia and Laos. The more significant 'third world' states comprise Mexico, Zaire, Cameroon, Ghana, South Korea and Morocco. The other states are arguably of even less military or strategic significance (ICRC, 1984). It is known in ICRC circles that the present Reagan administration will never ratify the Protocol, not simply because its nuclear strategy would be impaired but also because it regards other parts of the Protocol as offensive, as a charter for guerilla warfare. It is estimated that the Soviets would be willing to undertake a simultaneous ratification of the document with the US. Clearly the step to be taken is simple but the distance to be covered is enormous.

The conclusion of this argument is to endorse the view of Schwarzenberger that it appears impossible to state with any confidence that near total air and missile warfare will be avoided simply because of the contemporary customary laws of war (Schwarzenberger, 1968, p. 665). The rules of war are obsolete not because of the advent of especially destructive weapons such as nuclear weapons, but because they are incompatible with the total war assumptions underlying the strategic warfare doctrines of which nuclear weapons are an integral part.

It has already been noted that even 'conservative' lawyers, such as Meyrowitz, recognize quite clearly that a legal paradox exists concerning the context in which 'deterrence' fails, so to speak. He insists that the very idea of the law of war is that it is limited. Except for reprisals against an enemy population after one's own has been attacked, Meyrowitz excludes the whole concept of total war as incompatible with a law of war. In particular he rejects the argument that the overwhelming evil of an enemy can justify annihilation. This would be to ignore the fundamental principle that the law of war is neutral as to the justice of the belligerent's cause. Equally he rejects the idea that annihilatory use of nuclear weapons could be used to stave off an otherwise inevitable defeat. This would be to ignore the limited character of war and sacrifice future to present generations. Indeed he considers the strategic bombing of Germany, including the atom bombing of Japan, as incompatible with the law of war, and any application of similar policies in the context of future warfare would be equally illegal (Meyrowitz, 1983, pp. 178, 181, 183, and esp. 185–6).

There is a very simple logic in the paradox which perplexes Meyrowitz. As long as war does not break out, one may suppose that the devastating prospect of nuclear warfare helps to keep the peace. Once the supreme value of peace has been lost and war breaks out, the same devastating effect of nuclear weapons must be subordinated to the greater humanitarian value implied in the notion of the limit to war which the law of war implies (p. 178). This logic can also be translated into the speculation that once it is perceived that the breakdown of peace is inevitable western politicians, at least, will not have recourse to nuclear weapons, if only because this would serve no medium- or long-term political purpose, while exposing all those engaged in conducting the war to the charge of criminality, according to the view of 'conservative' lawyers such as Meyrowitz.

In my opinion this is the breaking-point of the argument surrounding the legality of nuclear weapons. The perspective offered here is to confront the positivist, that is practice-oriented, lawyer with the overwhelming evidence of a continuity in strategic practice and total war ideology on the part of the major nuclear powers since the 1930s. The paradox which Meyrowitz sees is purely logical and ignores the continuity which it will be the major weight of this chapter to establish. Nuclear weapons exist within the context of a concept of strategic warfare which itself rests upon the supposition of total war. The rigorous professional lawyer's insistence on the illegality of nuclear war-fighting is as unhistorical as his or her insistence upon the legality of the doctrine of nuclear deterrence.

Hence it is essential to dismiss as beside the point the frequent discussions of the legality of nuclear weapons which try to be purely hypothetical. One may conceive of circumstances where their unlawfulness is not clear, such as in submarine warfare where their military usefulness was not necessarily accompanied by disproportionate injury to civilians, and a precision use of tactical weapons on key communications points (Naval War College, 1966, pp. 174, 188). McDoughal and Feliciano may be correct in disapproving of arguments as to legality which are based on analogies between nuclear weapons and biological weapons, on the ground that reasoning from past precedents is worthless when not placed alongside an analysis of contemporary policies. However, it is equally disingenuous to argue that the use of nuclear weapons is not necessarily going to have effects disproportionate to their military value (McDoughal and Feliciano, 1961, pp. 659–64). Unless such remarks are accompanied by a detailed analysis of existing policies they can appear to leave in abeyance an issue which is in desperate need of clarification.

The same reservation must be had about the argument that the use of nuclear weapons need not be excluded where they lead to a weakening of the military in the general terms of the St Petersburg Declaration: for example, the common argument that nuclear weapons are becoming smaller and more accurate against military targets. While it may not follow that the use of weapons in this sense is always illegal a lawyer cannot be allowed to leave the matter so much in the air.

Equally the argument about reprisals should be referred to actual strategies. The Protocol prohibits reprisals. However, traditional law did not exclude a retaliation unlawful in itself if it was not excessive in severity. This reasoning would not preclude an attack on a city as a reprisal (Wortley, 1983, p. 159). As nuclear deterrence is presented as a conditional threat to respond to aggression, this appears to concede the whole argument as to the legality of existing nuclear strategies. Yet the significance of such a position can only become clear once the development of actual nuclear strategies is considered.

The impossible doctrines of nuclear war-fighting

Historically the doctrine of nuclear deterrence as such is an afterthought to the deployment and targeting of nuclear weapons. In 1954 John Foster Dulles, US Secretary of State, proclaimed the doctrine of 'massive retaliation'. To counter aggression, the US would 'depend primarily upon a great capacity to retaliate instantly by means and at places of its own choosing'. This was in a context where the Soviets had a superior conventional military force and the NATO Council decided that tactical nuclear weapons were needed to redress the disparity. At the same time the Soviets were just beginning to have the capacity to retaliate in turn against the US with nuclear weapons (Zuckerman, 1985, pp. 81–2).

Apart from the concrete issue of a preference for nuclear defence over conventional defence, none of this language of nuclear deterrence is concerned with how a war would actually be fought and what preparations are being made to fight it. It is political rhetoric which, as is seen in the case of Dulles, is an accretion to the history of nuclear strategies. These were well set out for all the nuclear powers by the late 1940s. It is the generally destructive consequences of implementation of such total war policies with nuclear weapons which has led to the significant attempts made by both of the superpowers to move away from the notion of total war to that of limited war.

This could be seen as a reflection of an elemental sense of legal obligation. Quite apart from the First Protocol there is virtual agreement that as a matter of customary international law the deliberate terror-bombing of civilians is illegal. For instance, both Wortley and McDoughal agree on this point, although the latter speaks of a prohibition of terrorization in the sense of an annihilation of the general civilian population (McDoughal and Feliciano, 1961, p. 668; Wortley, 1983, p. 157). Such a position was reached as long ago as 1952 by Lauterpacht. He was very doubtful whether any illegality attached to the use of nuclear weapons as such. It was the concept of total war and not the advent of nuclear weapons which rendered the distinction between combatants and non-combatants illusory. Area bombardment had already paved the way for nuclear weapons and, given the difficulty of distinguishing those who contribute to the war effort from those who do not, very extensive civilian casualties are inevitable. Nonetheless he goes on to express a reservation which has undoubtedly been reflected in the post-war strategies of the superpowers, namely that terrorization of civilians marks the end of the very idea of law. '[S]o long as the assumption is allowed to subsist that there is a law of war, the prohibition of the weapon of terror not incidental to lawful operations must be regarded as an absolute rule of law' (Lauterpacht, 1952, pp. 368–9). However, the crucial question remains whether it is possible to go for a piecemeal withdrawal from the concept of strategic war against a total enemy. The fate of the First Protocol so far is vitally significant. When the question of principle is raised the nuclear powers make their reservations plain enough. They do not appear to be able or willing to make a fundamental break with the past.

Three US and NATO doctrines

It is remarkable that McNamara's landmark Ann Arbor speech of June 1962 was an attempt to discard the basic feature of the wartime strategic bombing in its total war dimension, although in a context which was clearly ironic: that is the clear capacity of the supposed victim to retaliate; 'The principal military objectives, in the event of a nuclear war stemming from a major attack on the Alliance, should be the destruction of the enemy's military forces, not of his civilian population . . . We are giving a possible opponent the strongest imaginable incentive to refrain from striking our own cities' (Ball, 1983, p. 12).

According to Ball, the main reason why McNamara had to retreat from this policy in a matter of months was bureaucratic. The Services and particularly the Air Force, were using the new strategy as a basis for force development, for more missiles and bombers to hit the potentially much larger number of counterforce (that is, military) targets. However, he stresses equally the European fear that the removal of the threat to Soviet cities would remove the deterrent to a Soviet invasion of western Europe. At the same time the Europeans were not willing to accept the implications of a counterforce policy for a small nuclear force.

In the final analysis the question for McNamara was whether it would be possible to retain two elements in a nuclear strategy. The first was a capacity to inflict unacceptable damage on an attacker. The second would be to limit damage to US populations and industrial capacities. The final McNamara policy had, as well, to consider US operational potential. The outcome for US strategic policy involved one-quarter of the population and two-thirds of the industrial capacity of the Soviet Union. The language of the 1966 financial year budget statement is familiar: 'But, it seems reasonable to assume the destruction of, say, one-quarter to one-third of its population and about two-thirds of its industrial capacity . . . would certainly represent intolerable punishment to any industrialized nation and thus serve as an effective deterrent' (Ball, 1983, pp. 12–14, esp. p. 14).

PD 59 was made by President Carter in the autumn of 1980 and represents present US strategic targeting policy towards the Soviet Union. It has been the butt of criticism that the US is planning to fight a limited nuclear war. In fact it marks the second major US attempt to modify the strategy of total nuclear war. President Carter came into office with a programme of minimum deterrence, but met with resistance from the start.

According to Powers, military men are wary of the word 'enough'. Carter could not even obtain an answer from the military about what weaponry they needed to carry out official policy. Instead Brzezinski set the dominant tone early in the administration with the question: 'Where are the criteria for killing Russians?' In other words it was a matter of how to fight a war, not how to obtain deep cuts in arsenals (Powers, 1982, pp. 84–6).

Indeed there is abundant evidence of what Wright Mills and Nisbet call military metaphysics. Brzezinski's military assistant, General Odom, is described as a man who 'took a hard line'. The Soviets are expansionist. Arms controllers think that military confrontation can simply be negotiated away. These were views which Brzezinski shared. This would not have been enough, only Carter's own immersion in details led him to a fascination with the fact that technical improvements appeared to mean nuclear weapons could be used in a traditional military way.

In some measure the adherence to the Second World War strategic bombing approach had been necessitated by weapons as clumsy as Polaris. The US was organized for a short devastating war and the question was whether this organization could be changed. Matters were complicated by the fact that Soviet military targets were mushrooming and becoming harder to destroy. Soviet civil defence measures were 'eroding' American capacity to kill civilians directly. This capacity was now estimated to be well under 100 million (Powers, 1982, pp. 94–7).

Satisfied that the Soviets had developed a new front end for the SS-19, Carter went ahead with the decision to build an American hard-target killer. The war-fighting weaponry was to be created; there remained the need for a new strategic doctrine to match it. The political problem was seen to be that the American public had become accustomed to the idea that nuclear war was all the less likely the more horrific the strategy for fighting it. Odom pressed for a new PD. He drafted it at Brzezinski's request, and the latter persuaded Carter to sign it without a full National Security Council meeting (pp. 103–4). If it can be said that it was not until PD 59 that the emphasis in strategic thinking changed from the mechanics of all-out destruction to the techniques of actually fighting, this can only be because weapon technology preceded doctrine. Yet it continued to be strategic in the sense of hitting the immediate sources of the enemy's ability to fight (Powers, 1982, pp. 106–8).

It is the language itself as an indication of 'levels of consciousness' which it is intended to highlight here. Powers is anxious to impress his readers that the new selectivity of PD 59 rests, at least in part, on the fact that weapons will be directed to the structure of the Soviet empire. This is the significance of Brzezinski's remark about killing Russians. 'Leadership' targets include the hardened shelters of the Party bosses, not just the Politburo but 'the bureaucratic apparatus that runs the country'. It is hard to quote this language selectively. There is no question of leaving out anything targeted previously. As Powers puts it, by 1980 the number of targets had grown to 40,000. 'Now everything is on the list.' This 'everything' includes 886 cities with a population of more than 25,000. Apart from that, he can point to 50 per cent of key Soviet industry contained in 200 complexes (1982, pp. 108–9).

Where does this leave the doctrine of nuclear deterrence and its godfather, the morale-smashing strategic bombing? Powers points to what he sees as a considerable change, with PD 59:

The principal purpose of P.D. 59 . . . is still deterrence, but it is deterrence of the sort that prevailed before 1914. In the years after 1945, when the bomb was as cumbersome as it was destructive, the theory of deterrence emphasized the ghastly consequences – the holocaust – that would follow if deterrence failed. We did not build the bomb in order to deter war; we built it because we could build it . . . Deterrence was simply the best theory we could devise for its 'use', once we had it. But theory plods where technology sprints . . . The result has been regression to deterrence of the sort implied in the Roman maxim 'Let him who desires peace prepare for war'. This approach worked well for thirty years before World War I. (Powers, 1982, pp. 109–10)

It seems a fair interpretation of Powers' line of reasoning that he thinks we have come full circle since 1945. The most convincing moral argument for the RAF strategic bombing of Germany was that it would avoid a repetition of the slaughter of the trenches. Now it seems that new precision nuclear weapons will enable us to fight a war of attrition more like what took place after 1914. In Powers' words: 'When exhaustion set in, and the fighting dwindled, the two sides would be left to manage their recovery as best they could'.

Another attempt to reduce the dangers of total nuclear war concerns the suggestion of somehow raising the nuclear threshold in Europe. NATO's security has rested on the doctrine of flexible response. This involves a willingness to use a wide range of battle-field nuclear weapons in the event of a Soviet attack. The reliance upon such weapons has been largely at the insistence of the Europeans, who prefer the much lower budget and personnel implications which such reliance has appeared to afford. The Americans would always have preferred large European conventional forces well able to match the Soviets. Underlying European thinking seems to be the supposition that controlled escalation, based upon western nuclear superiority, would always be such as to prevent the Soviets from risking any war at all. In other words flexible response still rested upon the expectation that the Soviets would balk at any aggression so long as there was considerable likelihood of devastation of the Soviet homeland.

Calls for a rethink are based upon at least two considerations. The first concerns the battlefield nuclear weapons themselves. It is pointed out that they are now vulnerable to Soviet conventional artillery, and that they are equally vulnerable to well-known Soviet plans for troop deployment, the Operational Group Manoeuvres, to neutralize them in their forward positions close to the Iron Curtain. This puts a great pressure on their rapid use of abandonment at the initial stage of an attack, which is to defeat the whole sense of 'flexible response'. Second, it is remarked that any use of nuclear weapons in a battle on German territory could cost as many as two million German civilian casualties in the first days of battle alone. Given this situation, it is considered fortunate that improvements in the technology of conventional weapons, improvements now enshrined in NATO FOFA (follow-on forces attack) tactics, afford the possibility of an alternative to the functions which the battlefield nuclear weapons are supposed to fulfil. These are, essentially, the interdiction of second and third echelon Soviet forces before they become engaged, as well as the destruction of supporting Soviet airbases.

Proposals to introduce new conventional weapons would involve certain modifications of nuclear strategy but it is difficult to see how they are fundamental when put in the total context of post-war nuclear strategy. One view is that the ability to resist a conventional Soviet invasion of western Europe by conventional means would allow NATO to adopt a no-first-use declaration on nuclear weapons. It could alter its nuclear weapon procurement to reflect a minimum need for a survivable second strike capacity. This may be seen as a sensible reflection of the fact that one can only estimate how one's opponent will behave. As McGeorge Bundy puts it:

As long as each side has large numbers of weapons that could be used against an opponent, even after the strongest possible preemptive attack, existential deterrence is strong and it rests on uncertainty about what could happen . . . [I]t makes no sense to base procurement decisions on refined calculations of the specific kinds of force that would be needed for a wide variety of limited nuclear responses. (McGeorge Bundy, 1983)

This appears to be the strongest statement in favour of limiting the possible use of nuclear weapons. McNamara's own individual defence of a similar position is firmly within the logic of debate about the credibility of battlefield nuclear weapons. These are militarily obsolete now that there are other, equally satisfactory, conventional options. As he says:

The Alliance's tactical nuclear posture could be thoroughly overhauled, with an eye towards shifting to a posture intended solely to deter the first use of nuclear weapons by the Warsaw Pact. Such a shift would permit major reductions in the number of nuclear weapons now deployed with Nato's forces in Europe, no more and probably no less than 3,000 weapons would be sufficient. (McNamara, 1983, p. 78)

Indeed the Report of the European Security Study (ESECS), upon which McNamara also relies, points out how the most that can be expected of the new initiative is to de-emphasize the role of theatre, and particularly battlefield, nuclear weapons. This shift 'should not be interpreted as a renunciation of the role of nuclear weapons in

Nato strategy. Nuclear weapons will remain an essential component of Nato strategy in order to deter Soviet use of nuclear weapons, hold Soviet forces at risk, thereby ensuring their dispersal, and threaten retaliation against Soviet first use' (European Security Report, 1983, p. 199).

There is no doubt that the new weaponry does not have the same collateral effects as battlefield nuclear weapons. However, the main military proponent of the initiative, General Rogers, Supreme Allied Commander Europe (SACEUR), does not favour a no-first-use policy on nuclear weapons and there exists considerable controversy as to just how expensive procurement of the new weaponry would be (Stockholm International Peace Research Institute (SIPRI), 1984, pp. 144–7). So it seems that this so-called 'Rogers Plan' is open to all the speculation which is endemic to nuclear strategy (Rogers, 1984).

For instance, one might ask why the Americans want to improve their capacity to fight a conventional war in Europe. Does it not make it more likely that the Soviets will risk a conventional war, which might gain them important territories in Central Europe without running any risk of nuclear escalation? Alternatively, is the move intended to facilitate the possibility of, or the threat of, a strike into eastern Europe – given that the technology is 'deep-strike' in nature – with the attendant risk that the Soviets escalate to nuclear weapons, nothwithstanding their no-first-use declaration? Would it not be better to remain with weapons which would quickly cause a holocaust, and confine oneself to showing a determination to use them if necessary, dragging all of the Alliance in at the same time? Is this not the best guarantee of peace?

It seems that talk of raising the nuclear threshold does not afford much possibility of extricating Europe from nuclear menace, even in the limited theatre context, not to mention the problem of strategic targeting which has been discussed previously.

A footnote to the discussion of US nuclear strategies might be a brief look at some of the language of the SDI; Grey is an arms control consultant to Reagan on various Government agencies and Payne is in the Pentagon. They both defend US policy in foreign affairs in the language of 'military metaphysics'. There is what they call a moral imperative to develop defensive nuclear weapons. The reason is simply that no US President has the power to ensure that there will never be a nuclear war. 'It is beyond reason to believe that all nuclear armed powers would agree to ban the use of nuclear weapons and abide by the agreement under all conditions.' It is equally incredible that arms control could reduce the nuclear arsenal below what would cause climactic catastrophe. This does not mean that arms control has no value for the US pursuit of strategic stability, but rather that it can hardly be relied upon. So an emphasis on defence and nuclear disarmament are essential allies. For instance, a defence posture leads to easier prospects of verification. Huge numbers are needed to break through, whereas the verification of the small number of weapons one should have to support a posture of minimum deterrence would be much less difficult (Payne and Grey, 1984, pp. 840–1).

Payne and Grey become lost in their speculative meanderings about the advantages of the defensive policy which they advocate. They admit to being very unclear about the Soviet reactions to an effective acquisition of defensive technology. There could be a danger of a Soviet pre-emptive strike. There is bound to be a strong determination on the part of the Soviets to maintain the credibility of their offensive capacity, presumably by increasing it. If, as is likely, the Soviets go for a similar defensive capacity, this will force NATO into a purely conventional strategy. Indeed a 'defended' US will be freer to come to the rescue of western Europe (pp. 824, 829–31). Clearly covering the options of grave risk of proximate pre-emptive nuclear war and a forced return to exclusively conventional war involves a very wide sweep. Yet it does not amount to rational political analysis. Payne and Grey are simply second-guessing possible uses of nuclear weapons.

Two Soviet doctrines in the European theatre and the question of deterrence

There is one respect in which it is easier for the Soviets to argue that there is nothing inherently illegal about their present military build-up. It is well known that military strategy in the Soviet Union is the province of the military. It can possibly be argued that it is naturally their task to prepare for the waging and winning of war, rather than to aim for such an inherently political goal as providing a sufficient threat of punishment to states and societies which do not conduct themselves appropriately. It appears that Soviet political leaders do not work with a theory of deterrence as a way of 'keeping the peace'. According to Holloway, there is no Soviet equivalent to the American doctrine of deterrence. Prevention of war is achieved by a peaceful policy. Indeed, there is no precise Russian equivalent for the term deterrence. A distinction is drawn between the Soviet policy of holding back and the western policy of intimidation (Holloway, 1983, pp. 32–3).

Holloway is anxious to qualify the impression which some commentators have, that the US has a war-deterring policy while the Soviet Union has a war-waging policy. Inevitably the Soviets were less able to rely upon the deterrent impact of their weaponry until the late 1960s, although in Holloway's interpretation Khrushchev accepted in 1960 that a situation of mutually assured destruction existed (Holloway, 1983, pp. 38, 55–6). Meyer points out how just after Stalin's death Malenkov had seen in the vast destructive power of nuclear weapons a means to acquire a cheap arsenal to destroy the enemy while diverting most resources away from military to consumer goods, in other words a 'force de frappe' along French lines. It was Khrushchev who then rejected the idea that any absolute weapon could make war impossible. Only a 'balanced' development of Soviet armed forces could guarantee Soviet security (Meyer, 1984a, p. 12).

There have been further developments in Soviet thinking since the late 1950s. Perhaps inconsistently with his primary thesis about deterrence in Soviet thought, military or otherwise, Holloway draws out clear support for a theory of deterrence in Brezhnev's 'Tula speech' within the context of an argument that nuclear parity was the Soviet goal. At the same time he points to a clear Soviet awareness of the catastrophic dimensions of any new world war (Holloway, 1983, pp. 48–9, 53). Nonetheless this does not involve a fundamental change in the Soviet view that war must be fought with an appropriate combination of all military forces, whether nuclear or conventional. The Soviet Defence Minister Ustinov notes that a major consequence of Brezhnev's 'no-first-use' doctrine is to place increased demands on the combat readiness and technical equipment of Soviet troops (Meyer, 1984a, p. 30). This is in line with the view of Sokolovski, an authority quoted by Holloway as supporting the thesis that 'final victory' could only be achieved by the combined efforts of all services (Holloway, 1983, pp. 49–52).

Perhaps two features of Soviet theatre strategy deserve special mention: the attempt to devise a phase of purely conventional war, and the 'modernization' implications of the deployment of the SS-20s. The Soviets do not accept the concept of a limited nuclear war in Europe and they show no confidence that theatre nuclear war can be 'managed'. The only true 'firebreak' which is recognized is that between conventional and nuclear weapons, although the USSR continues to envisage sparing as much as possible of western Europe's industrial potential, no matter how much of the USA may have had to be destroyed (Meyer, 1984a, pp. 22–5).

So the Soviets have thought it worthwhile to devise a strategy for the elimination of NATO's theatre nuclear weapons through conventional means. This is a principal rationale for improvements in Soviet ground, naval and air forces. It appears a less menacing policy, and is to some extent a reaction to McNamara's 'flexible response' doctrine. However, it has two obvious defects in terms of any significant reduction in the risk of nuclear war. The Soviets expect that as the war progresses the theatre nuclear balance will move in favour of themselves.

In this context one should see how Soviet military writings link the decision to employ theatre nuclear forces (TNF) to an assessment of the likelihood of imminent use of nuclear weapons by the enemy. Meyer is not sure where the military writings leave Brezhnev's 'no-first-use' doctrine. The desire is to lengthen the conventional phase by waiting until the West indicates a preparation to launch a theatre nuclear strike, whereupon the Soviets will aim to be the first to employ nuclear weapons decisively. Meyer puts it: 'What will be important, however is that the subsequent use of Soviet T.N.F. should be decisive, seizing the initiative through pre-emptive nuclear strikes against enemy T.N.F. and other targets' (Meyer, 1984a, p. 28, also pp. 26–7).

In my view this particular debate merely reflects the Soviet philosophy held both by the politicians and the military since the early 1950s, to combine whatever nuclear and conventional weapons might be available to their maximum military effect without accepting that the 'nuclear age' has created any new dimension. How else could the Soviets overlook the fact that faced with losing their TNF the NATO states may well prefer to use them before the balance in that particular sector goes entirely in favour of the Soviets.

Nothing could do more to show the inextricable interweaving of conventional and nuclear weapons in West-East theatre strategy than an attempt to answer the question of whether the introduction of the Soviet SS-20s is a new destabilizing factor. There is, not surprisingly, no clarity as to when the Soviets might feel that they would have to move from a conventional attempt to neutralize NATO theatre nuclear weapons to a pre-emptive theatre nuclear strike. Nonetheless, should such a decision be taken, the new SS-20 force does not, in Meyer's view, alter the destructive capacity of Soviet nuclear forces devoted to attacks on NATO nuclear targets. The new forces simply make the operation more easy to manage than would be the case with continued reliance upon a much larger number of SS-4/SS-5, and the diversion of the ICBM SS-11 and SS-19. Where previously some 770 missiles were necessary, now 250 could be sufficient. Operational certainties are increased with weapons which are more manoeuvrable and accurate. The vulnerability of NATO in Europe to Soviet nuclear forces goes back decades, and has not been increased (Meyer, 1984b, pp. 25–7, 49).

However, none of this is any cause for relief about the extent of the nuclear threat. It is part of Soviet policy to reduce collateral damage as far as possible in western Europe so that the latter can assist in the post-war reconstruction of the Soviet Union. The use of the more accurate SS-20s, capable of low airburst against hard targets, may almost eliminate fallout. Lethal contamination could be reduced by 90 per cent compared to the use of the SS-11. Yet fallout may still reach between 15 per cent and 40 per cent of West Germany (Meyer, 1984b p. 28).

Nonetheless, the overall Soviet strategy of 'leaving something to conquer' is not, in Meyer's view, as significant as the much more destabilizing Soviet strategy of a conventional strike against western European nuclear forces. This has created a 'use them or lose them' situation, which cannot be affected one way or another by appeal to a no-first-use strategy. Whether NATO intends to use these weapons or not, the Soviets intend to destroy them (Meyer, 1984b, p. 50). In Meyer's view the only effective response to the Soviet policy would be a strengthening of NATO conventional forces, an already very familiar argument which usually indicates no intention to reduce reliance upon nuclear forces. This is not to mention the question whether the Soviet acceptance of a conventional phase of war was based upon the withdrawal of NATO land-based missiles capable of reaching the Soviet homeland. The reintroduction of such NATO TNF systems may lead the Soviets to abandon the ideal of a conventional phase and resort immediately to preventive or pre-emptive nuclear strikes in the event of a theatre war (p. 43).

The legal nihilism of nuclear strategies

The object of the historical studies in the previous chapter is to show that while the atom bombing of Hiroshima and Nagasaki followed directly from the prevailing strategic military logic, there was absolutely nothing inevitable about the decision to bomb in terms of either moral or military necessity. Therefore the moral dilemma posed by nuclear weapons is a quite recent historical creation of individual human beings. Moral philosophers and theologians speak often of the grip of the dilemma posed by the existence of weapons which cannot be disinvented. For instance the French Catholic Bishops consider that the moral law permits smaller powers to threaten intolerable injury to superpowers at a cost which is within their resources (Les Grandes Textes, 1983, pp. 7–8). They warn against abstracting issues from the complexity of the situations in which they are found. The world is a place of violence and sin, in which the politicians and military have a duty to defuse blackmail to which the nation could be submitted. Faced with two unavoidable evils, one chooses the lesser, without trying to make it appear good (pp. 9–10).

This is to ignore the historical responsibility which exists for the creation of the present crisis. It is not enough simply to start from where we are now. The recent history of the development of nuclear strategies shows that no piecemeal reversal of policies is conceivable. We are faced not so much with a moral dilemma as with baneful consequences of wrong actions. The extent of the crisis is expressed graphically by Nisbet. He concludes his study of what he calls the lure of military society with the hardly moderate words 'that only events presently unforeseeable in nature and scope – perhaps those constituting a major religious movement of worldwide proportions – could possibly arrest the present drive of militarism in the Western world or for that matter in the world at large' (Nisbet, 1976, p. 191).

The term legal nihilism signifies the absence of law. The customary international law which might appear to exclude terror-bombing of civilians can only rest upon the moral conscience of mankind. One has to face squarely the question of whether any such conscience exists, at least in the northern hemisphere. This is why it is so important not to play down the significance of the declarations which the nuclear powers have made with respect to the First Protocol. This is why one must take completely seriously the efforts which have been made by the superpowers to draw back from the full consequences of all-out nuclear war since the 1950s. At the end of all analysis one is left with a numbing sense of absence.

Keeny and Panofsky's claim that the relative lack of public response to the scale of casualties which it is certain a nuclear war would entail 'suggests a general denial psychosis when the public is confronted with the prospect of such an unimaginable catastrophe' (Keeny and Panofsky, 1981/2, p. 291). Garrison identifies the problem in a not dissimilar way with his mention of *hibakusha*, a concept used to signify 'without self, without centre'. It is focused upon the aftermath of the atom bombing of Japan and is supposed to reflect the replacement of a natural order of life and death with an unnatural order of death-dominated life (Garrison, 1982, pp. 69–71). It is immensely difficult to pin-point an absence, yet a suggestive line of historical enquiry is to trace the extent to which the German and Japanese aggression were the occasion for a radical dehumanization of their opponents. Garrison makes the following remarkable assertions:

The great tragedy of post-war Europe is that the willingness to own up to one's own guilt and recognize the inner existence of the shadow has not happened . . . The conflagration that broke out in Germany was the outcome of psychic conditions that are universal, only while the Germans threatened a single people with genocide, the nuclear arms race threatens the entire human race with extinction. (Garrison, 1982, p. 203)

The just war: a postscript

It may be worth noting in context of a study of the legal aspects of modern international conflict that there is at least one almost forgotten aspect of the classical theory of the just war. It appears that the decision of Christian philosopher-theologians to move away from a more extreme form of pacifism to an acceptance of a doctrine of the justified use of force was tied to a form of the 'demonization' of the enemy which we have been trying to pin down here.

Hartigan attributes to Augustine, 'an ideologically derived self-confidence in the rightness of one's cause, . . . a major characteristic of Western conflict justification'. Augustine was the first to define the concept of just war and it was to become enormously significant. Yet he required, from the very start, a notion of moral vengeance, justified wrath and intended punishment against an evil doer. His view of conflict in purely moral terms made it easy for him to ascribe a condition of communal guilt and universal evil to the enemy.

Augustine forbade massacres, wanton killing and attacks on women and children. However, the logic of his theory of the just war did not allow easily the notion that there were innocents among the enemy. Given his belief in the intimate link between individual and social responsibility, he did not suppose that there would regularly be many innocents in the enemy population. Even if there were, the innocence or guilt of those attacked did not matter in determining the guilt of the attacker. All that counted was the subjective matter of his own intent and his judgement of military necessity. This view of the just war held for a thousand years and even Thomas Aquinas did not question it (Hartigan, 1982, pp. 29–33).

These views were progressively modified by Vitoria, Grotius and Vattel. It may be possible to say that the less interest there is in justification for war, the more interest there is in its just conduct. The process of the theoretical development of the principles for the just conduct of war was directly related to a historical process of secularization. Indeed when one comes to the Enlightenment legal theorist of the eighteenth century, Vattel, the arch-proponent of the immunity of non-combatants, there is no hint in his doctrine of rightness or wrongness of the struggle against the enemy. The lawyer is not supposed to be able to judge what is seen as inevitably no more than a matter of opinion (Hartigan, 1982, pp. 43, 89–90, 96, 102, 108–9).

It has been stressed that there is a parallel in the development of the ideology of total war and of the concept of strategic warfare. Vattel notwithstanding, the French Revolution introduced to modern warfare an armed population with an ideal. Only a new weapons technology was needed to destroy the fragile immunity of the civilian (Hartigan, 1982, p. 112). It was not long in coming. Since the late nineteenth century leading nation states have been committed to the idea that defence requires the possession of the maximum amount of the most advanced weaponry (Gallie, 1984, pp. 183–91).

It is fundamental to the ideology of total war that the process whereby the enemy is demonized requires that one's own exercise of power is without guilt. In such a case any justified use of force can only be a holy crusade. This is how one contemporary German historian of ideas interprets the intellectual background to American foreign and military policy (Krakau, 1967, pp. 186, 189–92, 199–203). He traces a direct connection between the ideology of total war and the legal nihilism which has been described here.

Among American international lawyers, the movement to abolish war in the inter-war period was supposed to lead to the elimination of the need for rules relating to the conduct of war. The roots of total war were already present in the statement of Manley Hudson in 1928 that 'in cases of aggression no body of sea law is to restrain attempts to overcome the aggressor'. In 1930, two years after the conclusion of the Kellog-Briand Pact, which provided the legal foundation for the charge that Germany and Japan had waged an illegal war and hence were outlaws, Wright, Fenwick and Eagleton, leading American international lawyers, regarded war as beyond law. The aggressor had no rights and any attempt to develop a law of war could be interpreted as a pro-war move. These arguments were advanced by the US at the Nuremberg Tribunal, although they were not accepted (Krakau, 1967, pp. 357–60).

8

Nuclear Weapons in Europe: Political and Moral Considerations

David Holloway

In recent years Europeans have become much more worried by the prospect of nuclear war, and much more conscious of the 10,000 or so nuclear weapons based in Europe or in the waters around it. The worsening of political relations between the US and the Soviet Union, the deployment of new missiles in both western and eastern Europe, the publicity given to plans for the conduct of nuclear war in Europe: all of these have contributed to a profound sense of anxiety. Doubts about the wisdom of current policies have been accompanied by a growing concern about the morality of basing security on nuclear weapons. A sense of moral unease has been engendered by the fear of nuclear war, and by the inhumanity of making threats of nuclear destruction.

The churches have tried to respond to this unease by giving guidance on the ethical questions raised by nuclear weapons. They have set out principles to guide practical action, and offered specific policy recommendations on the basis of these principles. The level of moral awareness in the public debate about nuclear weapons has risen as a result, even if the moral content of our policies has not.

The Christian churches have traditionally adopted two approaches to the problem of war and peace. There is a strong pacifist tradition, which rejects any kind of war; this has been strengthened by the advent of nuclear weapons which, with their terrible destructive power, make the prospect of war so much more horrendous than before. But the dominant Christian tradition, which centres on the just war doctrine, has led to two diametrically opposed positions when applied to nuclear weapons. The first argues that no use of nuclear weapons could ever meet the conditions of a just war, and that consequently nuclear war is morally unacceptable. The second comes to a different conclusion, arguing that more discriminating nuclear weapons systems (for example, with lower explosive yield and greater accuracy) ought to be developed, and that strategies ought to be devised for using these weapons in a limited and controlled way, thus meeting the conditions of the just war doctrine.[1]

The churches, in their various statements and pastoral letters, have by and large rejected this second view. There is general agreement that nuclear war must be condemned in principle, and that international security should be based on something other than the threat to use nuclear weapons. But once one moves beyond this point, disagreement emerges as to whether deterrence – and hence the possession of nuclear weapons – is to be rejected unconditionally, or whether it can be given a conditional acceptance.[2] Some Church statements have taken the former position, on the grounds that if the use of nuclear weapons is wrong, then the intention to use them –which is implicit in deterrence – is also wrong, but other statements have argued that deterrence can be given a conditional acceptance. In his message to the Special Session of the UN General Assembly on Disarmament in 1982 Pope John Paul II said that 'in current conditions "deterrence" based on balance, certainly not as an end in itself but as a step on the way toward a progressive disarmament, may still be judged morally acceptable. Nonetheless in order to ensure peace, it is indispensable not to be satisfied with this minimum which is always susceptible to the real danger of explosion' (US Catholic Bishops, 1983, p. 54). Similar sentiments have been expressed in the pastoral letters of the German and American Catholic Bishops.

This position appears to be based on the belief that nuclear weapons have created such a great discontinuity in the issue of war and peace that traditional approaches may no longer be appropriate, or may need to be adapted. The American Bishops, for example, write that 'traditionally the Church's moral teaching sought first to prevent war and then to limit its consequences if it occurred. Today the possibilities for placing political and moral limits on nuclear war are so minimal that the moral task, like the medical, is prevention: as a people, we must refuse to legitimate the idea of nuclear war' (US Catholic Bishops, 1983, pp. 41–2). They are willing to give a 'strictly conditioned moral acceptance' to nuclear deterrence, in part because they believe that it contributes to the prevention of war.

The second draft of the American Bishops' pastoral letter stated that 'not only the *use* of strategic nuclear weapons, but also the *declared intent* to use them involved in our deterrence policy, are both wrong'. The draft went on to say, however, that deterrence could be 'tolerated' by Catholic moral teaching 'as the lesser of two evils', on condition that negotiations proceed towards the reduction and elimination of nuclear weapons. This argument was rejected in the final draft because of its consequentialism, which Catholic ethics traditionally rejects. Because Catholic teaching regards the intention to act as morally equivalent to the action itself, the only thing that makes deterrence acceptable in the final draft is the argument that, in certain very restricted circumstances, the use of nuclear weapons might be morally acceptable (Okin, 1984). But while this may provide a technical solution to the problem of consequentialism, many of the passages in the letter retain more than an element of consequentialism about them, particularly in the recognition that nuclear deterrence may be given conditional acceptance in part because it has, or may have, helped to prevent nuclear war.

These ethical issues are explored elsewhere in this book, and will not be examined in this chapter. Here it is appropriate to note that the American Bishops write: 'our arguments in this pastoral letter must be detailed and nuanced; but our "no" to nuclear war must, in the end, be definitive and decisive' (US Catholic Bishops, 1983, p. 43). They also say, however, that 'it is much less clear how we translate a "no" to nuclear war into the personal and public choices which can move us in a new direction, toward a national policy and an international system which more adequately reflect the values and vision of the kingdom of God' (p. 42). The aim of this paper is to look at some of the proposals advanced in recent years for reducing nuclear weapons in Europe, in the light of criteria drawn from the American Bishops' pastoral letter. I shall not look here at the policy choices facing individual countries such as Britain and France, but focus rather on the possibility of change within the framework of a divided Europe.

The evolution of nuclear forces in Europe

Nuclear weapons have been deployed in Europe as part of the conflict that emerged between the Soviet Union and the western allies at the end of the war with Nazi Germany. Nuclear weapons were not the cause of this conflict, but they soon became an important element in it. They were first introduced into Europe when the US deployed bombers in Britain in the late 1940s. These aircraft did not have the range to strike the Soviet Union from the US, but they could reach Soviet targets from forward bases in Europe. During the 1950s bombers based in Europe formed a substantial part of the US strategic force, and towards the end of the decade they were supplemented by intermediate-range ballistic missiles, which were

withdrawn some years later. In the 1960s the US deployed a large
number of ICBMs on its own territory, as well as a sizeable force of
missile-carrying submarines. But some forward-based systems remained in western Europe, and these were augmented by the
Ground Launched Cruise Missiles (GLCMs) and Pershing II
missiles, which began to be deployed in 1983.

The US introduced tactical nuclear weapons, with a short range
and a relatively low yield, into Europe in the early 1950s, and still
maintains a sizeable force of these systems there. NATO believed it
needed these weapons because it could not match the large Soviet
conventional forces. Most of these systems do not have the range to
reach the Soviet Union from western Europe.

NATO has based its policy on the premise that the US would be
willing to use its nuclear weapons in the event of a Soviet attack on
western Europe. This 'nuclear guarantee', which is the cornerstone
of NATO strategy, was clear and unambiguous in the first years of
the Alliance when the US could strike the Soviet Union but was not
itself vulnerable to a Soviet nuclear attack. Under these conditions
the US could credibly threaten massive nuclear retaliation against
the Soviet Union.

The Soviet Union detonated its first atomic bomb in August 1949,
and by the late 1950s it had deployed medium-range systems which
could deliver nuclear weapons to targets in and around Europe.
These were intended to strike command and communications centres, as well as enemy strategic forces and the bases from which they
could operate. In the late 1950s the Soviet Union also began to
deploy shorter-range tactical nuclear weapons for use on the battlefield. In the 1960s it too began to acquire a large force of ICBMs
capable of striking targets in the US.

As the Soviet Union's intercontinental forces grew in the 1960s,
the threat of immediate and massive resort to strategic nuclear forces
by the US began to seem less credible. As a result, NATO moved
towards a strategy of 'flexible response', designed to meet any aggression in Europe at the appropriate level. A conventional attack
would be met by conventional forces, and tactical nuclear weapons
would be used only if conventional defence failed. The use of tactical
nuclear weapons would carry the calculated risk of escalation to strategic nuclear war in which both superpowers would be engulfed, and
this risk would constitute the ultimate deterrent to the Soviet Union.

Flexible response, which was formally adopted in 1967, remains
NATO's strategy. It tries to link the forward defence of the Central
Front with the US strategic nuclear forces, and thereby to extend the
deterrent effect of those forces to western Europe. Through flexible
response NATO tries to reconcile the interests of West Germany,

which wants to link its security to US strategic forces, and of the US, which does not wish to risk its own survival by threatening to use its strategic forces in response to a low-level attack on western Europe.

Soviet military strategy in Europe has not had to accommodate the interests of allies in the same way. In the 1950s the Soviet Union assumed that a world war would be nuclear from the start and concentrated, therefore, on preparing for a war which would begin with massive nuclear strikes. It attached considerable importance to the pre-emptive strike which could break up an enemy attack before it got off the ground. In the mid-1960s, however, the Soviet Union began to take account of the possibility that war in Europe might begin with a conventional phase, and to prepare its forces for conventional as well as nuclear operations. This trend has continued to the point where the primary mission of the Soviet TNF may well be to deter NATO from resorting to its nuclear weapons in the event of war, thereby undermining the strategy of flexible response.

Soviet nuclear weapons policy has been designed to achieve important political goals. When the Soviet Union was unable to inflict nuclear strikes on the US, it held western Europe hostage by targeting it with nuclear weapons, and thus hoped to influence the policy of NATO as a whole. Now it tries to weaken the cohesion of the Alliance by making flexible response unworkable. Moreover, Soviet nuclear forces in eastern Europe (and in the European part of the Soviet Union) are part of a military posture that is designed to secure – and to signal the determination to maintain – the Soviet position in eastern Europe.

Britain and France also possess nuclear forces which, though much smaller than those of the superpowers, are sustained by the desire to assert national sovereignty as well as to deter a nuclear attack. The British forces, which are heavily dependent on US technology, are committed to NATO's integrated command, but the Polaris SLBMs (submarine-launched ballistic missiles) could be used independently if the government decided that 'supreme national interests are at stake'. The independence of the French forces is greater, since they rest on French technology and France is no longer a member of NATO's military organization.

The possibility that West Germany might acquire an independent nuclear force was a major issue in East–West relations in the 1950s and 1960s, but it lost much of its urgency when the West German government signed the Nuclear Non-Proliferation Treaty in 1969, thereby formally committing itself not to acquire nuclear weapons of its own. As it is, West Germany has more nuclear weapons per square kilometre than any other country in the world, though these are under the control of foreign governments.[3]

Unresolved issues

By the late 1960s the present shape of nuclear forces in Europe had been established, and the military and political rationales for these systems formulated, but a number of issues have remained controversial.

First, a major question mark hangs over the US nuclear guarantee, which is the central element in NATO's strategy. Many people in the West argue that the guarantee is no longer credible now that the Soviet Union has achieved strategic parity with the US. The Soviet leaders, they say, can no longer believe that the American President would expose the US to destruction in order to come to the aid of western Europe. In Henry Kissinger's words, US assurances to western Europe 'cannot be true . . . it is absurd to base the strategy of the West on the credibility of the threat of mutual suicide' (Kissinger, 1979, p. 266).

Others argue, however, that the US nuclear guarantee is as effective as ever, and that it rests not merely on particular types and numbers of weapons, but on the whole nexus of political, economic, social and cultural ties between western Europe and the US, not to mention the 300,000 US troops stationed in Europe. They point out, moreover, that while the Soviet leaders might not be certain that the President would retaliate with US strategic forces in the event of a Soviet attack on western Europe, neither could they be sure that he would not do so. Such uncertainty – the small risk of a large nuclear war – would be enough, it is claimed, to deter a Soviet attack (McGeorge Bundy, 1979, pp. 271–2).

However, the US nuclear guarantee, although it might be enough to deter the Soviet Union from attacking western Europe, is not always sufficient to reassure the West European governments, for whom it remains a central issue in the politics of defence. In a somewhat different way it has failed to reassure many West European citizens, who believe that the measures taken to reinforce the guarantee, far from reducing the risk of nuclear war, have in fact made it more likely.

Second, many Europeans now fear that the superpowers believe that a nuclear war could be limited to Europe, and that this belief might make them more willing to start such a war. This is an understandable fear, because each superpower accuses the other of thinking that it could make a major military gain in Europe without itself becoming embroiled in war. The US has expressed the fear that the Soviet Union might attack western Europe in the belief that the US would not resort to its strategic forces. The Soviet Union, for its part, has accused the US of believing that a nuclear war could be confined to Europe, and has warned that any attack on the Soviet Union by US missiles based in Europe would meet the same response as an attack by US-based missiles. Each superpower has tried to convince the other that a major military move in Europe would lead to a nuclear war between them.

Nevertheless, doubts remain in many European minds. The very efforts of the superpowers to get their message across have encouraged fears that they believe that a nuclear war might indeed be limited to Europe. Their protestations, moreover, are made less convincing by the fact that both sides acknowledge the possibility of a limted nuclear war in an oblique way. NATO's flexible response strategy allows a threshold between tactical and strategic nuclear weapons, and thus recognizes the possibility of limiting nuclear war to Europe. Similarly the possibility of a nuclear war limited to Europe, as long as the Soviet Union itself was not struck, is implied by Soviet warnings that the US could not escape retaliation if Soviet territory were attacked (Ball, 1981).

A third unresolved issue is how to think about tactical nuclear weapons: should they be regarded as complementary to conventional weapons, or as something qualitatively different? In NATO they are seen as a substitute for conventional forces. They are designed to provide a counterweight to the conventional superiority of the Warsaw Pact, and to play a special role in the policy of flexible response. In NATO doctrine the nuclear threshold – the point at which nuclear weapons are used – is an important step on the ladder of escalation; but it is not the only one, and escalation to general nuclear war is not seen as inevitable. Nevertheless, the risk of such escalation exists, and this risk, it is claimed, makes flexible response a credible deterrent.

Some retired NATO commanders have challenged this view, arguing that nuclear weapons are so destructive, so indiscriminate in their effects, and so difficult to control that they can have no real military utility. The only function they can have is to deter Soviet use of nuclear weapons, because any use of nuclear weapons, however limited, would very soon lead to an uncontrollable conflict which would probably escalate into general nuclear war. Since this is so, they argue, the threat to use tactical nuclear weapons first is not credible, because it is tantamount to a threat to commit mutual suicide; and consequently this element in flexible response is just as ineffective as Kissinger claims the US nuclear guarantee to be.

Different practical conclusions can be drawn from these arguments. If the nuclear threshold is only one of several steps on the ladder of escalation, then the need to keep the threshold high will not seem so urgent, because the use of tactical nuclear weapons will not automatically lead to general nuclear war. In this context a limited nuclear war in Europe becomes thinkable because there is another threshold between the use of nuclear weapons in Europe and their use against the territories of the superpowers. At the same time, however, NATO policy requires that some risk of escalation to general nuclear war be maintained, so that the deterrent effect of the US strategic forces is extended to Europe.

If, however, escalation to general war is seen as the almost in-evitable consequence of any use of nuclear weapons in Europe, then it becomes urgent to keep the nuclear threshold as high as possible and to avoid the deployment of weapons which might lower it. This was one of the chief arguments advanced against the neutron bomb, and it also underpins the argument that NATO should move towards a doctrine of no first use – or no early use – of nuclear weapons.

The fourth controversial issue is Soviet policy. NATO argues that it needs strong armed forces to deter a Soviet attack, but Soviet leaders deny that they have any intention of launching one, and few people in western Europe see an attack by the Warsaw Pact as a real possiblity in the present circumstances. Many believe that the primary, even the sole, aim of Soviet military power in Europe is to deter western intervention in eastern Europe. Those who do fear Soviet military power place greater stress on the Soviet ability to in-timidate western Europe and to sever its ties with the US, and urge that NATO maintain its cohesion and demonstrate its resolve through its own military effort.

Soviet leaders claim that their military power serves only defen-sive purposes, but they maintain large forces in eastern Europe, and their military strategy stresses the importance of seizing the initiative and achieving surprise in military operations. The apparent con-tradiction between an avowedly defensive policy and an offensive military strategy is the source of much concern and suspicion in western Europe. Many people support NATO's deterrent posture not because they believe that the Soviet Union is straining at the leash and needs to be restrained, but because they are uncertain about what the Soviet Union might do if the western European states were to reduce their defence in a significant way.

The INF issue

In the mid-1970s the Soviet Union began to deploy the SS-20 IRBM (intermediate-range ballistic missile) and the Backfire bomber in

Europe to replace those medium-range systems which had entered service in the 1950s and early 1960s. Western governments had regarded the earlier Soviet theatre systems as a stopgap, intended to hold western Europe hostage until an effective Soviet intercontinental force was deployed. They did not anticipate the deployment of new medium-range systems once the Soviet Union had attained strategic parity with the US, and saw the SS-20 and the Backfire bomber, therefore, as part of an attempt to tilt the balance of power in the Soviet favour.

NATO decided in December 1979 to deploy US GLCMs and Pershing II missiles in Europe because it feared that the Soviet Union would acquire superiority on the intermediate rungs of the nuclear ladder, and that this would deter NATO from escalating in the event of war. NATO was afraid that if that happened its threat to resort to tactical and then strategic nuclear weapons would be a much less effective deterrent to the Soviet Union. NATO's decision sprang also from the fear that strategic parity, by depriving the US nuclear guarantee of much of its credibility, might enable the Soviet Union to 'decouple' western Europe from the US. The new missiles were needed, it was argued, to strengthen the ties between the two parts of the Alliance.

The Soviet Union, however, claims that the new American missiles are part of an attempt by the US to regain strategic superiority, and sees in them not so much an addition to NATO's theatre forces as an augmentation of American strategic power (because they can strike the Soviet Union), and thus a means of upsetting the Soviet-American strategic balance. It regards Pershing II as especially threatening because it is a highly accurate missile and could reach targets in the western part of the Soviet Union with only four to six minutes' warning time.

The negotiating positions of the two sides reflected their different conceptions of the military balance: the Soviet Union argued that approximate parity existed, while the US claimed that the Soviet Union had a six-to-one lead in INF. The US wanted limitations on missiles, while the Soviet Union wished to limit bombers as well. The Soviet Union wanted to count the British and French forces, while the US and its allies insisted that these could not be taken into account. The US wanted global ceilings, which would cover Soviet deployments in the Far East, while the Soviet Union sought an agreement confined to Europe.

In spite of these differences, the two sides did move closer together during the negotiations. In the summer of 1982 the two chief negotiators worked out the principles of agreement (the so-called 'walk in the woods' deal) but this was rejected in both Moscow and

Washington. The two capitals regarded the negotiations as the focus of a political struggle in which Washington's main aim was to secure the deployment of the new missiles in Europe, and Moscow's goal was to stop that deployment; the pursuit of an agreement was of secondary importance. The talks ended when the Soviet Union withdrew in November 1983, as the NATO deployment began. The Soviet Union has since placed new missiles of its own in eastern Europe, and increased the number of submarines off the coast of the US capable of striking American targets with a very short warning time.

NATO regards the INF deployment as a success, because it showed that the Alliance could carry through a deployment in the face of considerable opposition. The Soviet Union suffered a political defeat, even though it had made some important concessions in its attempt to stop the deployment. It may be doubted, however, whether Europe as a whole is any safer as a result of the deployments (see Holm and Petersen, 1983).

Deterrence and morality

The central feature of the military relationship between NATO and the Warsaw Pact is nuclear deterrence: each side claims that it can prevent the other from attacking only by threatening retaliation with nuclear weapons. This policy of deterrence is complex: it is defensive in its purpose insofar as it seeks to prevent an attack, but it is offensive in its means inasmuch as it threatens 'unacceptable damage' to the attacker's society. It requires cooperation as well as mutual hostility, for it will not 'work' unless there is self-restraint based on a common interest in avoiding nuclear war.

Notwithstanding its defensive purpose, deterrence rests ultimately upon the threat to inflict widespread death and destruction. A distinction is sometimes drawn between deterrence by punishment, which threatens massive and indiscriminate destruction on the attacker's society, and deterrence by denial, which threatens to prevent the attacker from achieving his goals by destroying his military forces. Both kinds of deterrence may be found in the policies of NATO and the Warsaw Pact, which plan to use nuclear weapons against enemy forces but know also that the indiscriminate destruction these weapons would cause are important elements in deterrence.

Most of the statements issued by the churches in recent years have condemned the use of nuclear weapons as incompatible with Christian teaching on war. In line with the just war tradition, for example, the American Catholic Bishops state categorically that 'no

Christian can rightfully carry out orders or policies deliberately aimed at killing non-combatants', even in retaliation for an attack on cities (US Catholic Bishops, 1983, p. 47). They say that 'it is not morally acceptable to intend to kill the innocent as part of a strategy of deterring nuclear war' (p. 56). They also reject as morally unacceptable the intention to strike only military targets because they believe that, since many important military targets are located in populated areas, such an attack would kill horrendous numbers of innocents. 'We cannot,' they say, 'be satisfied that the assertion of an intention not to strike civilians directly, or even the most honest effort to implement that intention, by itself constitutes a "moral policy" for the use of nuclear weapons' (p. 57).

Nevertheless, the American Bishops allow a 'strictly conditioned moral acceptance' of deterrence, even though they reject deterrence as 'a long-term basis for peace' (p. 58). They accept deterrence because they believe that it has, or may have, played some role in preventing war over the last 40 years. They reject deterrence as a long-term basis for peace not only because they see it as morally questionable, but also because they judge that it is not a foolproof method for preventing war.

The American Bishops offer three criteria for assessing the moral acceptability of a deterrence policy. The first is that nuclear weapons should exist only to prevent the use of nuclear weapons by others, and consequently 'planning for prolonged periods of repeated nuclear strikes and counterstrikes, or "prevailing" in nuclear war' is not acceptable. Moreover, this criterion, in the Bishops' view, rules out a policy of possible first use of nuclear weapons. The second criterion is that the goal of policy should be 'sufficiency' to deter, rather than superiority in order to prevail in a war. Third is that nuclear deterrence should be used as a step on the way to progressive disarmament (US Catholic Bishops, 1983, p. 59).

It should be clear from the previous discussion that NATO's current policy is not consistent with these criteria. In the first place, NATO has a doctrine of possible first use of nuclear weapons. Second, NATO's policy of flexible response implies a need for superiority at different levels of escalation (this is sometimes called escalation dominance), and seems to require new weapons periodically to shore up its credibility. This seems not to be compatible with the Bishop's second criterion. Third, the requirements of NATO doctrine, and in particular the stress on flexible response, complicate arms control negotiations, and thus do not meet the Bishops' third criterion.

The Bishops condemn as incompatible with the just war tradition any strategy that would kill large numbers of innocent people, even as an indirect consequence of the targets struck. But they also see deterrence as resting on the assured capability to inflict 'unacceptable damage' in a retaliatory strike, and regard as impractical and ill-considered any attempt to devise war-fighting strategies that would try to limit casualties among non-combatants. They seem to accept that the destructiveness of nuclear weapons, which makes their use in war intolerable, is precisely what makes them particularly effective in preventing war. In giving a conditioned acceptance to deterrence, they apparently consider that the goal of preventing nuclear war is more important than the principle of discrimination in war.

The Bishops do not hide their dissatisfaction with the morality of deterrence, however, and they stress the need to move away from it. One of the great dangers in the provisional acceptance of deterrence is that this acceptance will become permanent, and here Duncan Forrester's chapter is particularly important in outlining the role of the churches in drawing attention to the evils of the present situation, and in stressing the contrast with true peace.

Yet even while an effort is being made to withdraw moral legitimacy from nuclear weapons, attention must be given to the practical steps which might lead to a sounder and more moral basis for peace. One has to move beyond the assertion of moral principles or the expression of a moral vision to consider the likely practical consequences of the actions being proposed. In assessing President Reagan's SDI, for example, it is essential to look beyond his vision of a world in which nuclear weapons have become 'impotent and obsolete' to ask how feasible strategic defence is, and how it is in fact likely to affect the prospects for peace. Similarly, it would be irresponsible, I think, in seeking to move away from the present situation, to refuse to exercise prudence in assessing the probable consequence of the action taken.

The American Bishops' pastoral letter suggests that the goal of preventing nuclear war must play a crucial role in guiding the movement away from deterrence. Little is to be gained if the steps taken increase the risk of war, even while, for instance, reducing the numbers of nuclear weapons. It is true, as Ian Thompson argues in his chapter, that long-term peace must be founded on justice, but in the search for this peace the immediate and pressing task of preventing nuclear war must not be neglected, for if there is a nuclear war there will be little opportunity for the struggle for justice.

Proposals and prospects

There are many who believe that the military-political situation in Europe is the most stable on our uneasy planet, and that the nuclear forces there have helped to prevent war for 40 years. The presence of large numbers of nuclear weapons on the continent has not, they say, precluded – and may even have facilitated – the peaceful resolution of difficult territorial and political disputes. For these reasons, they do not consider nuclear disarmament an urgent matter for Europe.

Yet even if stability exists, there are several reasons for regarding the present situation as unsatisfactory. First, the detonation of even a few of the existing nuclear weapons would cause immense suffering and destruction in Europe, and would carry a high risk of escalation to general nuclear war, with devastating consequences for the whole world. This means that there is no room for mistakes, no margin for error, in the present security arrangements in Europe.

Second, the fate of Europe is intimately bound up with the overall state of Soviet-American relations, and hence even if the situation in Europe is stable, the possibility cannot be excluded that war in Europe might be precipitated by a crisis or clash elsewhere in the world.

Third, the military doctrines of the two sides fuel the military competition by generating requirements for new weapons and new tactics. Soviet military policy, with its determination to dominate eastern Europe and its stress on the offensive, requires large forces in the region. NATO, with its commitment to forward defence and flexible response, also requires large forces on the Central Front and constant attention to potential gaps in the ladder of escalation. Each side justifies its new weapons as defensive in purpose, but they may be regarded as a threat by the other side and thus provoke a reaction. The net result may be, as in the case of INF, that neither side is made more secure.

The recognition of these problems has prompted numerous proposals in recent years for reducing the risk of war, and the numbers of nuclear weapons, in Europe. Some of these will be considered here in the light of the American Bishops' three criteria for the 'strictly conditioned moral acceptance' of nuclear deterrence.[4]

No first use

One of the most important and most widely discussed proposals for change has been that NATO should commit itself not to be the first to use nuclear weapons (Kaiser et al., 1982; McGeorge Bundy et al; 1982).

The main arguments advanced against the adoption of such a policy are, first, that NATO needs the threat of possible first use to counterbalance the Warsaw Pact's superiority in conventional forces. There is disagreement on the precise state of the conventional balance, but there is widespread acceptance that the Warsaw Pact does enjoy at least an edge, even though it may not be of great

military significance. A major issue in the debate about no first use
has been whether western Europe or the US would be willing to pay
for additional forces to maintain a conventional balance. It is not
clear how much NATO would have to do to create a viable conventional defence; it might be, for example, that reorganization of
NATO forces in West Germany might be more useful than new
weapons. In any event, this is not something that should be beyond
NATO's ability to do.

A second argument against the adoption of a no-first-use policy by
NATO is that it would increase the likelihood of war by making the
risk of attacking western Europe more calculable to the Soviet
Union. There may be some force in this argument, but it overstates
the calculability of a conventional attack. A large-scale conventional
war in central Europe would be unpredictable in its political consequences, especially perhaps in eastern Europe. Moreover, as long as
nuclear weapons exist, such a war would carry the risk that nuclear
weapons might be used no matter what policy had been adopted.
Consequently it is not evident that this is a very strong argument
against a no-first-use policy.

The strongest opposition to a no-first-use policy comes from West
Germany where many people fear what it would weaken security
ties with the US.[5] If NATO adopted such a policy it would need to
overhaul flexible response and perhaps to strengthen NATO's conventional forces, in order to maintain a credible military posture. It
might also be necessary to redefine the security relationship between
the US and western Europe, with the latter assuming a greater
responsibility for its own defence.

A no-first-use policy that did not increase the risk of conventional
conflict would lead to a more credible policy for NATO. It would
have the important benefit of raising the nuclear threshold and opening the way to further reductions in nuclear weapons. There is a
danger – which would have to be avoided – that a commitment to no
first use might merely lead to an increase in conventional forces
without reductions in nuclear weapons, since preparations would
still be made for nuclear war. The Soviet Union, for example, has
pledged that it will not be the first to use nuclear weapons, but
besides maintaining large conventional forces in eastern Europe, it
has increased its nuclear forces there since making its no-first-use
pledge.

Alternative defence policies

The Western European peace movement has looked beyond no first
use to alternative defence policies which would eschew both nuclear

weapons and conventional forces as they now stand. The chief argument against basing a reduction of nuclear weapons on a balance of
conventional forces is that when one side is satisfied with the
balance, the other will be dissatisfied and seek to redress it, thus
stimulating further military competition.

Most proposals for alternative defence policies advocate some
kind of territorial defence, delegated to militia forces. These would
be armed with modern anti-tank and anti-air missiles, which are
thought to give the defence an advantage. Proponents of such
schemes argue that defence of this kind would be effective against invasion or intimidation, and that because it would pose no threat to
eastern Europe, it would make a reduction of forces possible there too.

The real question is whether such a defence would be effective
against conventional forces of the type that the Warsaw Pact now
possesses: this is a matter for careful study, and these ideas have
aroused interest in official circles in western Europe. Because a territorial defence would offer no defence against nuclear weapons, and
no deterrent through the threat of retaliation, some proponents advocate that a nuclear force be retained. Such a force would be
designed purely for retaliation in the event of a nuclear attack and
could be much smaller than NATO's current nuclear forces.

An alternative policy of this kind, if it were effective from a
military point of view, could well complement a policy of no first
use. It would raise the nuclear threshold; provide an unprovocative
defence, and thus be less likely to fuel the military competition; and
reduce the salience of nuclear weapons in European politics, thus
helping to provide a climate in which non-military bases for security
might be pursued.

Arms control

The difficulties of negotiating an agreement on INF have already
been discussed, and many of the same problems confront other proposals for arms control. Because of major differences in geography,
technology and military doctrine, the two sides find it hard to agree
on what constitutes an equitable balance. Indeed, the Mutual and
Balanced Force Reduction (MBFR) talks, which have dragged on in
Vienna for more than ten years without an agreement, show that the
two sides may take time even to agree what forces each has. Nevertheless, arms control can play an important part in making Europe
more secure, and it is not inconceivable that new agreements could
be reached: the outlines of an INF agreement were formulated during the 'walk in the woods' in 1982, while the basic elements of an
MBFR Treaty have been clarified at the Vienna talks.

The idea of a nuclear freeze runs into some of the same problems as other arms control proposals. To someone who thinks, as I do, that there are more than enough nuclear weapons in Europe to make a military adventure by either side extremely risky, and that the existing 'balance' will not be easily upset, a freeze now would be a good starting-point for reductions in the present excessive levels of nuclear weapons. NATO has in fact reduced significantly the total number of nuclear weapons it has in Europe in the last five years, without any adverse effect on the stability of the existing military balance.

What makes a freeze difficult to arrange is that governments are sensitive to inequalities in the military balance. At any given time it is likely that one side considers the other to be ahead, or sees some gap in its own forces which needs to be filled, and consequently will be reluctant to agree to a freeze. Moreover, the terms of an agreement need to be defined carefully, and the agreement has to be verifiable. The main advantage of a freeze is that it would halt the momentum of deployment and counterdeployment and thus provide a breathing-space in which to work out a scheme for the reduction of forces and the stabilization of the military balance.

Another approach to arms control is being pursued at the Conference on Disarmament in Europe, which is now being held in Stockholm. This is part of the Helsinki process, and is seeking in the first instance to expand the confidence-building measures adopted in the 1975 Helsinki Final Act. Its main aim is to lessen the risk of military conflict in Europe by devising measures – for example, the exchange of military information, constraints on the deployment of forces and agreements about the non-use of force – that will increase mutual confidence and security. Measures of this kind would not affect the existing military situation in a radical way but they could help to stabilize it, and to lessen the salience of military power in European politics.

Arms control is a bilateral or multilateral exercise, but it could provide a more favourable context in which NATO could undertake unilateral measures to reduce its reliance on nuclear weapons. An MBFR agreement, for example, could be helpful in maintaining a stable conventional balance at a lower level than at present, and thus make it easier to adopt no-first-use policies.

Political measures

No-first-use, alternative defence and arms control policies could all contribute to making Europe safer, but they would not tackle the underlying political conflict. Both sides have said that they wish to reduce the level of military confrontation and move towards a greater degree of cooperation in political, economic and cultural relations. It has been difficult to achieve these goals, but there have been important successes, such as the Austrian State Treaty of 1955 and the Four Power Agreement on Berlin of 1971, and the pursuit of détente through such mechanisms as the Helsinki process has been a crucial element in the search for peace and security in Europe.

The worsening of Soviet-American relations in recent years has made the pursuit of cooperation in Europe more difficult than before. This has engendered a growing feeling, at least in the West European peace movement, that Europe will be made more secure not by changes in the policies of NATO or the Warsaw Pact, but by disbandment of the military alliances and disengagement by both of the superpowers. Disengagement would still leave the problem of constructing a European security system which would restrain the growth of military forces and reduce the risk of war, for although it might lead to a reduction of forces, it might also lead to a 'Gaullist' Europe with more states acquiring nuclear weapons in order to assert their national sovereignty.

Disengagement is unlikely at present. In spite of the strains in NATO, the US is not likely to abandon western Europe to its own devices. Nor are there any signs that the Soviet Union is willing to relinquish its position in eastern Europe: for all its trials and tribulations, it still seems to regard domination of the region as central to its own security, and bases that domination on military force. West European countries face the problem of what to do about Soviet military power, and most feel that some kind of military alliance with the US is needed to maintain a balance of power on the continent.

Conclusion

Religious images are to be found in much of the discussion about nuclear weapons. The development of the atomic bomb by the US has been seen as a kind of Fall, with the consequences of which we now have to live. The prospect of nuclear war is often portrayed in apocalyptic terms as Armageddon, the last great battle of good and evil. The use of these images underlines the profound significance of nuclear weapons and the urgency of the choices they force upon us.

I have tried in this chapter to outline some of the questions raised by nuclear weapons in Europe, to point to some unresolved issues, and to assess some proposals for change in the light of guidelines drawn from the American Bishops' pastoral letter. Not all Church statements have taken the same position on nuclear weapons, and some have been clearer in rejecting nuclear deterrence as morally unacceptable. But the pastoral letter is especially interesting for its attempt to combine moral principles and policy issues in a single detailed analysis. It is a real effort to 'engage' theology with policy.

This survey suggests the following conclusions. Because nuclear weapons policies are ultimately rooted in the political conflict which divides the continent, their elimination will be possible only if action is taken in both parts of Europe. It is therefore essential to pursue arms control and disarmament through negotiation, and to continue to search for a sound political basis for peace and security on the continent as a whole.

Even within the constraints of a divided Europe, however, western Europe has considerable scope in devising its own policy: in deciding what relationship to have with the US, how much reliance to place on nuclear weapons, and what kinds of conventional forces to deploy. It should therefore be possible for western European governments to move unilaterally towards a policy more in conformity with the guidelines in the pastoral letter, without upsetting the stability of the military balance and thereby increasing the risk of war. They could do this by adopting a no-first-use policy while ensuring that adequate defence against conventional attack was provided, perhaps by so-called alternative means. The policy of flexible response, which seems to generate constant requirements for new weapons to sustain its credibility, needs to be rethought, and this may make it necessary to redefine the military relationship between western Europe and the US. Arms control agreements should be pursued, both for their own sake, and because they could provide a helpful context in which to pursue unilateral measures.

Only after measures of this kind were implemented would it be possible to give 'strictly conditioned moral acceptance' to NATO policy, in line with the criteria set out in the pastoral letter: and that acceptance would be conditional upon further efforts in the direction of progressive disarmament.

9

The New Cold War

Howard Davis

In all the complexity and confusion of current debates about defence and disarmament one thing is certain. There is no evidence that the Soviet Union is planning any immediate attack on western Europe or the US. Some take this to mean that the Soviet Union has successfully been deterred from threatening or actually attacking the countries of the NATO Alliance. Others would argue that the evidence can be taken at face value: that there is no political objective which might conceivably be in the Soviet Union's interest which could usefully be served by the direct threat or actual use of military force in western Europe.

This universal acknowledgement that the Soviets are not about to invade is a clear reminder that the military preparedness and strategic doctrines of NATO – and, one may presume, the Warsaw Pact countries since the possibility of western invasion is equally remote from their thinking – has to be justified in other terms. These justifications, which are rooted in historical events of the Cold War period and subsequent developments in technology on both sides, have an important moral dimension. In particular, they depend on a stance towards the adversary which identifies the highest qualities of virtue with one's own system, ideals and way of life. The converse of this is that negative qualities are attributed to the alternative social system almost regardless of its objective properties. This social self-justification or self-righteousness tends to demonize the adversary and make an idol of national security. It is not simply a question of political rhetoric; it can change dramatically in tone, for example, between a presidential election campaign and the mid-term of the presidency. There is a more constant source of enemy images in the weapons, strategies and philosophies of deterrence.

Deterrence

The doctrines of nuclear deterrence, a cornerstone of NATO defence policy, have been through several phases of revision and reinterpretation. Both Tony Carty and David Holloway refer to military, technological and political aspects of the process (see chapters 6 and 8, above). The present analysis begins at the conceptual level. Morgan (1983) describes deterrence as a kind of decision-making theory based on the calculations, actions and reactions of supposedly rational military planners and political leaders. This aspect is well reflected in the majority of official statements on defence policy such as the following:

> The essence of deterrence is that, to prevent war, or use of the threat of war, a country must itself maintain the instruments of war and make clear to any potential aggressor that it is willing to retaliate against aggression . . . Unless a potential aggressor believes in a country's capability and willingness to defend its territory, he may be prepared to start a war or to threaten an invasion to pursue his goals.[1]

But the generality of such a statement, which makes it superficially plausible, hides a very specific assumption about the adversary. As Morgan points out, the circumstances in which pure deterrence operates (that is, when at least one or two hostile states is seriously considering an attack but desists primarily because of the retaliatory threat of the opponent) are rare indeed.

There are of course many other considerations which will tend to deter an attacker, but pure deterrence implies that the inhibitions arise entirely from the threat of retaliation. Although this is a situation which is unlikely to be found in such a simplified form in reality, the analysis and justification for deterrence (and nuclear deterrence in particular) begins with the assumption that an 'attack' is planned and that a credible deterrent must match the enemy's capabilities if it is to deter. The policy of deterrence, according to this description, involves a specific adversary and is meaningless without one. Deterrence also has a more general meaning. It applies to a context in which states face each other with mutual suspicion and hostility. A sense of insecurity arises because of the conviction that leaders in at least one country would consider resorting to force to advance their interests if the opportunity arose. The other side, being persuaded of the first's willingness to consider the use of force, maintains forces of its own and threatens to respond in kind. Deterrence in this situation 'works' if decision-makers are inhibited from considering an actual attack because of the expectation of counterattack. The 'general deterrence' which this situation represents is significantly different from the pure deterrence which may correspond to a crisis situation. Nevertheless, the vagueness of the threats, and the reluctance to specify the exact conditions which might provoke an armed response, does not modify the basic requirement of the deterrence posture: that it must be directed towards a specific adversary or adversaries. Thus the document quoted above describes the nature of the 'Soviet threat' in military and historical terms:

The threat of conflict in Europe springs from the fact that the Soviet Union continues to maintain massive military forces in Europe, conventional, chemical and nuclear, well in excess of those required for its own defence. These forces are constantly being improved, particularly in their mobility and firepower . . . Britain and her NATO allies *cannot afford to base their defences on the assumption that the Soviet leadership is essentially benevolent and concerned only with Soviet security* . . . The Soviet Union has shown a willingness to use force in and outside Europe to secure its political ends on many occasions since the Second World War against countries which could not defend themselves. (my emphasis)

The characterization of the adversary in these or similar terms is intrinsic to deterrence theories. Deterrence assumes not just that there is a need and a government responsibility to maintain defences against possible aggression by parties which have not yet declared themselves but that there is a specific 'threat' from a known, hostile opponent. This feature of deterrence is essential to its 'justification' and at the same time one of the greatest obstacles to more secure and stable East-West relations. It overrides the subtle distinctions which are often made in debates on the morality of deterrence between 'declaratory policy' (the public expression of strategic intentions and capabilities) and 'action policies' (the military planning and targeting policies to be followed in a nuclear war) or between 'minimum' and 'extended' deterrence, for example. The argument here is not that weapons systems themselves are the cause of war but that the spirit and logic of deterrence tend to reproduce the conditions which make conflict more rather than less likely. The 'worst case' assumptions of military planners become the received wisdom of politicians and the public.

The Cold War

The key to the current identification of the problem of security in western countries with the problem of containing the Soviet Union is the immediate post-war period. The history of the Cold War, 1946-53, is a series of events and circumstances which made deterrence appear both plausible and justified but which institutionalized enmity in a peculiarly intractable form.

Deterrence thinking did not, of course, originate in August 1945. It is a part of policing and child-rearing as much as military strategy, but it developed a new form and vocabulary. As Tony Carty explains (above, chapter 6), there was close continuity between the thinking which informed the Allies' decision to bomb German cities, the US decision to bomb Hiroshima and Nagasaki, and subsequent strategic doctrines which relied on the threat of indiscriminate and near-total destruction. But increasingly the new weapons posed a strategic problem: did they have a practical military use?

After 1945, the military and political significance of nuclear weapons came to be understood in terms of the emerging international system of eastern and western 'blocs'. Thus the weapons which were intended to bring about the total defeat of an enemy in a time of war were now deployed in the contest between capitalism and communism, where the 'enemy's' intentions (seen from either side) were much less transparent. It is hardly surprising to find a contrast between the simple, if questionable, military logic behind the destruction of German and Japanese cities, including Hiroshima, and the convolutions of deterrence thinking as it evolved in the 1950s and 1960s. As Hinsley (Martin and Mullen, 1983, p. 59) points out, strategic studies in this period had a curious air of unreality: 'they possess all the cogency, all the intellectual rigour and all the irrelevance of the scholastic writings of the middle ages'. Professor Laurence Martin in his 1981 Reith Lectures remarked on the lack of appreciation of the political and psychological dimensions of these strategies as they were evolved: 'there was certainly no psycho-political analysis of what it takes to deter' (1981, p. 597). At least this unreality was acknowledged by those politicians and members of the public who saw the new thermo-nuclear weapons as 'unusable' as weapons of war and scarcely justifiable even as the last resort threat against the aggressive intentions of the Soviet Union.

Yet how *were* Soviet actions and intentions to be interpreted? With the defeat of Germany in 1945, Soviet policy in Europe – which in effect meant the policy of Stalin – was directed against the revival of German economic and military strength and towards the consolidation of its own power as far to the West as was possible. Since the Russian Revolution of October 1917 and the years of civil war which followed, the Soviet Union had felt profoundly insecure as a single socialist country surrounded by capitalist countries with superior economic and military forces. The whole effort to build 'socialism in one country' and militarization during the 1930s has to be understood in terms of this drive to catch up with and overtake these hostile powers.

In the event, preparations for war failed to prevent Germany's surprise attack in June 1941 and the occupation of most of western Russia. The indelible impression of this near-defeat and the vast scale of human casualties and physical destruction which it involved are at the root of the Soviet determination never again to allow economic or technical inferiority, especially in military affairs.

The defeat of Hitler and the Soviet occupation of eastern Europe and part of Germany in 1945 gave the Soviet Union greater security and more political influence than was imaginable before the war. It also led to the contest over the future of Germany and Poland which developed into the Cold War and continued well into the 1950s. The most acute crisis occurred with the Berlin blockade in 1948 and the consolidation of political power by communist parties in all the eastern European countries at the same period. The simultaneous development in western Europe was the revival and reconstruction of capitalism under the Marshall Plan, the mobilization of anti-communist movements and forces against communist parties in France, Italy, Greece and other countries.

The stabilization of European frontiers and the formation of NATO and the Warsaw Pact laid the foundations of the alliance system which survives to this day. However, this did not appear to be the likely outcome at the time. On the Soviet side, there was a general belief that the conflict between capitalism and socialism would eventually lead to a new world war (Holloway, 1983, p. 27). On the western side, there was the conviction that the Soviet Union was firmly committed to world communism, achieved by force if necessary, and that sooner or later it would have to be resisted in like manner. In 1949, when a degree of accommodation had been reached in Europe, the focus of international conflict moved to the Far East and to hostilities in China, Korea and Indo-China. There was still more than sufficient evidence, in other words, to feed the conviction that the 'Free World' and 'Communism' were locked in mortal combat.

The possibility of change occurred with the military stalemates in Korea and Indo-China and with the death of Stalin in 1953. Despite the continuing use of Cold War terminology since then and by current western and Soviet leaders, there was a major discontinuity at this time. The Cold War did actually come to an end. This was recognized at the time and hindsight reinforces the impression that essential Cold War postures were abandoned by both sides. In his 1957 Reith Lectures, George Kennan, the former US ambassador to Moscow, voiced the kind of liberal understanding of international conflicts which had helped, along with the objective changes in the Soviet Union and western countries, to bring about the 'thaw' in East–West relations and paved the way for the period of détente in the late 1960s and 1970s. He spoke of the 'over-militarization' of thinking in the West on the nature of the Soviet threat and called for a more mature understanding of it.

The Soviet design has consisted . . . primarily of the determination to exploit every element of disunity, of confusion, of shortsightedness in our
society, with a view to causing us to eliminate ourselve as rivals to Soviet
power and influence everywhere . . . Armed force has, to be sure, been
cultivated on a major scale by the Soviet Government. In has been
cultivated partly as a precaution, partly as a psychological weapon, partly
because it was always envisaged that the Soviet armed forces might some
day be called upon to play a subsidiary role in the final phases of the decline
of capitalism. But it has never . . . been looked to as a major instrument by
which our undoing was to be accomplished. (1958, p. 18)

Subsequent events and assessments have tended to confirm the
view that the Soviet Union's military strength is directed more
towards the maintenance of political influence, especially within
neighbouring territories, than towards the continuation of a global
political strategy by means of armed force. This applies to both conventional and nuclear weapons. According to Holloway,

The Soviet leaders have treated nuclear weapons like conventional weapons
in regarding them as instruments of military power and political influence,
and at the same time have recognized the qualitatively new character and
devastation they could bring. The Soviet Union has built up powerful
nuclear forces not only in preparation for a possible nuclear war, but also to
deprive the United States of any political advantage that superiority might
bring. (1983, p. 179)

The years of the Cold War between 1946 and 1953 were, then, a
period during which the Soviet Union both attempted to guarantee
its security by matching the capabilities of the US, including its
nuclear strategic forces, and used military force to maintain control
over allies and subordinate states within its sphere of influence. The
US was similarly attempting to guarantee its security by military,
economic and political means and succeeded in acquiring global influence far greater than that of the Soviet Union. To that extent, the
US and the western democracies can be said to have gained more,
even to have 'won' the Cold War, although both superpowers
emerged with more strategic influence, political cohesion and
economic strength as a result.

The place of nuclear weapons in the capitalist-socialist conflict
was less significant than today, and not entirely because of the
smaller numbers of weapons, their smaller yield or cumbersome
delivery systems. The Cold War was not the outcome of military accumulation *per se*, let alone the early nuclear arms race. In fact, the
strategic implications of nuclear weapons were not fully considered
in the Soviet Union until after Stalin's death: the Soviet bomb was
built to deprive the US of the political advantages of its nuclear
monopoly. And there is no Soviet equivalent to the theory of deter-

rence developed in the US in the later 1950s and early 1960s, in spite of the rapidly increasing Soviet nuclear arsenal (Holloway, 1983, pp. 31–3). The identifiable forces behind the Cold War were not technological but primarily political and economic. Both sides were pursuing long-term goals which had been evolved during the War and were exploiting the opportunities for influence and domination which the immediate post-war situation provided. The Cold War would have occurred with or without the bomb.

Following the thaw in East-West relations between 1953 and 1969, acceptance of the other side's right to exist and the eventual recognition of the inviolability of national frontiers in Europe, if not always in other parts of the world, there was a deceleration in the arms race and a significant measure of arms control. This took place against a background of numerous agreements on trade and other non-military matters, regular communications, summit meetings and attempts to defuse tensions between countries outside the spheres of direct influence of the superpowers. Détente, marked by the SALT 1 agreement in 1972, the Helsinki Conference on Security and Cooperation in Europe (CSCE) between 1973 and 1975, and a general commitment to negotiation on matters of dispute, prevailed until the end of the 1970s. In retrospect, it turns out to have been a relatively brief respite from a generally high level of East–West conflict in the post-war period. The recent accelerated military build-up on both sides, intense propaganda campaigns, negotiating difficulties, and internal economic and political problems within both camps, has been on a sufficiently broad scale to justify the use of the term the 'second Cold War' (see Halliday, 1983).

The new Cold War

There are close similarities in the climate of international relations between the first Cold War and the current levels of hostility. The most significant new element, however, is the pattern of military expenditure and new forms of nuclear deterrent policy. This is a vital difference which has done more than anything else (including hostile rhetoric) to transform the general propensity for political and ideological contestation into a new Cold War with increased risks of US–Soviet military confrontation. This new Cold War, in contrast to the first, is the product of a (nuclear) arms race as well as the other economic and political tensions in the international system. It can be argued that technical innovations and military spending have shaped deterrence, and that the assumptions of deterrence have become embedded in western perceptions of Soviet society and its leaders' intentions.

The most threatening images of the new Cold War have little to do with waves of tanks and troops rolling across the plains of Germany. They are the images of all-out nuclear bombardment leading to the 'end of the world' as we know it. The public mood is increasingly conditioned by the knowledge of the vast scale of the nuclear arsenals held by the superpowers and the understanding that strategists on both sides have begun to prepare for the possibility of 'fighting' a nuclear war. Overtly hostile propaganda and posturings by political leaders are but a sympton of these developments. The origins lie deeper even within the period of détente, in the development of more accurate and versatile weapons systems. This process has a technical, military and economic logic of its own and is only indirectly related to the multitude of other factors which shape the course of international relations. The same logic, with certain variations which stem from the differences between the capitalist democracies and one-party state socialist systems, applies to both East and West.

The multiple independently-targetable re-entry vehicle (MIRV) was the most significant development in missile technology in the 1960s. It is an example of the logic at work, unfolding almost regardless of the political and ideological climate. The US and Soviet arsenals of single-warhead ICBMs established during the 1950s were sufficiently accurate to destroy the others' missiles so that the 'pre-emptive strike' was not a possible option for either side. The strength of deterrence was therefore perceived to lie in the scale and numbers of missiles. Paradoxically, 'security' meant being mutually vulnerable. This was hardly a stable situation, however, because a number of possible countermeasures, including more ac- curate delivery systems and anti-missile defences, were conceivable. In fact the feasibility of some of the relevant technologies was already under examination in the space programmes and weapons research on both sides. In 1964, against this background of concern about the instability of deterrence based on Mutual Assured Destruction (MAD), the US Secretary of Defence, Robert McNamara, took the key decision to develop the MIRV multiple warhead technology for the Poseidon missile and, in the following year, for the Minuteman. As Greenwood (1975) and others have shown, this decision was not made in response to an objective assessment of Soviet capabilities and intentions at that time (see also Tammen, 1973; Carlton and Shaerf, 1975; Kaldor, 1982; Nincic, 1982). There was a fear that the Soviet Union would acquire more accurate missiles and anti-ballistic missile (ABM) defences but intelligence could neither confirm that the Soviets were ahead in the competition nor, supposing that they were, how they intended to deploy such a capability. Like many other decisions about military technology which can take up to ten years to make operational, the MIRV decision was taken in a context of uncertainty.

In a competition where uncertainty prevails, the typical response is to hedge and keep future options open. The argument runs as follows.

Where threat information is adequate, we invest in amounts sufficient to meet the threat. Where information is inadequate and uncertainty high, we run some risks of over-investment to insure that our capability will be adequate, that it is sure to fulfil our strategic objectives . . . to avoid technological surprise, we must carry out vigorous, broadly-based research and exploratory development. We attempt to discover new ideas potentially relevant to national security. We test the feasibility of ideas to anticipate the worst that potential enemies could bring against us. (Dr John Foster, Director of Defence Research and Engineering, quoted in Greenwood, 1975, p. 87)

Decisions may therefore be taken without a clear understanding of the 'threat' posed by the adversary. A process of development is set in train which then becomes highly inflexible. The US MIRV led to eventual deployment in June 1970. The Soviet MIRV was initially tested in 1973 and deployed on land-based SS-18 missiles two years later. The Soviets were evidently not as far ahead as some had supposed. It is more than likely that their lack of success with ballistic missile defence in the 1960s contributed to their support for the 1972 ABM Treaty. However, the mounting evidence of Soviet technological inferiority and time lag made no impact on the US MIRV development. By the time the Treaty was signed the decision was irreversible and the new technology was providing the impetus for a new phase of strategic revisionism.

The relationship between weapons acquisition and security doctrines in the MIRV case is not unusual. Today, the US SDI appears to be developing in a similar fashion, although the multi-billion dollar programme is for research and development, not deployment. Both the US and the Soviet Union have had research programmes underway for many years into the technologies (satellites, computers, lasers and so on) which would be the components of a potential strategic defensive system. However, the Soviet Union appears to be trailing, as it was in the 1960s. It is all the more surprising, then, that in 1983 President Reagan initiated the massive 'Star Wars' research programme. The appeal of the initiative is partly a 'moral' one, that it is pure defence (see above, p. 8), but it also attracts the military argument that the Soviet ballistic missile defence programmes could lead to a 'breakout' from the present balance of forces. The argument runs: 'It would be imprudent and destabilizing to fail to respond to Soviet offensive and defensive investment.'

But the scale of the proposed US research (which will involve some UK scientists) is out of all proportion to the presently perceivable 'threat'.[2] According to the logic of superpower competition, the 'threat' can only come closer as the Soviets attempt to close the gap which they perceive to be opening up as a result of SDI. Once again, we can expect to see new strategic doctrines developed to justify the latest weapons. Deployment is then certain to follow.

These examples illustrate the effects of new generations of weapons on strategic thinking and the tendency for changes in weapons technology to precede changes in doctrine and not *vice versa.* This applies even more to the USA than to the USSR, which has shown greater doctrinal consistency over several generations of weapons. Developments are justified in military terms in the name of 'upgrading', 'modernization' and the need to find ways to respond to the other side's actual, perceived or anticipated capabilities. This is not an argument based on a deterministic view of technology; rather it resembles Galtung's view of the 'military-bureaucratic-corporate-intelligentsia' (MBCI) complex. He says that 'the power of this basic nucleus around which modern societies are built is of such a magnitude that . . . it will be capable of regenerating any interrupted military preparation process' (1984, p. 129). He would presumably agree with Powers' analysis of the shift in defence policy under President Carter. 'Shifting to "realistic" planning for limited war, so alarming to the general public, was not anything Carter or his advisers chose to do. They were pushed every step of the way by the weapons themselves' (Powers, 1982, p. 2). Once this stage was reached, deterrence policies which reflected a stalemate of 'unusable' weapons and a rough balance in capabilities were obsolete. The search for an alternative still continues, accompanied by the revitalisation of the ideas and rhetoric of the first Cold War. But the inappropriateness, ritual quality and moralistic tone of the rhetoric do not render it either harmless or implausible.

Deterrence and 'the focus of evil'

In several widely reported statements, President Reagan described the Soviet Union as an 'evil empire' and 'the focus of evil in our time'. They have all the religious and dogmatic flavour of the earlier Cold War crusade against Soviet communism. Other aspects of Cold War thinking are reproduced as though the 1950s had turned straight into the 1980s. For instance, the domino theory of communist subversion and take-over appears unchanged. Reagan is quoted as saying 'Let's not delude ourselves. The Soviet Union underlies all the unrest that is going on. If they weren't engaged in this game of dominoes, there wouldn't be any hot spots in the world' (*New Yorker,* 9 March 1981). The lessons of three decades in which it had come to be learned that Soviet foreign policy was aimed at reinforcing power and influence in countries bordering the Soviet Union and farther afield as a means to preserving the security of the Soviet state, were quickly unlearned or simply ignored. The supposedly escalating threat from new generations of Soviet weapons was allowed to obscure the fact that Soviet influence on a global scale is by no means unlimited and may actually have diminished in much of the Third World. The focus on weapons does, however, give new salience to deterrence. Whereas in the first Cold War, deterrence through nuclear weapons was a somewhat underdeveloped military strategy with little immediate political significance, the situation is now reversed. The political aspirations and intentions of the superpowers are more and more likely to be deduced from the development and deployment of their weapons systems and strategies for their use.

Anti-Sovietism in the US, and President Reagan's rhetoric in particular, present an easy target for criticism. Many remarks made in his first term of office will go down in history as those of a novice in international affairs. Official statements in Britain have been muted by comparison but they still tend to rely heavily on 'commonplaces' about the Soviet Union which, it must be assumed, have remained firmly embedded in the public's consciousness from the earlier Cold War period. According to Gittings (Chomsky et al., 1984, p. 12) five major debates were held in the House of Commons during 1980 and 1981 to discuss foreign and defence policy. On only one occasion, he says, did a government minister offer any sort of 'scenario' for the Soviet invasion of western Europe against which we are supposed to keep our guard, and that involved the implausible suggestion that the growing ethnic imbalance of the Soviet population would eventually bring about the disintegration of the Soviet state which, in desperation, might act as a 'dying giant lashing out across the central front' (John Nott, *Parliamentary Debates,* 7 July 1981). A scrutiny of debates and speeches during the 1982–3 session of Parliament reveals a corresponding lack of substance to the official publicly declared view of the Soviet Union. The recurring themes are the need to 'negotiate from strength', 'military power is the only language the Soviets understand', 'the Soviets cannot be trusted', and 'deterrence policies have been effective in keeping the peace in Europe'. Debates about Cruise missiles in the UK, the 'dual key' problem, the defence estimates and other matters rely heavily on such assumptions which surface only occasionally because they appear to be so widely accepted. For example, Mr Peter Blaker, Minister of State for the Armed Forces, replied to criticisms of government policy on INF deployment as follows: 'If Britain had adopted the Labour Party's policy, or if the Soviet Union believed it likely that we would do so, the Soviets would not be negotiating now . . . Only by remaining resolute in our approach shall we have a chance to obtain the agreement that we want' (*Parliamentary Debates*, 1982–3, vol. 35, p. 878).

In a later debate, the Liberal MP Mr David Penhaligon urged that discussions be held with the Soviet Union with a view to mutual arms reduction. He hints at the possibility of an alternative language: 'If the USSR has the peaceful intent that many believe it to have – I must put a question mark against that intent – then there are offers that it can accept' (*Parliamentary Debates*, 1982–3, vol. 36, p. 746). But Mr Blaker's reply eliminates the uncertainty by simply reiterating that: 'It is only the West's resolute approach – preserving peace by maintaining adequate defensive forces – which includes modernising them when necessary, coupled with consistent support for disarmament by both sides – which offers any prospect of ensuring our security and persuading the Soviet Union to engage in meaningful negotiations on arms control. It has brought the Russians to the negotiating table' (*Parliamentary Debates*, 1982–3, vol. 36, p. 755).

In the opening sentences of another debate on military bases, Conservative MP Alan Clark told the House: 'I accept the self-evident fact that the Soviet Union will negotiate in a significant manner only when it is confronted by strength and resolution and that the best chance of forcing a reduction in Soviet theatre weapons is represented by a counter deployment, or a threat of so doing, by the West of an equivalent system' (*Parliamentary Debates*, 1982–3, vol. 38, p. 217). The assertion was not challenged.

There was one occasion when the nature of the 'Soviet threat' was directly addressed. Mr Eric Deakins (Labour) asked the Secretary of State for Defence what evidence was available to his Department about any aggressive intentions of the USSR toward the UK. In a written answer (12 May 1983) Mr Blaker replied:

The size and disposition of Soviet forces in Europe are far in excess of what is necessary for defence alone. The massive and continuing effort to build up these forces, Soviet readiness to use force – as in Czechoslovakia and Afghanistan – and their commitment to an ideology that envisages the ultimate triumph of the Soviet version of communism constitute a threat to the security of this country that cannot be ignored. (*Parliamentary Debates*, 1982–3, vol. 42, p. 473)

The nature of Soviet political objectives and the means for achieving them is not spelled out and appeal is made to apparently self-explanatory cases. One alternative view was summarily dismissed by Mr Heseltine, Secretary of State for Defence, in the debate on the defence estimates: 'There are those who see the Russians as a deeply conservative people who feel threatened by an aggressive and alien Western culture . . . We cannot give them [the leaders in the Kremlin] the benefit of the doubt' (*Parliamentary Debates*, 1982–3, vol. 46, pp. 180–1). The alternative is not, as this remark implies to be gullible but to understand the dynamics of the superpower confrontation in all its cultural and political as well as military complexity. So long as the judgement of politicians and the public depends on untested, reflex responses of the sort we have illustrated, the clichés and stereotypes will continue to do their corrosive work.

Since these debates at the time of the Euro-missiles crisis, there have been definite signs of a desire in official circles to tone down the anti-Soviet rhetoric and, on occasions such as Mrs Thatcher's visit to Hungary, Mr Gorbachev's visit to the UK, and the 1985 Geneva Summit, to reaffirm some of the principles of détente. The question remains: are those countries, including Britain, which are actively developing and deploying new nuclear weapons systems able to combine indefinitely those policies which assume the worst at the military level and simultaneously encourage dialogue, trade and cultural contacts? The answer depends to a considerable degree on the non-military consequences of the deterrence posture, and the extent to which it is more than just an instrument of policy but an experience in itself for those who adopt it. What effect does it have on those who practise it, irrespective of whether its aims are realized?

Some consequences of deterrence

The effects of a country's commitment to deterrence (meaning here nuclear deterrence) can be analysed at several different levels. They include the effects on the user in terms of perceived moral superiority, distortion of values, the militarization of politics, and the fear felt by individuals.

The posture of deterrence necessarily implies an opponent with intentions which are presumed to be hostile. If this presumption proves to be even partly mistaken, and if it carries over from military planning into the political sphere, the adversary is dehumanized. If this assumption is not made, the need for deterrence disappears. Thus small neutral countries like Sweden and Switzerland have relatively strong defence forces but no need for a 'deterrent'. Deterrence on the other hand systematically overrides other interpretations of the adversary's behaviour as the product of that adversary's own genuine fears, different perceptions, special interests or difficulties. It downgrades rational discussion and compromise by encouraging a belief in the inevitability of response and yet uncertainty about the scale and type of response to perceived hostile behaviour. It involves a double standard of evaluation: the adversary's military capabilities and intentions are measured on scales which bear little resemblance to those applied to oneself. In the extreme case, brought into the realm of discussion by Reagan's musings on Armageddon, there is the simple identification of one side with good, the other side with evil.[3]

Adherence to the view that the Soviet Union is out to rule the world and must be deterred from achieving this allows history to be written in a simple, almost preprogrammed way. Any action, whether cultural, commercial, diplomatic or military, can be interpreted as a move in a deliberate plan of world conquest. Objectively quite different circumstances, such as East Germany in 1954, Hungary in 1956, and Czechoslovakia in 1968, are all interpreted as expressions of the same political ends. The same applies to direct and indirect Soviet involvement in revolutionary movements throughout the world. One by-product of this is that those who do not share the same anti-Soviet stance – whether they are liberals opposed to 'friendly' dictatorships, marxist intellectuals or socialists – tend to be seen as clients of Moscow or fellow-travellers when their real allegiance is to western democratic traditions.

Cold War conditions mean that the facts of a particular situation are typically viewed through military and strategic spectacles. Gittings (Chomsky et al., 1984, p. 14) gives an example in terms of the Soviet Union's reserves of fossil fuels and minerals. These have considerable political as well as economic significance because the Soviet Union, unlike many western countries, is largely self-sufficient in these materials. The West often depends on external sources of energy and raw materials in areas in which the Soviet Union has its own commercial and political interests. Soviet involvement, however, is judged as activity designed to subvert these areas and to expand its influence at the expense and to the detriment of the West. Another example is the tendency to regard the Soviet Union's internal social and economic problems not as phenomena which the state socialist system can accommodate and eventually adapt to, but as the prelude to an aggressive foreign policy designed to divert attention away from these problems. The extent to which the western countries have used the East–West conflict as a diversion away from their own internal difficulties is rarely considered.

There are many signs of fear, hopelessness and despair in the public's response to the new Cold War, although support for government defence policy has remained generally high. The rhetoric from many quarters in the nuclear debate plays on the fears and builds them up into a form which is like the primitive fear of natural catastrophe. The opinion polls, which report that very significant numbers of people, especially young people, believe that there will be a nuclear war before the end of the century, show that confidence is low and that circumstances are felt to be out of control, including the control of governments. This feeling is one of the most damaging and dehumanizing effects of deterrence; it comes from believing that although we should not need or can scarcely contemplate using our nuclear weapons, the diabolic greed and aggressiveness of the adversary compels us to behave in this way. With this fear comes the removal of a sense of responsibility and the will to act.

The nuclear debate shows every sign of suffering from all these consequences of deterrence thinking. Discussion rarely envisages the possibility that the 'other side' may have its own language of morality which we could understand; that history can be written from more than one perspective; that peace is destroyed by fear, 'theirs' or 'ours'. The conduct of the new Cold War shows clearly that the meaning of nuclear deterrence extends far beyond military science and technology. From being a fact of life, deterrence has become a way of life for those countries which seek to secure themselves by its means. The fateful question 'What is to be done when deterrence fails?' must now be turned on its head by the admission that deterrence has failed and continues to fail.

10

War, Peace and Power

John Eldridge

Politics will, to the end of history, be an area where conscience and power meet, where the ethical and coercive factors of human life will interpenetrate and work out their tentative and uneasy compromises. (Niebuhr, 1960, p.4)

Society has no justification if it does not bring a little peace to men – in their hearts and peace in their mutual intercourse. (Durkheim, 1957, p. 60)

I see these two statements, one by a theologian and one by a sociologist, as a challenge. Niebuhr, in *Moral Man and Immoral Society*, wanted his theological insights to be tempered with realism. The special difficulty we now face is that the conduct of politics may lead to the end of history, given the unparalleled forces of destruction which nuclear states now possess. The twentieth century is not only the century of total war, but also carries within it the potential to be the century of total annihilation of the planet. Consequently, questions concerning the role of conscience and its influence on the structures and exercise of power need to be pursued with an ever sharper sense of what is at stake. Durkheim saw in modern industrial societies the potential for new forms of social organization which could benefit people materially and enlarge their personalities in a diversified, interdependent, pluralist society. But what he saw happening was the breakdown of social cohesion, a centre which did not hold. This threat and incipient presence of collapse he referred to as the condition of anomie. I want to suggest as a signal of what is to follow that when we think of the danger of nuclear war sometimes it is in terms of the actions of powerful groups – control, as it were, is in the wrong hands – and sometimes in terms of a situation that has got out of control: no one is in control and that is the problem.

We cannot imagine a society in which power is absent, but we can ask sociological questions about the structures of power and domination in particular societies. In the process we may be able to contextualize some of the ethical questions that have to do with the use and abuse of power. Since much of what is to be said here concerns the superpowers, it may be helpful to recall the words of Senator William Fulbright writing about the arrogance of power. They are applied to his own country (he was writing in the 1960s) but with suitable adjustments they apply to the Soviet Union also:

There are many respects in which America, if she can bring herself to act with the magnanimity and the empathy which are appropriate to her size and power, can be an intelligent example to the world. We have the opportunity to set an example of generous understanding in our relations with China, or practical co-operation for peace in our relations with Russia, of reliable and respectful partnership in our relations with Western Europe, of material helpfulness without moral presumption in our relations with developing nations, of abstention from the temptations of hegemony in our relations with Latin America, and of the all-round advantages of minding one's own business in our relations with everybody. Most of all, we have the opportunity to serve as an example of democracy to the world by the way in which we run our society. (Fulbright, 1970, p. 246)

Since the contemplation of the dangers of war leads us into dark areas and critical comment, it is as well to observe the brightness of that image of peace and to glimpse it as a real possibility. We want to recapture the language by insisting that the things which make for peace are more realistic than the things which make for war. If Wright Mills is correct when he claims that the causes of the Third World War are the preparations for it, then the justifications of our present practices are indeed what he terms 'crackpot realism'. The appeal to common sense, pragmatism and realism in seeking support for the continuing and ever-increasing arms race is the ultimate absurdity.

C. Wright Mills was an American sociologist, most of whose work was published in the 1940s and 1950s. His writing on the subject of power and its application to the theme of war and peace continues to have resonance for our times. In defining power, he offers a three-fold distinction.

1 Coercion is power which involves the use of force to obtain what is wanted against the will of the other person or group. He sometimes refers to this as ultimate power in the sense that in the last resort the powerful can use physical sanctions against the powerless.
2 Authority applies to the more or less willing obedience of those who are given commands.
3 Manipulation is the secret exercise of control in which those influenced are not explicitly told what to do, but are nevertheless subject to the will of another. Manipulation exists where the powerful seek to rule without showing their powerfulness.

Such a distinction invites the question, what kind of power mix exists in a society? In what direction is that society moving and what significance do we attach to it? Writing in the 1950s, Wright Mills argued that manipulation was the prime way in which power was exercised in the US.

No longer can the problem of power be set forth as the simple one of changing the processes of coercion into those of consent. The engineering of consent to authority has moved into the realm of manipulation where the powerful are anonymous. Impersonal manipulation is more insidious than coercion precisely because it is hidden; one cannot create the enemy and declare war upon him. (1956, p. 110)

In Wright Mills' writing there is a pervasive sense of ordinary men and women being at the mercy of forces they can neither understand or govern. They are powerless. But over and above these masses stands a power elite:

The power elite is composed of men whose positions enable them to transcend the ordinary environments of ordinary men and women; they are in positions to make decisions having major consequences. Whether they do or not make such decisions is less important than the fact that they do occupy such pivotal positions: their failure to act, their failure to make decisions, is itself an act that is often of greater consequence than the decisions they do make. For they are in command of the major hierarchies and organisations of modern society . . . They occupy the strategic command posts of the social structure in which are now centred the effective means of the power and the wealth and the celebrity which they enjoy. (Wright Mills, 1959, pp. 3–4)

Wright Mills' general argument was that the centralization of the means of power has given rise to an interlocking political, military and economic elite able to make decisions which are enormous in their consequences for world history. This he contrasted with the democratic ideal in which a community of publics can respond to and in some measure control its rulers. The trend he identifies in this process is towards a mass society governed by elite power that is irresponsible in the sense that it is not accountable for its actions. Wright Mills offers us the following schematic image of American society:

The top of American society is increasingly unified, and often seems willfully co-ordinated – at the top there has emerged an elite of power. The middle levels are a drifting set of stalemated, balancing forces: the middle does not link the bottom with the top. The bottom of this society is politically fragmented and, even as a passive fact, increasingly powerless: at the bottom there is emerging a mass society. (Wright Mills, 1959, p. 324)

From the standpoint of a critique grounded in a commitment to democracy Wright Mills' portrayal of this situation is one of organized irresponsibility. The implications are enormous in that the power elite impose their definitions of reality upon the people. Clearly, if this is near to the mark, when it comes to the questions of war and peace the consequences can be momentous. Reasoned debate loses out to the official secret, the trivializing campaign and the techniques of public relations. In *The Causes of World War III* (1960) Wright Mills develops the power elite thesis in relation to the nuclear threat and the arms race. Against the old precept, 'If you want peace prepare for war', Wright Mills saw military preparations as the cause of our precarious situation: 'Both the Russian and the American elites, and intellectuals in both societies, are fighting the cold war in the name of peace, but the assumptions of their policies and the effects of their interactions have been, and are, increasing the chances of war' (Wright Mills, 1960, p. 62). We encounter what Wright Mills terms a military metaphysics with its commitment to seeing East-West relations in terms of rivalry expressed in an arms race. Hence economic, political and military decisions promote technological developments. War is bureaucratized: the instrument of rational control becomes the apparatus which is the embodiment of deadly possibilities: 'The first cause of World War III is, obviously, the existence of these bureaucratic and lethal machineries. Without these there could be no war' (1960, p. 58). Whether or not the deliberate intentions to go to war is present, the machines themselves are triggered and ready to go, so the risk of accident is ever present and increasing:

Never before has there been an arms race of this sort – a scientific arms race, with a series of ultimate weapons, dominated by a strategy of obliteration. At every turn of this 'competition' each side becomes more edgy and the chances become greater that accidents of character or of technology, that the US radar man in Canada, or his Russian counterpart in Siberia will trigger the sudden ending. (1960, p. 61)

In discussing these tendencies, Wright Mills distinguishes between 'drift' and 'thrust'. The first relates to the unforeseen consequences for human societies and people of innumerable decisions. It is not related to structured intentionality of identifiable individuals and groups and in that respect signifies absence of control. Thrust does concern the outcome of structured intentions and it is here that Wright Mills sees the concentration of power in the USA and the Soviet Union as a coalescence of interests that deliberately promotes the arms race. This is done in the name of 'necessity', 'realism' and even of peace. For Wright Mills, however, as already indicated, it is a negation of the values of liberalism and socialism. In Wright Mills' view the drift and thrust of events are interacting together towards a Third World War. One result of this is that men and women feel powerless to do anything and exhibit a spirit of fatalism. They may come to feel, albeit with some unease because they are powerless, that what is being done ostensibly in their name is regrettable but necessary. Although Wright Mills emphasizes the role of manipulative power, which certainly plays its part in the propaganda war, there are also elements of power-as-authority and power-as-coercion involved. Clearly the concern for the secure state can lead to the practices of policing and surveillance. Although some of these are hidden, others are overt displays of force. Insofar as societies become orientated towards the preparation of war it is difficult to see how such practices will not develop alongside.

Wright Mills does paint a bleak picture although he is not without constructive suggestions as to what might be done. Before turning to that, however, it is worth reflecting that his general diagnosis does, in my view, find support from what has happened since he wrote. On the American front Mary Kaldor has written of the 'baroque arsenal': the development of weapons systems and the continuing attempt to improve performance characteristics independently of strategic thinking (Kaldor, 1982). Indeed, strategy and tactics may come to be influenced, if not determined, by these developments rather than the other way round. Underpinning this is the Department of Defense seeking to maintain or improve its budget, military services doing likewise, and defence contractors fighting for contracts. The technical developments which take place are seen as functional for the survival of the military-industrial structure. The whole complex is big and costly with complicated sets of relationships established between soldiers, sailors, office managers, designers, bureaucrats and workers. It has a cumulative effect of establishing the arms race, yet at the same time leaves unanswered, or taken for granted, fundamental questions as to what it is all for and why it is necessary. Occasionally writers like Robert Aldridge break cover and show up some of the contradictions (1983).

Aldridge, a former design engineer for Polaris and Trident missile systems, claims that a Trident submarine commander will have at his fingertips an explosive force equal to 2,000 Hiroshimas. He describes Trident, with its long-range capacity to hit hardened Soviet missile silos, as the ultimate first strike weapon. He points out that President Carter feared that this capability would create further instability and make future strategic arms limitation more difficult if the Soviets responded to this threat. The movement towards first strike capability will, in Aldridge's judgement, become more reciprocal and more deadly if present policies continue: 'Once the two superpowers face each other in a first strike stand-off, with weapons systems and decision-making highly automated, an international crisis, such as we have every few years, may prove disastrous' (Aldridge, 1983, p. 251).

We are talking about very big business. In 1978 ten US companies each did more than one billion dollars' worth of business with the Pentagon. These included General Dynamics, McDonnell Douglas, Lockheed, General Electric and Boeing, the last of these being responsible for the production of Cruise and Minuteman missiles. James Fallows writes of the 'culture of procurement' and suggests that through threat inflation the public and its representatives are encouraged to allow the Pentagon to embark on expensive, complicated projects. He cites the well-known case of the heavily overestimated capacities of the Soviet MIG 25, the Foxbat. To counter its alleged combat range of 2,000 miles and speed of Mach 3.2 the case for the American F-15 was established. As a result of a Soviet pilot's defection to Japan the Foxbat was shown to have an effective range of 186 miles and a speed of Mach 2.5 (Fallows, 1981, pp. 70–1). Fallows also points out that the development of the MX missile system at enormous cost (which at one time seriously envisaged digging 4,000 silos for 200 missiles and rotating the missiles from silo to silo in random fashion so that the Russians would never be quite sure which silo they were in) is based upon the premise of 'the window of opportunity' which the Soviets are alleged to have now, giving them the capability of attacking American Minuteman missiles. All of this is based upon hypothetical and dubious assumptions, which provide the breeding ground for threat inflation and, as we are now observing, leads directly on to the Star Wars scenario which is all about closing the window of opportunity completely. But given these dynamics of weapons procurement and development it is easy to see why arms control, let alone arms reduction and disarmament, is resisted by some interest groups. It goes some way to explaining the statement that surrounds arms talks very frequently, 'We must re-arm (modernize) in order to disarm.' This is precisely what is happening today; the support for the MX missiles programme accompanies the Geneva talks because, say the Americans, we must have something with which to negotiate.

These institutional pressures can scarcely be underestimated. Indeed, although so far as the USA is concerned we have the image of the powerful President, whose finger is on the button, there is a sense in which he also is caught up in a network he cannot easily control. The ambiguity of the presidential role is perhaps encapsulated in the kind of things they say in their farewell addresses. As far back as 1961,

President Eisenhower spoke of his fears of the military-industrial complex:

In the councils of government, we must guard against the acquisition of unwarranted influence, whether sought or unsought, by the military-industrial complex. The potential for the disastrous rise of misplaced power exists and will persist. We must never let the weight of this combination endanger our liberties or our democratic processes. We should take nothing for granted. Only an alert and knowledgeable citizenry can compel the proper meshing of the huge industrial and military machinery of defence with our peaceful methods and goals, so that security and liberty may prosper together. (Pursell, 1972, pp. 206–7)

Those are impressive words and the reference to the need for an alert and knowledgeable citizenry is worth underlining, with reference to the Wright Mills thesis on the apathy in mass society. Yet we have to recall that is was President Eisenhower who admitted responsibility for the U2 flights over Soviet territory in clear violation of international law. In the dramatic incident in 1960, when the Soviets shot down the U2 plane and captured the pilot Gary Powers, the whole of the Paris Peace Summit came to nothing and Krushchev withdrew the invitation to Eisenhower to visit Moscow. Indeed we also know that during the attempted Summit period, which was aimed at a thaw in the Cold War, the US had ordered a worldwide military alert, a 'pre-combat readiness test'. From the standpoint of the Soviet Union the U2 incident had, and continues to have, symbolic significance.

Roy and Zhores Medvedev maintain that the American approach to East-West relations remains the same. The preservation of a clear US military technological lead is a precondition to any serious negotiation.

Looking at this from another angle, *every* significant new technology of nuclear warfare – nuclear missile submarines, MIRVs, Cruise missiles, the neutron bomb and so on – has been introduced into the arms race by the United States. Rather than viewing the negotiation process as one of preventing the development of further systems of annihilation, the United States has traditionally seen new strategic weapons as bargaining counters to force the Soviet Union to ratify the permanence of the post-war imbalance of military and political power. (Medvedev and Medvedev, 1982, p. 162)

Now clearly Eisenhower was a part of the military-industrial complex which he indicted, yet it is difficult to conclude that he was in charge of it. The momentum of arms development was cumulative and remorseless. He saw this and offered comment on what he believed to be the illusion on which it was based. What he said retains relevance on the whole issue of the closing of the window of opportunity:

No matter how much we spend for arms, there is not safety in arms alone. Our security is the total product of our economic, intellectual, moral and military strengths. Let me elaborate on this great truth. It happens that defence is a field in which I have had varied experience over a lifetime, and, if I have learned anything, it is that there is no way in which a country can satisfy the craving for absolute security – but it easily can bankrupt itself, morally and economically, in attempting to reach that illusory goal through arms alone. The Military Establishment, not productive of itself, necessarily must feed on the energy, productivity and brainpower of the country, and, if it takes too much, our total strength declines. (Pursell, 1972)

What Eisenhower would have said about the Star Wars project can well be imagined. He might even have joined Generals Against The Bomb!

Much more recently the experience of President Carter in the White House also taught us something about the difficulty of connecting conscience with power. Clearly exercised by the nuclear issue and a signatory to SALT II, he was unable to get the agreement ratified in Senate; he found himself embroiled in the Iranian hostages event and attempted a dangerous and abortive rescue mission; and he will be remembered for his support of the neutron bomb. Thomas Powers claims that Carter came to office with a rooted dislike of nuclear weapons (1982). In early meetings with the Joint Chiefs of Staff he advocated a policy of minimum deterrence, suggesting that the US could make do with a retaliatory force of 200 nuclear weapons. Yet by 1980 he was to issue PD 59, which enunciated a strategic doctrine for fighting a nuclear war and laid the groundwork for Reagan and Bush to talk about winning a nuclear war. How far this simply articulated what was already a deeply embedded operational policy is another matter. If that is the case then deterrent philosophies take on the character of *post hoc* rationalizations and do not accurately represent the role of nuclear weapons in military planning. After all this Carter's farewell address signalled his sense of the danger of the nuclear arms race:'It may only be a matter of time before madness, desperation, greed or miscalculation lets loose this terrible force . . . For this generation, life is nuclear survival; liberty is human rights; the pursuit of happiness is a planet whose resources are devoted to the physical and spiritual nourishment of its inhabitants' (Powers, 1982).

Although I have written primarily of the USA, partly because I do think that the historical record must attribute to them a particular responsibility for the arms race, the reactions and responses of the

Soviet Union are clearly also part of the picture. The overriding consideration is that since Wright Mills and Eisenhower the arms race has continued unabated. I want to resist the inference that this has been inevitable. What has happened can in principle be explained by a no doubt complex disentangling of social processes and human action. But, if the outcomes are as irrational as many commentators believe, we must also see this as a history of lost opportunites. Such disarmament negotiations as have taken place have in practice been accompanied by ever-increasing stockpiles of nuclear weapons. This does not increase our collective security but diminishes it. This is precisely the point made in Alva Myrdal's classic text on the subject. We may bear in mind that it was written some 16 years after Wright Mills' *The Causes of World War III*. Her comment on the arms race constitutes an extrapolation of Mills' fears:

This element of instability in the arms race is a pending world danger. The dangers of a collision are accentuated by technological development itself, as warning times steadily decrease, thus making it more and more probable that war might occur through technical accidents and errors. This is illustrated by the fact that the time required for interhemispheric delivery of nuclear bombs by missiles has shrunk to about ten minutes. The missile has also drastically shortened the warning time and heightened the surprise element possible between neighbouring nations on a continental land mass. The mechanical complexity and increasingly automated functioning between signal received and attack released makes national security more and more threatened by technical hazards. (Myrdal, 1980, p. 8)

What Wright Mills had called organized irresponsibility Myrdal describes as the reign of unreason. For both of them it is a betrayal of Enlightenment and humanist values. This betrayal of humanist values, sometimes in the name of civilization, not only heightens our collective and national insecurity, it makes it increasingly difficult to escape from the predicament. If, as Marx had it, we make history but not in circumstances of our own choosing, then the circumstances become ever less of our own choosing. If we wanted to work for world disarmament we would not choose to start from here. Yet that is where we are and that is what we have to do.

Pessimism of the intelligence; optimism of the will. From Wright Mills to Myrdal and now on to E.P. Thompson, that is the stance. In his extraordinary essay, 'Notes on Exterminism, the Last Stage of Civilisation', Thompson references Wright Mills' comments on 'drift' and 'thrust'. Is control or absence of control the most serious problem?

What if events are being willed by no single causative historical logic ('the increasingly aggressive military posture of world imperialism', etc.) – a logic which may then be analysed in terms of origins, intentions or goals, contradictions or conjunctures – but are simply the product of messy inertia? This inertia may have drifted down to us as a collocation of fragmented forces (political and military formations, ideological imperatives, weapons technologies): or, rather, as two antagonistic collocations of such fragments, interlocked by their oppositions. What we endure in the present is historically formed, and to that degree subject to rational analysis: but it exists now as a critical mass on the point of irrational detonation. Detonation might be triggered by accident miscalculation, by the implacable upward creep of weapons technology, or by the sudden hot flush of ideological passion. (Thompson, 1982, p. 1)

Between the two great powers Thompson traces the reciprocal deadly logic, the logic of exterminism. Politics has become militarized. The hair-trigger military technology itself eliminates the moment of politics in which human choice can intervene. Weapons build-ups are not more of the same, but generators of greater instability and great destruction. The reciprocal logic into which the world is locked through great power rivalry takes on, for Thompson, the character of addiction. The question is, where is deliverance to be found?

Any answers offered to this question are likely to be contested. This is because no analysis in this area can be value-free. Concepts and categories are value-impregnated. Moreover, prescriptions and views on appropriate policies necessarily entail speculations about outcomes and consequences which, in the nature of the case, cannot be known in advance with certainty. Consequently whatever is advocated carries with it connotations of risk. So it is that discourse in this domain constitutes a mix of empirical, moral, calculative and hypothetical statements. Still the discourse itself can be subjected to careful scrutiny.

For example, those who support a policy of nuclear deterrence sometimes tell us that nuclear weapons cannot be disinvented. Therefore, unpleasant and uncomfortable though it undoubtedly is, we have to live with this knowledge. We cannot return to a prenuclear Eden. Those who remind us of this do not necessarily want or advocate a nuclear arms race and indeed may seek for 'rational' approaches to arms control. Michael Howard argues in this vein when he maintains: 'The problem of controlling nuclear weapons, at least for our generation, is not one of abolishing them but of exploiting their contribution to international stability and minimising their threat to it, especially their threat to stability under conditions of acute crisis' (Howard, 1983, p. 165). But he goes on to express worries about the instability introduced by technological changes in weapons systems. Their accuracy has, he suggests, led American analysts to speculate on Russian willingness to launch a first strike and on the possibilities of the US fighting a nuclear war in which they might 'prevail'. Both views he castigates as a combination of great military and political naiveté.

Howard is a notable academic student of war, yet his position is not without problems. Having identified the problem of instability in adversarial relations which has been induced by technology and amplified by military and political naiveté, he is nonetheless content to assert: 'What technology has made unstable, technology will one day render stable' (Howard, 1983, p. 166). Clearly this is speculation, not an empirical fact. It is also a good illustration of the work which a concept like stability can play in discourse. Despite his worry about technology, Howard also claims: 'Even today . . . the underlying balance remains fundamentally deeply stable' (p. 166). Each of the terms in that clause does its reinforcing work. This is the heart of Howard's value position. And yet that perspective is partially challenged by some of the key actors in the situation and thereby qualifies Howard's own judgement. He writes:

But the military analysts have only themselves to thank for the violent passions they have unleashed. If the balance is really so unstable as they suggest: if there is a 'window of opportunity' so wide as to tempt the Soviet Union to risk its own destruction in a wild bid for world conquest; if technological hubris is so great as to tempt the United States into engaging in what they foresee as a 'limited' nuclear exchange with 'only' a few score million deaths on each side: then the Peace Movement is right to express its concern, even if the particular issue they have chosen is relatively trivial and the remedies they propose are worse than the disease. (Howard, 1983, pp. 167–8)

Howard's position expresses the argument that nuclear weapons cannot be disinvented and that provided we can maintain stability in weapons systems we can maintain peace and, in some respects, more effectively than with conventional weapons. The inference is that political, diplomatic and military power should be deployed to that end. This argument, like others taking different positions, cannot be disproved save in the event of nuclear war. Even then, assuming anyone were around to consider it, the claim might be made that the cause of the war was the failure to maintain the necessary weapons stability and/or that we were victims of political and military naiveté. The optimistic assumption, of course, is that we can identify and practise weapons stability in nuclear terms.

It is worth noting how the argument begins with the factual statement that nuclear weapons cannot be disinvented and then moves on the considerations based upon their continuing presence. We should, however, pause long enough to note the simple point that the things we invent can also be dismantled. At a much simpler level of technology we know that concentration camps cannot be disinvented, yet we can, as an international community, choose to say 'never again' and use our power to destroy that which is against the human interest precisely because it can consume us and human values and culture with it. Power, after all, is the facility to get things done. To Howard's position there is a counterconsideration that working towards the diminution and abolition of the means of total destruction is less risky than working to maintain weapons stability.

Behind such differences of perspective are competing views as to what is 'realistic' or 'prudential'. So it is that those who in the name of power politics and the role of nation states in world affairs espouse nuclear weapons and deterrence doctrines as ways of coming to terms with reality will tend to oppose nuclear disarmament as an idealistic fantasy. Yet the 'realism' of deterrence contains its own risks. Jonathan Schell suggests that there is a strategic defect in this realism:

> For, if we try to guarantee our safety by threatening ourselves with doom, then we have to mean the threat; but if we mean it, then we are actually planning to do, in some circumstance or other, that which we categorically must never do and are supposedly trying to prevent – namely extinguish ourselves. This is the circularity at the core of the nuclear deterrence doctrine; we seek to avoid our self extinction by threatening to perform the act. According to this logic, it is almost as though if we stopped threatening ourselves with extinction, then extinction would occur. (1982, p. 201)

Is it then rational or realistic to rely on nuclear deterrence as a means of maintaining peace? For Schell, the doctrine of nuclear deterrence is based on a monumental logical mistake: 'One cannot credibly deter a first strike with a second strike whose *raison d'être* dissolves the moment the first strike arrives. It follows that, as far as deterrence theory is concerned, there is no reason for either side not to launch a first strike' (Schell, 1982, p. 202). Schell's view is that the reason for the continued possession of nuclear weapons is not their military credibility but their role in protecting national sovereignty. It is this which leads those with power to the inconsistent position of threatening extinction in order to avoid it. Of course the extent to which nuclear weapons are simply built for deterrence purposes is another question. After all, nuclear war fighting is part of the concern which many in the peace movement have about NATO's flexible response strategy. Recently Donald Mackenzie has convincingly argued that nuclear weapons have never been conceived in wholly deterrent terms either by the USA or the Soviet Union. In their war plans both great powers take into account the possibility of pre-emptive strikes. Counterforce targeting is one of the signs of this (1984). That would at least help to explain why the nuclear powers appear ready to live with the contradictions of pure deterrence theory.

In any event such considerations bring us back to the role of nation states in power politics. Do we not have to conclude that, so long as nation states remain, the power politics they embody demand that we have to come to terms with the continued role of nuclear weapons? Is that not realistic? Those who come to such a conclusion sometimes cite Max Weber's now famous distinction between the ethics of conviction and the ethics of responsibility. After all, the nation state and its interests were a key element in Weber's sociology of power. Absolute values and personal ideals, however admirable and exemplary, could not suffice in the practical business of power politics. The ethic of responsibility required a prudential concern for the consequences of action. Hence Weber's unglamorous description of such politics as 'the strenuous slow drilling of hard boards' (Weber, 1948, p. 128).

Guenther Roth, a distinguished Weber scholar, has recently pointed out that in the US and in West Germany the distinction between the ethics of conviction and responsibility has surfaced in disputes about the realism of the peace movement (Roth, 1984). Opponents of the peace movement argue in this respect that its idealism is misplaced and does not come to terms with the real complexity of international relations. The flavour of this disagreement was well brought out in an exchange between the then West German Chancellor, Helmut Schmidt, and a former Mayor of West Berlin, Rev. Heinrich Albertz. Schmidt, citing Weber's two ethics, chided those who advocate the laying-down of arms for equating the sincerity of their motives with the success of their policies: 'They adhere to a naive ethic of conviction, which forgoes reason and experience, and are content with the feeling that they face the future with good intentions and leave to God, the Lord of History, the consequences resulting from their actions for which they don't want to be held responsible'.

Albertz, in reply, claimed that Weber's distinction was wrong and dangerous: 'With it one can ultimately justify every political decision. I fear that those lose increasingly their grip on reality who support the production, stationing and use of atomic weapons as a means of defence and saving the peace' (Roth, 1984, pp. 503–4).

We can see that there is a struggle going on over the very categories and concepts in which the debate is structured. Naiveté and responsibility clearly carry with them different resonances but the appropriateness of applying these labels to different positions will depend on our interpretation of a cluster of moral, practical, empirical and political judgements. The extent to which these judgements are implicit or explicit is itself worthy of scrutiny. Reason may not lead us to certainty in our judgement of political realities but its role in critically appraising assumptions, our own as well as those with whom we disagree, is important. Roth, for his part, has made an instructive comment on the concept of political responsibility. In the age of nuclear weapons, he maintains, the survival (and therefore specific interests) of the nation state is no longer the fundamental issue, as it was for Weber, but the survival of human populations. War in such circumstances cannot be legitimated as a matter of 'honour', of a nation 'meeting its responsibilities before history'. The danger of a potential for nuclear holocaust has changed the nature of the human situation and with it our ethical responsibilities:

Weber could take it for granted that there would be generational succession and hence history in the future. We cannot do so any more. This has created a special kind of responsibility not *before* our descendants but *for* the very possibility that the new generations will be able to live – a totally new ethical situation. Saving whole populations and even having to ensure the continuance of life has become a new 'ultimate value', transcending the salvation concerns of religious virtuosi and the political utopias of revolutionaries as well as the traditional interests of nation states. Before this situation Weber's distinction between the two ethics loses its political applicability. (Roth, 1984, pp. 508–9)

To say that the politics of peace cannot ignore the realities of power is then to open discussion, not to close it. At the level of understanding these realities there is a continuing academic task of clarification, which may also have political relevance. If, for example we use concepts like power elite, it still becomes important to assess not only who the members of this elite are but how cohesive or fragmented such a grouping is. Conflicts of interest may after all occur within elite groups, and coalitions may shift on particular issues. In the US disagreements as well as agreements may emerge between the business corporations and Congress, between the State Department and the Pentagon, between the various branches of the armed forces and so on. To delineate these structurally and ethnographically will tell us something about the contours of power. The same point holds by extension to discussions about the military-industrial complex. Studies have indeed been undertaken in this area (Pursell, 1972; Rosen, 1973).

From time to time business practices do become visible and a matter of public interest. In mid-1985 General Electric was fined one million dollars by a US court for fraudulent dealings in its defence contracts with the Pentagon. General Dynamics was fined $676,283 by the US Navy Secretary for 'pervasive' business conduct, its chairman was retired and Admiral Rickover was publicly censured. The company had two defence contracts worth $22 million cancelled and two of its divisions will not be able to bid for new contracts until $75 million in overcharges have been repaid. The report of the Pentagon's Inspector General, made public in June 1985, claimed that the Pentagon had wasted $1.6 billion through inefficiency. Eye-catching examples of ashtrays costing $500, lavatory seats at $600 and a coffee pot at $9,000 were cited. The *Observer's* correspondent, Robert Chesshyre, argued: 'The essential problem has been inattention by Congress in the face of a collusive and reinforcing relationship between the 53,000 officers and civilians charged with permanent responsibilities and their 170,000 customers, the defence industry.' And he referred to 'knowledgeable critics' who fear that 'the structural failings that led to the insane escalation of defence costs will remain uncured' (*Observer,* 25 June 1985). This is perhaps why so much business excitement has been generated by the SDI programme. This is not simply internal to the US since the British and German governments have intervened to support business interests in their own countries by signing agreements on participation.

Detailed analyses of this multifaceted set of activities may lead us to a more sensitive appreciation of the many conflicts and contradictions within the interlocking world of politics, technology and bureaucratic organization. This perspective, with its emphasis on contests whose outcomes are uncertain, does have anti-determinist connotations. This does not, on the other hand, imply that the contests taking place reflect a kind of pluralism in which power is equalized between contending groups. Nor should we miss the wood for the trees. There is after all clear evidence that in the USA (and in the USSR, though differently organized) there is a general culture of weapons procurement. J. K. Galbraith observed:

Reflecting an intelligent concern for the threat of nuclear devastation, legislators from New England and along the East Coast have been generally critical of the more promiscuous aspects of the arms build-up of the last few years. They have strongly supported the nuclear weapons freeze movement. Nearly all voted against the MX. But these convictions were extensively set aside a year ago in the competition to win the basing of an ancient and now missile-armed battleship with the accompanying and exceedingly modest prospects of jobs and revenue. It was a uniquely visible, evenly slightly bizarre, example of the compelling character of the compensatory power of the military establishment. (Galbraith, 1984, p. 201)

Since then, of course, the decision has been taken to go ahead with the production of MX missiles as well. There is still political space which makes it possible to think of alternatives such as nuclear freeze, but the culture of weapons procurement has a momentum of its own.

An awareness of these deep structures will properly minimize any tendency to think of disarmament as a matter easily accomplished, whether at conventional or nuclear levels. But it is an important social scientific and political task to understand the cultures which produce weapons systems and the mechanisms and networks by which they do so. Powerful though the organizations and institutional structures which sustain them undoubtedly are, we can remind ourselves that they are also human constructions and not immutable. Only if we think they are a product of some determinist theory of social change can we think otherwise. This is the significance of Donald Mackenzie's contention:

Nuclear militarism is not a rational, functional prerequisite of a socio-economic system; nor is it an irrational technologically determined Behemoth. It occupies an uneasy, difficult to specify, theoretical middle-ground of partial, local rationalities and of organisational and political conflict. It is shaped more by the exigencies of politics than of technology: but that does not imply it is a coherent, rational creation, even of an evil ruling elite (Mackenzie, 1984, p. 45)

If space exists to be contested then hope lies in the political and cultural struggle for peace, which is still possible, so that competing definitions of reality may be expressed and argued over. This, we may recall, is why Wright Mills argued for the importance of a community of publics, because it could provide the foundations of a politics of responsibility. He specifically identified religious leaders, scientists and intellectuals as those who could stimulate and sustain public debate and enquiry on the peace issue. Such people cannot only challenge those at the commanding heights of power about the direction in which they are going, but can also point to other options. The hope is precisely in that kind of struggle even if the outcome cannot be known.

Wright Mills wrote:

If we as intellectuals, scientists, ministers do not make available, in such organs of opinion as we command, criticisms and alternatives, clearly we have little right to complain about the demise of publics themselves. Given our own continued default, we cannot know what effect upon either publics or elites such public work as we might well perform and refuse to perform might have. Nobody will ever know unless we try it. (1960, p. 157)

Even at the time Wright Mills wrote some members of the scientific community had broken down ideological barriers of form the Pugwash conferences, which continue to meet. Today there is a growing body of scientists whose voices are heard more frequently, warning the nations of the world about the medical, ecological and physical effects of nuclear war. Where they judge it appropriate they are prepared to counteract official government propaganda. Journals like the *Scientific American* and the *Bulletin of Atomic Scientists* are important channels of communication. In the social sciences the International Union of Anthropological and Ethnological Sciences has established a Commission on the Study of Peace and publishes a newsletter. In Britain SANA includes natural and social scientists among its ranks and seeks to promote informed scientific opinion about the causes and consequences of the arms race.

Recently, for example, the Union of Concerned Scientists in the USA has attacked President Reagan's SDI arguing that it will have a destabilizing effect on NATO and make arms control agreements more difficult to secure. This is also a view shared by the Institute of Strategic Studies in London. We should not assume that the powerful are deaf to or unaffected by such voices. To do so would be to define them as being in a permanent state of bad faith, not seriously concerned with the peace of the world. Certainly statesmen are prepared to question the SDI and this was notably illustrated in Sir Geoffrey Howe's speech to the Royal United Services Institute in March 1985, *Defence and Security in the Nuclear Age* (Howe, 1985). He pointed out:

> The history of weapons development and the strategic balance shows only too clearly that research into new weapons and study of their strategic implications must go hand in hand. Otherwise, research may acquire an unstoppable momentum of its own, even though the case for stopping may strengthen with the passage of years. Prevention may be better than later attempts at cure. We must take care that political decisions are not pre-empted by the march of technology, still less by premature attempts to predict the route of that march. (Howe, 1985, p. 13)

This led him to ask a number of fundamental questions: will the supposed technology actually work? If it does, what will be its psychological impact on the other side? What are the chances that there would be no outright winner in the everlasting marathon of the arms race? Would political control over nuclear weapons and defensive systems be maintained or might we find ourselves in a situation where the peace of the world rested solely upon computers and automatic decision-making? Although Howe still holds to a deterrence theory, the questions he raises are of the kind which concerned scientists and informed members of the peace movement have helped to put on the agenda. This is no mean achievement.

Nor are such scientific initiatives to be found only in the West. In 1984 scientists from communist countries met under the auspices of the Scientific Council on Peace and Disarmament Research. In its address from Moscow to scientists of the world the conference recorded the view:

The world is now threatened with a danger unprecedented in history. The research of scientists in different countries, as well as the authoritative experts of the UN testifies that the use of even a small fraction of the stockpiles of nuclear weapons will lead to truly monstrous destructive consequences for humanity and the entire living nature of the planet.

In these extremely dangerous conditions the responsibility of scientists increases. The authority of science must be used first of all for the purpose of giving world public opinion the real picture of the scale of the impending catastrophe and the dangers of the continuing arms race, to show the hopelessness of the policy of strength and the urge towards military-strategic superiority, to demonstrate the inhuman character of militarisation of the economy and social consciousness, the policy of building up the atmosphere of mistrust, suspicion and hostility between peoples and states. Relying on the UN General Assembly on the right of the peoples to life and on condemning the use of nuclear weapons as a crime humanity, we call upon the scientists of the world to raise their voice in support of the proposal on the non-first use of nuclear weapons, the prevention of the militarisation of outer space, the complete prohibition of nuclear weapon tests and the freezing of nuclear armaments quantitatively and qualitatively as the first step on the way to their gradual reduction all the way to their total elimination, on the impermissibility of the use of force for settling disputed international problems.

The scientific community does cross national and ideological boundaries and can be used to restrain the militaristic forces within nation states rather than enhancing those forces. These are real choices where scientific activity gives to its practitioners special responsibilities in defining their vocation.

What about the role of religious leaders in the politics of peace? Wright Mills offered what he called a pagan sermon directed at Christian leaders. Do not these times, he asked, demand a little Puritan defiance? 'You will not find in moral principles the solutions to the problems of war, but without moral principles men are neither motivated nor directed to solve them' (1960, p. 171). But what about the objection that the Church should not be involved in politics?

The world *is* political. Politics, understood for what it really is today, has to do with the decisions men make which determine how they shall live and how they shall die. They are not living very well, and they are not going to die very well either. Politics is the locale both of evil and of good. If you do not get the church into politics, you cannot confront evil and you cannot work for good. You will be a subordinate amusement and a political satrap of whatever is going. You will be the great Christian joke. (1960, p. 172)

The willingness of the Church to be involved in peace politics has increased in many countries since Wright Mills wrote, including the USA. The level of its serious engagement there has perhaps been most notably expressed by the US Catholic Bishops' 1983 pastoral letter, 'The Challenge of Peace: God's Promise and Our Response'. In the course of a far-reaching discussion and evaluation of the arms race designed to raise the level of awareness in the Christian church, the report called among other things for an ongoing moral debate about nuclear deterrence policy. It recognized that this would require a substantial intellectual, political and moral effort. It argued that the dangers of the nuclear age called for new concepts of security and defence.

What is worth underlining is the way in which interventions of this kind can help to challenge, and even rewrite the political agenda. In doing so the public can be reminded of issues which are sometimes overlooked. The relationship between the arms race and development is a case in point:

We are aware that the precise relationship between disarmament and development is neither easily demonstrated nor easily reoriented. But the fact of a massive distortion of resources in the face of crying human need creates a moral question. In an interdependent world the security of one nation is related to the security of all. When we consider how and what we pay for defence today we need a broader view than the equation of arms with security. The threats to the security and stability of an interdependent world are not all contained in missiles and bombers. (US Catholic Bishops, 1983, p. 76)

Unless we think that the management of public opinion is wholly in the hands of governments, then the struggles in the value sphere can influence the ways in which material and ideal interests are interpreted. We can envisage the creation of new ways of thinking and acting which can permeate the community of nations and help to transform their relationships. Not the national interest as traditionally understood but the human interest, yet to be realized and pursued, can become the powerful goal of the politics of peace. Thinking will not make it so, but imagining other options gives us the possibility through public debate and political action of discovering what is feasible. We should not be ashamed to hope.

Part *III*
Defence Policy and the Public

11

Public Opinion and the Media

John Eldridge

Since wars begin in the minds of men, it is in the minds of men that the defences of peace must be constructed.

This statement forms part of the preamble to the constitution of UNESCO when the organization was set up after the Second World War. UNESCO statements and declarations over the years have frequently emphasized the role that the mass media can play in strengthening peace and international understanding. They can sensitize public opinion to the major problems confronting the world, many of which are global in character. In general terms a clear value position is taken up. Incitement to war and the use of propaganda which jeopardizes peace is seen as morally wrong. This position meshes in with the Final Document of the UN Special Session on Disarmament (1978). In the light of the present dangers of the arms race it was thought to be essential that:

Member states should be encouraged to ensure a better flow of information with regard to the various aspects of disarmament to avoid dissemination of false and tendentious information concerning armaments, and to concentrate on the danger of escalation of the arms race and on the need for general and complete disarmament under effective international control. (paragraph 105)

In 1980, UNESCO published the MacBride Report, *Many Voices, One World*. This included some discussion of the responsibilities of the media in relation to the goal of peace. In a key paragraph we read the following:

The primary function of the media is always to inform the public of significant facts, however unpleasant or disturbing they may be. At times of tension, the news consists largely of military moves and statements by political leaders which give rise to anxiety. But it should not be impossible to reconcile full and truthful reporting with a presentation that reminds readers of the possibility – indeed, the necessity – of peaceful solutions to disputes. We live, alas, in an age stained by cruelty, torture, conflict and violence. These are not the natural human condition; they are scourges to be eradicated. We should never resign ourselves to endure passively what can be cured. Ordinary men and women in every country – and this includes a country depicted as 'the enemy' – share a yearning to live out their lives in peace. That desire, if it is mobilised and expressed, can have an effect on the actions of governments. These statements may appear obvious, but if they appeared more consistently in the media, peace would be safer. (p. 177)

What comes through in the MacBride Report is a view that stresses the goal of peace as transcending other political and national interests and the need for an active rather than passive acceptance of the goal: 'The spirit of peace and the will to preserve peace must be tirelessly cultivated and consolidated' (p. 175). The mass media then are called to a constructive and responsible role in this respect. The response to the call is another matter.

Peace talk in the media

The problems as well as the possibilities were what the UNESCO conference on the media and disarmament met to discuss in Nairobi in April 1983. In her background paper, *UNESCO Mass Media Declaration and Disarmament,* Dr Breda Pavlic pointed out that the military-industrial-political complexes in all parts of the world have a self-preserving and self-reinforcing character:

They are powerful, resourceful and pervasive coalitions that have developed around the common purpose: the continued expansion of the military sector, irrespective of actual (and not perceived) military needs, and most of all irrespective of their society's real human needs. How much do the world's mass media assist them in this, either through business links or more-or-less concealed submission to the state-bureaucratic apparatus, remains an open question for the moment. (1983, pp. 29–30)

This reminds us that the mass media are not free-floating institutions independent of the societies in which they are located. They have to survive in an environment that can include a variety of constraints: commercial, political, economic and ideological. So we can recognize that in practice news about disarmament may be neglected whilst news which emphasizes the need for strong defence may be promoted. For example, the evidence available suggests that both the 1978 and 1982 UN Special Sessions on Disarmament were not well reported in the world's Press. On both occasions, however, NATO chose to have its own conference and this was widely reported. On the other hand, if Press and broadcasting are tied too closely to a state or party apparatus, then, while it may offer plenty of peace talk, its interpretation of events may be narrow, even dogmatic: adversaries within and without the society may be treated as identikit caricatures. Still in all modern societies the mass media are a site for cultural struggle. Those who produce the output may be constrained by powerful forces but they are not necessarily determined by them. They have the opportunity not only to reflect official definitions of reality but to point to other possibilities and proposals. What happens in the space where media messages are articulated matters very much. There can be trivialization, chauvinism and misinformation. Journalists can be on the receiving end of censorship, disinformation and propaganda campaigns from powerful pressure groups. But if the issue of peace is as significant for the future of the world as the UNESCO position maintains, then all of this is a challenge to owners, producers, editors and journalists. This guiding principle in fact enabled the Nairobi conference consisting of academics and representatives from the mass media from a large number of countries – East, West, North and South – to reach some general conclusions. The fact that consensus was achieved among a disparate group of people with differing interests and political perspectives was, in a small way, encouraging.

What were some of these conclusions? It was argued that the media have the capacity to influence perceptions of threat and contribute to the formation of attitudes concerning security. There is, for example, a strong contrast between the doctrines of deterrence espoused by the great powers and the views expressed in the UN Special Session on Disarmament in 1978 which stated that the accumulation of nuclear arms led to greater insecurity and that a programme of disarmament was needed to promote lasting international security. If the deterrence view becomes part of the taken for granted reality which the media portray, then perceptions of threat will be shaped by that assumption. Similarly the conference drew attention to the Palme Commission's report *Common Security* (1982), since it challenges received notions of deterrence, mutually assured destruction and first-strike capacity. Palme was quite specific about this, arguing that international security must rest on a commitment to joint survival rather than on a threat of mutual destruction, and the programme contained developed proposals for reducing the arms race and establishing new collective security procedures. Unless these kinds of proposal are also seriously covered in the media we may lose sight of what Gwyn Prins has recently called the paradox of security:

The paradox of security is not only that in the nuclear world those habits of mind and expressions of power to which we are accustomed are no longer consistent with security, even in its restricted form of defence. Were it merely so, the situation would be only unfortunate rather than grave, and it would be stable. The paradox is bitter because the relationship between nuclear weapons and security is volatile and corrosive. It is an inverse relationship: the more that people and states seek to increase their security by the old methods, but with new atomic power, the less security they have; and the more that heightened insecurity is sensed, the faster the arms race becomes, the heavier its burden, and the more hateful, aggressive, expansionist and devious the enemy appears. In this way the spiralling accelerates viciously and the hope of escape recedes as the nuclear presence spreads over the whole political landscape. (Prins, 1984, p. xv)

It was because of this recognition of the general capacity of the media to influence perceptions of threat and conceptions of security that the Nairobi conference argued the need for pluralism both in relation to sources of information and approaches to the coverage of disarmament issues. It was stressed that the media must have free access to the diversity of relevant sources of information, including peace and disarmament research institutes, in accordance with the rights of the public in all countries to know and to communicate about the causes and the consequences of the arms race and the obstacles to disarmament. Moreover, journalists everywhere should be enabled to explore disarmament from many approaches, including the links between disarmament and development and emerging new concepts of security. In the exercise of their professional responsibilities they should be enabled to use a variety of relevant sources and to apply their critical awareness to them in their constant search for the highest level of accuracy and truth.

The importance of access to diverse sources of information is worth emphasizing. If restrictions are imposed through Press censorship or through journalists relying too extensively on official statements, then limits are clearly being placed on the public's right to know. In the Falklands conflict, for example, foreign correspondents in Britain complained bitterly about their exclusion from Press briefings. Many British journalists were deeply unhappy with their treatment by MoD officials and the military. More generally, the lobby system, which gives special privileges to some correspondents in exchanges for non-attributable comments, has been much criticized both for its secrecy and for its exclusiveness. These and many other aspects of media coverage of the Falklands dispute have been well documented by Richard Harris (1983).

What this points to is the need for critical journalism, that is, an approach to issues and stories which does not take the official line or the Press handout for granted. Alternative sources of information provide some check on the reliability of the information. In the field of defence and disarmament, for example, there are research institutes with specialist academic knowledge. The International

Institute of Strategic Studies in London, the Stockholm International
Peace Research Institute, the UN Institute for Disarmament
Research, the New Delhi Institute for Defence Study and Analysis
and the Armament and Disarmament Information Unit of the
University of Sussex provide the kind of detailed and technical information which can serve the press and, for that matter, the public
and non-governmental organizations with an interest in these issues.
What the informed or sceptical journalist knows is that he or she is
likely to be on the receiving end of claims and statements, some of
them seeking to gain an advantage in a propaganda war of words. It
is not always easy to recognize this but the ability to put
the knowledgeable question or check the relevant sources so that
contradiction, inconsistencies or factual errors may be exposed is important. Even to be aware of the technical problems in counting
weapons or the linguistic problems involved in distinguishing between strategic, theatre and tactical weapons (with their hidden ambiguities) is to be able to avoid some pitfalls which politicians or
official spokespeople may create. For example, the whole discussion
relating to INF has been beset with these problems. Definitions of
which weapons are to be, or should be, included differ between the
states and this can lead to different tabulations and inferences. Thus
the Soviets claimed that before the deployment of Pershing II and
Cruise in Europe something like rough parity already existed,
whereas the Americans claimed that deployment was necessary to
restore parity against acquired Soviet superiority. Clearly we are not
just dealing with matters of simple arithmetic here. But, apart from
an awareness of the political game being played, it is important to
appreciate what other parameters are relevant when comparing the
operational capabilities of different systems. Paradoxically, this may
generate an awareness of the spurious concreteness which underlies
much apparently factual discussion. As the SIPRI Yearbook for
1982 points out: 'Any comparison of NATO and WTO [Warsaw
Treaty Organization] forces should, ideally, be dynamic and
qualitative, based on assessments of survivability, penetrability,
reliability, targeting options and employment doctrines, accuracy,
exchange scenarios and the endurance of Command, Control, Communications and Intelligence. However, attempts at quantifying
these factors are bound to be arbitrary and the whole exercise of very
uncertain validity' (p. 9).

It was for these kinds of reason that the Nairobi conference stressed the need for journalists with high qualifications to deal with complex matters of disarmament. Relevant training could include
foreign languages, law, economics, history and international relations as well as an appreciation of the methodology of news collection

and dissemination. This is something that needs to be fed back into schools of journalism. These may be high demands to make upon the profession of journalism but the issues are too great to permit less. And they are of course ethical issues as well as technical, economic and political. To live with these complexities is not easy and one cannot suppose that journalists will all resolve them in the same way. Nevertheless, the experience of Andrew Wilson, former defence correspondent for the *Observer,* is worth recalling:

As I explained in an article in the *Observer* (1st November, 1981), my change of views was further advanced by my frequent confrontation, as a defence correspondent, with items of nuclear hardware, and more particularly the people who operate them. This was not – and it bears repeating – because such people very often correspond with the caricatures drawn by much 'peace' propaganda. (In the British services, at any rate, I found many of them moved by the same instincts that I was, but believing – albeit with growing difficulty – that they would never be called upon to 'press the button'.) Rather it was because I recognised that this very 'decency', like the technical fascination of the hardware itself, provided the essential framework within which to pursue peace-time planning for operations involving the death of millions.

My conviction is that, however much I might not wish to undergo the consequences of a nuclear attack on this country (or perhaps the no less deadly consequences of a more distant exchange), I would find it even harder – indeed intolerable – to live with the responsibility for having unleashed such an event on the other people. In short, I would not want to press the button, even in retaliation. Anyone holding this conviction, and believing, as I do now, that the occasion for 'pressing the button' may indeed arise, must in honesty cease to support the doctrine of deterrence. (Aubrey, 1982, pp. 36–7)

Incidentally, Wilson's *The Disarmer's Handbook of Military Technology and Organisation* (1983) is now a useful sourcebook for journalists and the public.

Wilson's comments are important because they represent a journalist speaking to fellow-journalists. I should like to couple them with those of another journalist, Jonathan Dimbleby, who has an impressive record in this field. Writing in 1982 he declared:

If the media were now to display a little more zeal in pursuit of nuclear truths they could transform our understanding not only of the Geneva talks, but of their relationship to other, no less urgent issues: the controversy about flexible response; the doctrine of limited nuclear war; the concept of 'balance' in a world of nuclear overkill; the prospect of another dangerous spiral in the arms race; the risk of an accidental holocaust that begins ludicrously from miscalculation or misunderstanding; and, finally, to that gravest of all, question of whether the prevailing strategies are protecting the peace of driving us towards the abyss. It is surely not too much to insist that commonsense requires the debate to begin in earnest without delay.

Professionalism under scrutiny

The Nairobi conference included journalists and media researchers. Bearing in mind the fact that the relationship between the two is sometimes adversarial – there is perhaps a natural reluctance to expose one's professional activities to external scrutiny – it was the more impressive that a unanimous agreement was reached on the need for systematic research into media coverage of disarmament issues. UNESCO itself was asked to promote international cooperation between researches in this area. There have always been journalists – certainly going as far back as Walter Lippmann in the early part of this century – who have seen the value of research into media output. Lippmann (1922) recognized that the reporting of events was a complex matter and could lead to misunderstanding and even misrepresentation:

Just because news is complex and slippery, good reporting requires the exercise of the highest of the scientific virtues. They are the habits of ascribing no more credibility to a statement than it warrants, a nice sense of the probabilities, and a keen understanding of the quantitatives importance of particular facts . . . Some time in the future, when men have thoroughly grasped the role of public opinion in society, scholars will not hesitate to write treatises on evidence for the use of news-gathering services.

Journalists are also capable of writing in a critical and illuminating way about their own profession. Harris's book on the media coverage of the Falklands war has already been cited. Much more wide-ranging is Phillip Knightley's book, *The First Casualty* (1982). The title, derived from the comment of Senator Hiram Johnson, in 1917, 'The first casualty when war comes is truth,' looks at the role of the war correspondent as hero, propagandist and myth-maker from the Crimean to the Vietnam War. This is not to imply that all such reporting glorified or romaticized war, though problems of distortion, selective reporting, censorship and editing abound. However, a case has been put that in the case of Vietnam the media in the US helped to stop the war, though in all conscience it took a long time to do so. The role of television was seen as particularly influential by some observers. Air Vice-Marshall S. W. B. Menaul thought that television had 'a lot to answer for [in] the collapse of American morale in relation to the Vietnam war' and Brigadier F. G. Caldwell was of the view that, in the light of the American experience over Vietnam, if Britain went to war again, 'We should have to start saying to ourselves, "Are we going to let the television cameras loose on the battle field?"' (Knightley, 1982, p. 379). Attitudes of this kind go some way to explaining the difficulties experienced, notably by television, in the Falklands conflict.

From the standpoint of disarmament issues it is worth recalling that one of the first studies initiated by SIPRI was on Press coverage of the Eighteen Nation Disarmament Committee held in 1968. The method adopted was to work from verbatim transcripts of the meetings and then look at what was actually reported in the international Press. The author, Loyal N. Gould, concluded that the Press coverage of the issues was very limited and that papers in the various aligned countries gave little attention to the proposals from the other side (Gould, 1969). The documentation for the Nairobi conference drew attention to a number of studies carried out in various parts of the world.

In his review of West German research Jörg Becker came to the general conclusion that Press reporting in that country was insufficient to help the public appraise in any critical way military and strategic decisions (1983). Among the examples he cites are Kalka's study of three national dailies, covering the period 6 June 1977 to 9 April 1978, looking particularly at the approach to the neutron bomb. While the papers took up different positions on the issue, Kalka concluded that there was an absence of adequate critical consideration of political and strategic questions. Thus the question as to what the neutron bomb meant in terms of the security of the Federal Republic and whether its political price was justified was scarcely mentioned. This was in line with earlier studies conducted in the 1960s and also with Guha's 1980 study of the NATO twin track decision of December 1979 (that is, NATO's intention to deploy Cruise and Pershing II missiles in Europe unless the Soviets dismantled their SS-20s and SS-4s and 5s). He concluded that figures cited for arms comparisons between East and West were selected and manipulated and that studies which did not support the predominant doctrine of deterrence were ignored. In his view the Press reporting of these complex problems had to be regarded as a failure. Again, Kister's study published in 1983 looked at Press coverage of first-strike capability since 1977. He noted that *Die Welt* and *Frankfurter Allgemeine Zeitung* were the only national dailies to approach a real strategy debate and that all the main dailies were in favour of the NATO doctrine of flexible response and did not discuss alternative defence concepts.

A case study of the Press coverage of the Indian dailies entitled *Loud on War, Soft on Peace* was undertaken by Chanchal Sankar (1983). This was based on a sample of 276 articles drawn from nine

Indian dailies for the week 22–28 March 1983. He observed that there was far more attention given to preparations for war than for peace and noted that the Indian Press is almost totally dependent on the major international agencies such as AP, UPI, Reuters and AFP. In this view an important weakness in the Indian coverage was the lack of explanation. Sankar writes:

The ordinary reader, for instance, would be quite unable to understand whether the Pentagon publication *Soviet Military Power* is an objective and accurate statement of the Soviet position or whether it is aimed at convincing the American public that the Russians are very far ahead in armaments and therefore the Americans must spend very much more to catch up. It also needs expert analysis to determine whether American policy is moving from deterrence to the concept of fighting and winning a nuclear war. In all this the Indian papers are quite backward with their explanations. (1983, p. 4)

Sankar goes on to point out that there is not only the absence of explanations but a failure to present new ideas for ending the arms race, such as a nuclear freeze, cutting existing nuclear stockpiles by half, renouncing first use of nuclear weapons and negotiated moratoria. The absence of interest in disarmament questions is surprising given the legacy of Gandhi's philosophy of non-violence. This is not explained in terms of censorship and leads rather to another solution:

There is a big task of education, a big need to reach out to the gatekeepers of copy, to editors, reporters and others who decide the content of papers. The defence establishment does something to teach journalists about weaponry, tactics and war but no one does anything to teach them about the horrors of war, the destructiveness of weapons, the fabulous cost of the arms race and about people and movements which have stood squarely against war. The thirty or more Journalism schools – in universities and outside – have no special course linking media people to disarmament and peace-mongering. (1983, p. 28)

Research is, then, going on in a number of countries into media coverage of defence and disarmament issues and there were other contributions from Nigeria and Japan. But it is limited and does not constitute anything like the systematic work that is required if prevailing standards and practices are to be challenged.

War and peace news in the UK

In the UK, the Glasgow University Media Group have undertaken a series of studies of television news. The latest study, *War and Peace News* (1985), bears most directly upon our present concerns. Television news is a major source of information for large numbers of the population and is supposed to offer us impartial news. In this respect it is held to be different from newspapers with editorial lines. Nevertheless, it is possible to show through the analysis of news programmes the routine technical, visual and linguistic practices which permeate the production of news and give us the taken-for-granted news values. These values are visible, when pointed out, but are not always noticed. If, however, they are explicity brought to the attention as a result of systematic research, this can create the conditions for self-examination and possibly for change.

In *War and Peace News* it is pointed out that in matters of defence and disarmament the mass media are at the centre of a struggle to define and influence public opinion. The superpowers seek to use the media to promulgate their viewpoints. The British government, for its part, has waged a campaign which sought to defuse the message and impact of the growing peace movement. It is against such a background that organizations like CND have tried to convey their message to the British public.

How did television journalism relate to such campaigns? There are certainly times when we are told that a propaganda war is going on. For example, when President Reagan called a press conference to announce his 'zero option' in November 1981, television news interpreted what he was doing as part of a propaganda campaign. 'It was' said an ITN correspondent, 'aimed at calming the growing European peace movement protesting at the risk of nuclear war.' The careful management of the event was also wryly commented upon: 'It was interesting to note that, since Mr Reagan's *faux pas* have usually been in response to journalists' questions, today he wasn't allowed to answer any.' The BBC correspondent described the occasion as the President's 'peace offensive'. 'It was intended,' he said, 'to demonstrate to his European allies that the administration is serious in its search for arms control.'

A similar awareness could be seen in the coverage of Reagan's announcement of START talks in June 1982 and of his subsequent European tour. Commenting on this, and on the West German situation in particular, Charles Wheeler, on BBC 2, 'Newsnight', told us:

President Reagan's courtship of his European allies has been well prepared in a series of speeches and political moves towards arms control. These have been received here with relief. But to many West Germans his conversion from re-armer to disarmer has been too sudden and too slick to be convincing. There was a vivid example of President Reagan's over-anxiety to please in his speech today at the Bundestag, the lower house of the German parliament. There he came close to aligning himself to a German peace movement which only four months ago he was condemning as financed by the Kremlin.

Despite evidence of the awareness of the propaganda war on the part of television journalists, it is still possible for them to be sucked in by the undertow. So on the Reagan European tour there were many visual treatments of ceremonies, parades, state banquets and the like. The artificial, non-informative character of this kind of news was again candidly stated by Charles Wheeler when Reagan was in West Germany: 'To catch a glimpse of their American visitor Germans must turn to television with its narrow view of a few carefully controlled events and non-events like arrivals and departures of the glamorous and the great.' The broadcasters themselves might well choose to blame it on 'news management'. The BBC's Brian Wenham wrote in June 1984: 'We find today a growing and dangerous tendency for those in authority to seek to bend television, on the one hand to contrive events that are pre-cooked and synthetic, on the other to keep cameras at bay in matters that are true and of importance.' This is a good point but, unless we want to think of those responsible for news broadcasts as cyphers, or unthinking agents of the powerful and hence simply and solely representing the *status quo,* this does leave open the question as to what the broadcasters choose to do about it.

Wenham was writing at the time of the fortieth anniversary of D-Day. This event illustrated very well the pressures that are placed upon the mass media by powerful political interests. The commemoration of the event itself has of course been quietly going on year after year. Quite why 40 years after was selected for massive publicity and where the idea came from is not immediately clear. But, as Peter Fiddick, the *Guardian's* media editor, pointed out:

There will be scarcely a journalist, television commentator, producer, or cameraman, of whichever nation and whatever political persuasion, unaware of being trapped in the classic media bind: as they assist in the celebration of a major event, a noble cause, they risk becoming yet again helpless victims of a political hijack. It is Ronald Reagan's election year. Francois Mitterand is deep in a political trough and badly needs a distraction which could evoke popular support. So what is a nice neutral head of state like Elizabeth R. doing on a beach like this? In whose honour are we gathered? (*Guardian,* 28 May 1984)

The reference to a political hijack is apposite. The significance of the event was, as it were, reinterpreted by the West. This entailed not inviting the Soviet Union to the celebrations and decontextualizing D-Day by ignoring what was happening on the eastern front. A celebration of an event which contributed towards the defeat of fascism can in practice be used to bolster Cold War politics.

Let us take an earlier example. In Easter 1983 there were widespread peace demonstrations in western Europe expressing concern about the possibility of Cruise missiles and Pershing II being deployed in Europe at the end of the year. The British government was, to put it mildly, unhappy with these proceedings. As part of its propaganda campaign against the movement Mr Michael Heseltine went to the Berlin Wall, at the taxpayers' expense. This raises the question of what we are to make of news values which choose to cover what was palpably a public relations exercise. No doubt it could be argued that this was done in the name of balance, but peace demonstrators do not have the routine access to the media that the powerful in our society can command. In fact Heseltine had more than one bite of the cherry. When he came back from Berlin he called a Press conference to say what he thought of the peace demonstrations. Since the broadcasters chose to top and tail their news accounts with extracts of him speaking at that conference, the reports of the peace demonstrations were sandwiched in between Heseltine negatives. The juxtaposition of events and comments in this way is not inevitable. What comes out is a reflection of choice. Given that some broadcasters acknowledge the potential pitfalls, this is reason enough for scrutinizing the organization of news output.

There is a more general problem about covering the peace issue on television news. Demonstrations are in themselves ritualized events, expressions of deep feelings which thousands of people have about the nuclear issue: deep enough to make them want to identify with the movement. However, it is not an obvious vehicle for the expression of rational argument, especially if coverage of the speeches is very limited, as it usually is. If coverage of CND tends to be restricted to such occasions on television news, along with such incidents as Bruce Kent's address to the British Communist Party, or his supposed difficulties with his Church, or Cardinal Hume, then the central argument of the peace movement – that the system of deterrence is unstable and precarious – is unlikely to be articulated consistently or clearly in any regular way. Deterrence may be a simple idea but it has a range of connotations and implications which are rarely unpacked on television news. Perhaps its axiomatic status overstates its credibility. It certainly diminishes the consideration of alternative possibilities.

An alternative agenda?

What the informed, sceptical journalist knows is that he or she is likely to be on the receiving end of claims and statements, some of them seeking to gain advantage in the propaganda war of words. The ability to put the knowledgeable question, or to check relevant sources so that contradictions, inconsistencies or factual errors may be exposed, is important. Even to be aware of the technical problems in counting weapons or the linguistic problems in distinguishing between strategic, theatre, tactical and intermediate weapons – with their overlapping elements and hidden ambiguities – helps to avoid some of the pitfalls which politicians and official spokespeople wittingly or unwittingly create.

It is worth stressing that critical journalism will lead to a news agenda much more pluralistic in its implications. Concepts of deterrence, threat and security would be open to more, not less, scrutiny. Since enormous consequences flow from the application of these concepts in policy making, this has to be a gain if the public's right to know is to be anything more than a slogan.

Those who trade in Cold War rhetoric may object that to allow such critical scrutiny in this 'sensitive' area is dangerous and even subversive. But there is a growing belief in some parts of broadcasting that such an approach should be developed. The programme *Kabul Autumn,* shown on Channel 4 in December 1984, is a good example. It contrasted television images of the Afghan war in the West with those in the Soviet Union.

Back in the USSR, viewers get an entirely different perspective of the Afghan war. While the West sees pictures of gunships and Mojahadeen attacks, Soviets are shown a war against poverty, ignorance and disease . . . We in the West don't hear much about the torture and mutilation of civilians by the Mojahadeen. By the same token Soviet television doesn't broadcast the fact that, while many children will live because of Soviet doctors and nurses others will die from Soviet bombs. The media are locked into their respective cold war attitudes.

In the British context a particular critical responsibility is placed upon broadcasters. Given a popular Press which shows little sign of responding seriously to public issues, the broadcasters with their large audience especially for news programmes, are presented both with a challenge and an opportunity. A pessimistic view would argue that the constraints on broadcasters are so powerful and their own professional codes so deep-rooted that any change is impossible. Other do not agree. Those who produce media output may be constrained by powerful forces but they are not totally determined by them. They do have some opportunity to point to other possibilities and proposals and not simply to reflect official definitions of reality. Some evidence of the readiness to do this is to be found in current affairs and documentary programmes; most notably, by screening *Threads,* the play about the effects of nuclear war on Sheffield, the

BBC redeemed its failure to show *The War Game*. At long last that too has been shown, revealing that policies can shift on such matters. Such shifts can never be taken for granted. They have to be argued and struggled for.

The way issues of peace and war are presented, analysed and evaluated will help to shape public perceptions of our situation and what can be done about it. Nuclear weapons, we are often told, cannot be disinvented; although, like concentration camps, they can be dismantled and the causes and consequences of the arms race be critically exposed.

Public opinion East and West

I want to conclude this chapter by touching upon the issue of the mass media and public opinion. The role of public opinion in relation to defence and disarmament policy and practice is both a puzzle and a challenge. All I can hope to do is illustrate what I mean.

I want to suggest that it is facile and misleading to equate public opinion which what public opinion pollsters produce. The opinion poll is a social invention which has its origin in market research and election studies. It has typically operated in the context of doing work for client organizations such as political parties, businesses, Press and broadcasting. There are many problems, well known to social scientists, about the methodology of polling: the wording of the questions, the interview setting and relationship, and the inferences drawn. Moreover, when the polls are made public through the media, they can be subject to various other filtering processes. From the original findings (with all their methodological problems which are usually left unremarked) more selection, simplification, compression and re-emphasis can take place. In this way we learn what 'the public', in which we are included, is supposed to think about this or that. It thereby plays a part in the social process which it purports to describe and refine. It becomes part of the social milieu within which issues are discussed and evaluated. We do not know in what ways this influences subsequent judgements or perceptions. At a Quaker organized British-Soviet conference on the media and public opinion (in Sochi, December 1983), one of the Soviet contributors suggested that if phrases like 'better dead than red' are used in poll questions, or if phrases like 'enemy state' are used as so-called barometer questions, they can feed back into public consciousness. Consequently questions can themselves create or reinforce stereotypes, and this puts a great responsibility upon pollsters.

While members of the public as individuals often feel themselves to be helpless in the face of forces they cannot control, there is no doubt that governments and various interest groups, including the media, see public opinion as important. It is there to be sought, massaged, reported on, appealed to, or, if it is defined as going against you, changed. When President Reagan announced his zero option, interim zero option and START proposals, these were identified in parts of the media as part of his peace offensive to persuade 'European public opinion' of his seriousness and credibility on arms control and disarmament. As we have seen, when Mr Heseltine, as Secretary for Defence, went to the Berlin Wall in Easter 1983, it was an explicitly acknowledged public relations exercise to counter the influence on public opinion of the growing peace movement. Here the media have a difficult job. They can either operate as sceptical or critical journalists and identify such activities in their own terms or they can collude and endorse particular positions. What research can potentially do is sensitize us to ask the question, what do the media do when they mediate? In general terms, they select information, they tell stories, they report 'opinion', they take sides and they set agendas. Sometimes agendas are set by what the current state of public opinion is thought to be. For example, a number of current affairs programmes on defence questions begin with a public opinion poll as a way of defining a problem and then proceeding with an enquiry. Thus, in an enquiry into dual control of Cruise missiles in Britain, 'Panorama' began with the poll finding that 76 per cent of the population thought there should be a physical device to prevent firing without British consent (21 November 1983).

When the members of the SRT study group visited NATO, we were told by the British Press Officer that public opinion in the West was subject to disinformation campaigns from the Soviet Union. Examples cited (without evidence) were the Vietnam War and the decision about the neutron bomb. This of course carries with it a mechanistic view about how public opinion can be manipulated. Against this was set the electoral mandate as the true expression of democracy and public opinion. This presumably was not manipulated but free. The *NATO Review* is a magazine published under the authority of the Secretary General intended to contribute to a constructive discussion of Atlantic problems. In the April 1984 issue there is a cartoon accompanying the article by Hans-Georg Wieck on 'The Soviet Union and the Future of East-West Relations'. It depicts a map of the USSR and Europe with a Soviet General standing against a stockpile of missiles releasing a flock of doves across to the West. And *NATO Review*, Nos 3/4, 1983 has a cartoon cover of a peace demonstration with two placarded slogans:

'No to Pershing II in Europe' and 'Join the Passivists'. It merges in the front into columns of SS-20 missiles. Inside is an article by the Norwegian Member of Parliament, Grethe Vaerno, called 'A Public Opinion Strategy'. His expressed view is that there is a need to struggle with public opinion, to analyse why the 'peace movement' has gained such widespread support and to develop a strategy designed to regain public support for the Alliance. This means reinforcing the view that there is a Soviet threat, both military and political. He suggested that a mental barrier has been constructed in many peoples' minds by expectations of peaceful cooperation and goodwill which did not take account of the Soviet military build-up. This had enabled what he called the anti-NATO campaign to criticize NATO nuclear doctrines and the low nuclear threshold in battlefield weapons. Vaerno argued that there is a leadership crisis in the NATO countries which has been the most serious obstacle to consensus over security. The essence of his position and prescription is as follows:

The mood of the day is *distrust*. Leaders have been proved wrong, everybody's opinion is equal to the next man's. Nobody accepts authority and nobody is believed, particularly not the elected politicians, establishment figures and the military. There is a marked desire for direct influence and participation even outside the normal political system. This is hard to change, perhaps impossible. It may be countered by creating a more informed public. It is, however, paramount that political leaders should not abdicate responsibility for taking the lead in shaping public opinion. When they stop insisting on what they feel is right; when they start to follow what they perceive as a popular trend; when they refrain from using their position to explain; and deprive those who still believe in them of a positive lead, then they have started a vicious circle of dwindling support both for themselves and their policies. (Vaerno, 1983, pp. 28–9)

The call for an informed public is appropriate although the assumption that members of the peace movement are not well informed in many instances is questionable. Indeed, later in his article Vaerno makes two points to which members of the peace movement have drawn attention. The Alliance has to demonstrate that its long-term goal is a peaceful relationship, not confrontation, superiority or an offensive capability, otherwise it will get no support for its defence plans. This is precisely what debates about Trident, Pershing II and MX missiles are all about. Second, the Alliance has to show that it is genuine in its attempts to lessen the dangers of nuclear war and Vaerno points out that it is not enough simply to assert that NATO's policy of deterrence has kept the peace for more than three decades:

The fear will always be there – the fear of deterrence failing, of being a target for nuclear weapons. Other questions cause confusion – those concerning a moral refusal to be the first to use such weapons; theological discussions about deterrence as a means of righteous defence; logical questions about the credibility of a suicide strategy (for both sides, by the way). These are serious dilemmas for quite a lot of people. We should not be afraid of a more open discussion about nuclear doctrine. It would be meaningless to pretend that the problems are not there. (Vaerno, 1983, p. 31)

Of course Vaerno hopes that a more open discussion will lead to a restoration of faith in NATO and its strategy but, if the questions which he admits cause confusion are rigorously explored, then it involves in principle the possibility that NATO will have to respond to new thinking from below, including parts of the peace movement which are very well informed as a burgeoning literature bears witness to. In other words, public opinion is not something which in a democratic society is shaped from above, but requires the political and military leadership to be responsive to informed argument and discussion. Clearly the mass media can play a crucial role in facilitating such a dialogue.

At the Sochi conference the relationship between the mass media and public opinion was much discussed. A respected British journalist with experience of East and West felt that there was sometimes a problem of reporting defence questions in the British Press. It is not always easy to qualify criticisms because of shortage of space so what comes across after editing might give the impression that the Soviet economy is on the verge of collapse. On the other hand, he thought that if one regularly watched Soviet television it would be difficult to understand how the Thatcher government survived. He also thought that there was a problem for foreign journalists in the USSR, particularly in how to write about the Party. Access to Party officials is difficult and only very rarely on their travels will Party Secretaries receive them. This leads the journalist to rely on written sources, gossip and suchlike. Yet if an adequate image of the Soviet Union were to be conveyed abroad this needs to be attended to, for part of the problem is that people are scared of what they do not understand.

He also made an interesting distinction between different kinds of public opinion. There is 'ordinary' public opinion which journalists report as news but which they play a part in forming. This, he thought, was very noticeable on arms questions. There was 'professional' public opinion, made up of the well-informed and educated groups in society, of which the quality Press was certainly conscious. There was also the public of the paper's readership, which raises the question, who is whose prisoner? There is the obvious feedback of the letters column. Only in special circumstances do journalists and newspapers feel the weight of the readership's opinion, as in the case of the Suez crisis. The anti-government position of the *Guardian* and the *Observer* caused both those papers difficulties.

The Soviet contributors drew attention to some of the things which affected their public opinion. Soviet fears of the West were rooted in tradition. After both the First World War (following the October Revolution) and the Second World War with the policy of military encirclement, they felt themselves to be threatened by the West. Naturally, they said, this gives feelings of great insecurity. The more nuclear weapons there are, the more insecure everyone feels. One Soviet sociologist pointed out that history is complicated in all countries and particular experiences can give rise to fears, mistrust and stereotypes. Thus the effect of the Second World War in which 20 million were killed in the Soviet Union was very great but it could be reflected in contradictory tendencies. On the one hand was the feeling that military strength was needed in order to prevent the Soviet Union ever being invaded again; and on the other hand there was the desire to build a peace-loving movement, based on a deep sense of the value of human life. Both responses were understandable but the first he thought was 'neurotic', whereas the second was realistic. The history of the USA was different, but it also had its neurotic and realistic elements. The neurotic element plays upon fears and generates mistrust. So, when the Soviet Union reached parity in the arms race with the USA, from the Soviet point of view from inferiority to parity is a way up, but for the Americans it was a way down.

Into this framework were put some thoughts about the role of western public opinion. This was a 'third force' which could restrain the aggressive tendencies of western governments and the Americans in particular. But are the people in the West active enough and clear-sighted enough to solve this problem? What influence did the mass movements for peace have? How could an anti-Soviet person like E. P. Thompson be a leader of the peace movement when he does not believe in Soviet intentions? It seems that one of the underlying problems here was the prevailing assumption of the Soviet contributors that rough parity in arms is a sufficient basis upon which to construct peace and the task is to convey the message to world opinion that is now exists. Consequently the deployment of Cruise and Pershing II was seen as both aggressive and destabilizing. At the same time the concept of parity is not only definitionally complex but also in practice carries a commitment to modernization. This has multiplied the number of nuclear weapons in existence many times over the past 15-20 years. It is here that public opinion as represented in the peace movement parts company with the superpowers, both East and West. Indeed, what our Soviet colleague had labelled a 'neurotic' response was manifested after the conference in the Moscow offices of *Izvestia,* when again we were reminded of the 20 million war dead and told that the Soviet Union must negotiate from strength. This was Casper Weinberger in mirror image. Moreover, we were told, members of the unofficial peace movement in the Soviet Union were a fifth column in the pay of the West. No doubt this would be food for thought for those who claim CND is in the pay of the Kremlin.

The peace movement and the opinions it represents are a threat to all those who are led by thoughts of negotiation from strength, which in practice means modernization and continual arms build-up. If the Soviet Union were really determined to influence the peace movement in the West then it would also have to examine critically its own policies. Whatever the horrors of the Second World War, if their fears lead them to look to nuclear weapons for security then they are as mistaken as their western adversaries. The search for non-nuclear, non-offensive forms of defence must become as central for them as it should for the West. Even if with some justice they see themselves as responding to American modernization, they too have responsibilities to initiate non-nuclear peaceful coexistence. Journalists and 'public opinion' will surely spare time to celebrate it.

12

Professional Voices

Helen Zealley

The unleashed power of the atom has changed everything except our thinking. We need an essentially new way of thinking if mankind is to survive. (Einstein, 1946, quoted in Nathan and Norden, 1960)

Issues of justice, peace, defence and disarmament demand to be considered within a systematic ethical framework, yet the emphasis during vocational and professional education on specific knowledge and skills leaves many of those with professional involvement in decision-making ill-prepared for this. Conversely, those trained to explore issues from a moral standpoint frequently lack the detailed scientific knowledge to question technological decisions. Conditions are ripe for confusion about the nature of personal and professional responsibility.

The professional ethos

Most professional people are conscious of an underlying moral code and an obligation to pursue their work within its framework of rules. The code of medicine, for instance, derives from Greek philosophy and the teaching of the Greek physician Hippocrates. As defined in the *Dictionary of Medical Ethics* (Duncan and Dunstan, 1981) it comprises three main themes: beneficence or service to humanity; justice; and respect for persons and confidences. In addition, emphasis is placed on the importance of loyalty to the doctor's teachers and colleagues. This oath is still sworn by many graduating medical students and provides the foundation on which medico-moral decisions are made. Over the centuries, the original themes have been expanded to take account of other values so that doctors, in treating patients, are expected to disregard religion, nationality, race, party politics or social standing. Since 1948, with the Declaration of Geneva, the focus for defining and clarifying the international ethical code has been the World Medical Association. Gillon (1985a) summarizes the Declaration, revised in 1968 and 1983, and its requirement for the doctor to 'consecrate his life to the service of humanity' and 'not to use his medical knowledge contrary to the laws of humanity'. Detailed specific advice is provided in this, and subsequent Declarations, and only in regard to the code on abortion has there been some relaxation of the basic principles laid down over 2,000 years ago. Nurses, who have more recently been organized as a distinct profession, also emphasize the universality of their obligations and the requirement to respect life, dignity and the rights of mankind (Campbell, 1972).

Although many professions lack such an explicit code, their practitioners recognize an implicit ethos in their work, sometimes having to balance these against conflicting pressures if they work for employers with other priorities. For example, lawyers may refuse to act as state prosecutors. Prison warders and doctors may refuse to force-feed hunger-strikers. Psychiatrists may refuse to treat those whose only symptom is non-compliance with state directives. Public servants may draw attention to facts which governments have deliberately kept secret from the people.

Changes which affect the environment of professional practice most abruptly are those which arise from a significant shift in social values and from major scientific discoveries, or from interaction between the two. For example, developments in scientific knowledge sometimes challenge traditional beliefs and provoke action or reaction from the Church and other 'moral guardians'. Similarly, as the scope of professional practice is extended by innovations in technique and organization, there is a need within the professions themselves to question the status of traditional goals and moral values. The rate at which new ideas can be assimilated will vary. For instance, while incestuous relationships have always been considered wrong, the tiny risk of an incestuous half-brother/sister liaison arising inadvertently through the use of artificial donor insemination was accepted by the majority of the members of the Warnock Inquiry (1985). Similarly, the introduction of life-support systems has changed the concept of killing for the medical and nursing staff involved in their use (Gillon, 1985b). The rigid code of the past relating to abortion has been relaxed not only because of legal changes but because many health staff found themselves torn between the present and future health and wellbeing of the parents, siblings and potential child.

Thus the categorical imperatives of the past are transformed and individuals come to review the ideals by which they practise. Defence policies, civil defence planning and the deployment of nuclear weapons in vast numbers are causing such a transformation. Since 1980 in particular, there have emerged in Britain a number of identifiable professional groups which are opposed to nuclear weapons and place their members' skills at the disposal of others working for peace.[1] SANA issue up-to-date factual information that is used to challenge many of the assumptions on which present day nuclear policy is based. Lawyers for Nuclear Disarmament, and a parallel Scottish group, have made public the inconsistency of current nuclear policies with existing international treaties. Psychologists for Peace (PfP) draw attention to the possible consequences of illogicality, inconsistency and invalidity in the conceptual systems of those who defend the massive, highly sophisticated and technocratically guided defence industry. Architects for Peace (AfP) emphasize the ineffectiveness of civil defence protection measures within a state committed to nuclear weapons. Generals for Peace and Disarmament (1983) propose a package of measure to reduce the defence systems of all nations to a level that is consistent with their national defence requirements. In addition, members of these and other groups have identified common themes which transcend professional boundaries.

Those whose professional work involves them directly in the work of government departments may find themselves confronted with other complex personal moral issues. How can they separate 'moral integrity' from 'subservience to authority' when one component of their moral duty must be to work within the system that operates? When Sarah Tisdall was convicted of passing information to a newspaper about the arrival of Cruise missiles in the UK, she found herself in this position. Resignation from her post – although widely advocated in the Press – would not in practice have resolved her moral dilemma because her commitment to 'maintain secrecy' should extend beyond her resignation. A further, more detailed illustration of the dilemma for civil servants is Clive Ponting's release of information to Tam Dalyell, an elected Member of Parliament, about the decisions leading to the sinking of the *Belgrano* at the start of the Falklands Campaign (Ponting, 1985). His argument that this duty was to the elected Parliament – as representing the people – rather than to the Government of the day was upheld by a jury despite a direction to the contrary by the judge. Current efforts to clarify an ethical code of pratice for civil servants may reduce uncertainty in the future.

Those who are only too well aware of the limitations of knowledge and expertise within their own profession must view with considerable alarm the findings of studies of so-called 'expert' information. Steadman (1981) has drawn attention to the discrepancies between British data used for calculating blast casualty rates following a nuclear explosion and those prepared by the US Office of

Technology Assessment (1980), discrepancies which seriously underestimate the likely number of such casualties. Prins (1983) and others from the Cambridge University Disarmament Seminar describe a number of nuclear accidents and near accidents that have already resulted in nuclear contamination of the environment. Ford (1985) shatters the illusion – carefully created by certain statesmen and generals – that, for better or worse, the defence and deterrence system is deeply thought out, technologically reliable and under the control of people who know exactly what they are doing. The reality, painstakingly researched in interviews with defence strategists and visits to American research establishments, demonstrates major flaws in the system, including technological breakdowns, incompetence, political ignorance and neglect.[2]

Thompson (1985) points to the dangers of the ultimate in technical expertise: completely automated military systems. He argues that an 'infallible automated decision-making system can *never* [his emphasis] be built because of the inherent limitations of expert systems technology'. He does not doubt the possible construction of totally reliable hardware, although like any mechanical object this will be difficult to achieve: nor does he question the possible construction of 'correct' software. His contention is that the systems specification is dependent on the prior *exhaustive* characterization of all possible scenarios that could ever arise. This is impossible. Those who imply that our present system of defence and deterrence is under the complete control of cool-headed professional experts need to recall that the conduct of military operations in accordance with fixed plans or agreements is impossible. In warfare the unexpected is the norm and no one can anticipate how an opponent will react to the unexpected. To imply that this would not be the case in the event of a war involving the nuclear powers is profoundly naive or irresponsible.

The response of doctors and other health professionals

Given their long-standing and explicit commitment to the service of humanity it is not surprising that doctors – as a professional group – were among the first to develop a group identity within the peace movement. As long ago as 1951 the Medical Association for the Prevention of War (MAPW) was founded to unite the profession's efforts to prevent war by formulating ethical principles; studying the causes and results of war; examining the psychological mechanisms by which people are conditioned to accept war as a necessity; urging that the energies and money spent in preparation for war be diverted to fight disease and malnutrition; and seeking the cooperation of all doctors in all countries having the same aims. In recent years MAPW has concerned itself particularly with the nuclear threat and the ultimate relationship between expenditure on arms and lack of expenditure on health and social development, especially in the Third World. MAPW has always been a rather discreet organization and was unknown to many of the doctors who, during the 1970s and 1980s, were developing their individual commitment to the peace movement. This involvement – or, for many, reinvolvement – developed a particular momentum following the issuing of a warning by the Medical Working Group of the Thirtieth Pugwash Conference (1980) that medical disaster planning for nuclear warfare is futile. An extraordinary lecture tour of the UK by Dr Helen Caldicott – based on her book *Nuclear Madness* (1978) – drew attention to developments in the nuclear industry and their medical implications. The result was powerful and within weeks the MCANW had been established with active branches throughout the UK. The Campaign was deliberately more visible than MAPW – although they work jointly on many issues – with the additional aim of alerting colleagues, and through them the public and policy makers, to the disastrous consequences of a war fought with nuclear weapons.

Within months there was widespread awareness of the Campaign and it was joined by many eminent members of the profession. At the same time there was an awakening of interest in nuclear issues with scientific articles in most of the major medical journals, for instance a series in the *British Medical Journal* on 'Medicine and the Bomb' by Smith and Smith (1981). In the national media there was widespread discusson of the view that a 'limited nuclear war' in Europe was winnable without escalation. Civil defence planning was being promoted and medical staff in every health authority were being required to make preparations 'to meet the effects of any major (nuclear) attack on this country' (Home Defence Circular HDC 77/1). Understandably, doctors from different parts of the country looked to the British Medical Association (BMA), their main representative professional body, for guidance in relation to such work. Many sensed the possible dilemma that a home defence programme might increase the likelihood of the very event it was designed to mitigate. In 1981 the BMA had no policy by which to guide its members and its Annual Representative Meeting – a well-attended body representing the profession throughout the UK – asked the Association's Board of Science and Education to review the effects of nuclear war and the value of civil defence in order that the BMA might form a policy. A Working Group was established, whose Report on the Medical Effects of Nuclear War (1983) was published 18 months later. The Report described in detail the probably immediate and long-term medical consequences of the use of nuclear weapons. It included a critical analysis of possible responses and drew attention to the total inadequacy of any potential medical response. The Report explores the weight of scientific evidence concerning the nuclear aftermath and identifies key factors, such as firestorms, that had been omitted from official British calculations of casualty rates. It also provided disturbing comparisons between rather low official British casualty estimates and those derived from the widely respected American scientific data, comparisons that were rapidly criticized by the Home Office. Having stated the facts and given their informed conclusions, the Working Party stated that 'each reader will make up his or her own mind on matters connected with the nuclear weapons debate'. Despite this carefully worded neutral statement, a subsequent Home Office letter (1983) to all Regional Scientific Advisers stated that the BMA Report 'reflected a high degree of bias towards the CND case'.

This Report came not from a radical splinter group within medicine, but from one of the most traditional and longest-standing representative medical bodies. It has received widespread recognition and explicit support from a number of the Royal Colleges and Faculties within the profession. Subsequent reactions have varied. For many doctors the scientific analysis and factual conclusions are sufficient. They assume that the implications will be understood and the detailed findings wisely used. Some seem to wish that the Report – and its conclusions that there can be no effective response to a nuclear war – would go away. This might allow them to return to the comfortable view that survival is possible. Others argue that if a medical response is not possible it seems pointless to waste precious resources planning for such a possibility. Indeed some argue that doctors participating in such planning would be acting unethically towards the public by implying that protection and survival would be possible; and many doctors have been disturbed to find that one of the main purposes of planning for the aftermath of a nuclear war is to provide a façade to maintain morale, an objective that has been confirmed by those who were involved in the early days of such planning. The contrary view is also expressed: the very participation of doctors provides them with an opportunity to ensure that the wider public realizes that survival, as we understand it, will not be possible and to urge the need to avoid any risk of such a war. The Faculty of Community Medicine (1984) advised those of its members involved in war planning to respond in this way.

Debate continues in the medical profession on whether it is appropriate to state conclusions, based on scientific evidence and professional values, which appear to be political. The definition of the word 'political' is, of course, not clear. Similar arguments surround the extent to which the medical profession could and should press for the implementation of recommendations in the Black Report (1980) to reduce the inequalities in health caused by poverty; or seek greater legislative and fiscal control to reduce smoking and alcohol abuse; or express collective support for the NHS. Such debates are not new for doctors. In the recent past considerable anxiety was expressed by some over the extent to which doctors became involved in the movement to introduce seatbelt legislation. Those in support of public statements argue that it is equally political to stand apart from the important issues of the day and remind their colleagues that doctors have been involved with many of the great debates which led to the introduction of major sanitary reforms and much of the social legislation over the past 150 years, often to the great consternation of their colleagues.

A number of arguments are put forward by doctors in support of further professional action in relation to nuclear weapons, recognizing that consciousness-raising about the potential medical consequences of their use is not enough. Given that the explicit purpose of nuclear weapons deployment is to deter aggression and thereby maintain peace, many are disturbed to find so much evidence of the very fragile nature of international relationships around the world. Richter (1983) drew attention to the need for doctors to assist in the process of achieving the 'psychological disarmament' – the change in our thinking – that is essential if we are to avoid replacing today's fearsome weapons with others. Not only is a peaceful world far from a reality but the growing cost of the arms race is a major obstacle to the fulfilment of basic human expectations and social development, now even affecting the richest nations of the world. This, of itself, creates gross injustice and results in power struggles which lead to increased tension and fear.

Doctors researching the psychological consequences of nuclear weapons have concluded that fear and tension increase in direct proportion to the increase in weapons. They have searched in vain for evidence to refute this conclusion. The growing number committed to the promotion of health and the prevention of disease would echo Ian Thompson's observations relating to the low priority accorded to both health and peace promotion (above, p. 97). Both are, of course, potentially threatening to the traditional medical and political establishments respectively because they depend for their success on active participation by the people. But doctors who have learned to recognize the value of an active partnership with their patients describe the very real value of such a change.

The BMA Report on the potential medical consequences of nuclear war has acted as a starting-point for a deeply disturbing enquiry about peace, justice, power, conflict, resource distribution and the arms trade. However, despite the widespread debate, it is probable that the full implications of the Report may not be properly understood because they are too disturbing. Doctors are well aware that individual patients suppress information they find too disturbing to cope with when it is first presented to them. Many people find it virtually impossible to contemplate that, in the UK, at least 17 million (Home Office estimates, Butler, 1982) or as many as 27 million (Openshaw and Steadman, 1982) people will be killed in a nuclear exchange using only 200 megatons of the estimated international stockpiles of 18,000 megatons. The effort to understand can, of itself, lead to additional tension and this raises a further moral question for doctors, nurses and scientists. If the risk of nuclear war were negligible there would be little or no reason to create additional fear amongst the public. On the other hand, if the risk is so great that such an outcome seems inevitable, there again seems little purpose in denying transient peace of mind to those who are able to suppress the awesome findings.

The possibility of a major international conflict leading to the use of nuclear weapons is real; but not inevitable. Preventive action is still possible: action – like that required to combat many of today's major diseases – by many different people, the most important being a determined commitment to change long-standing and often gratifying patterns of behaviour. Some of these changes may even carry their own risks, particularly if attempted too soon or too fast. Doctors who advise individual patients know that risks often have to be balanced against each other. Similarly, the risks of accepting the spiraling arms race as inevitable must be balanced against those risks inherent in searching for new ways of sharing the world's resources or in learning to resolve conflict between nations.

When doctors suggest that they might have a role to play in helping to assess such risks many, including some within the profession, would say that they are already too deeply involved in trying to change pattens of behaviour, and diagnose such an ambition as intractable arrogance. But, for those who believe preventive action is possible and urgently required, how else are they to 'consecrate their lives to the service of humanity'?

Working for peace

For many doctors, scientists and other health workers their initial search for information about the medical efforts of nuclear weapons has led to a realization that beyond the technical issues there are moral imperatives. One group, assuming that many of their names are on the estimated list of 20,000 held by MI5 referred to by Campbell (1982) for arrest during the early stages of international conflict, responded by 'giving themselves up' during a nuclear alert exercise. Others, with a particular role as 'medical war planners', have argued for a conscience clause to entitle them to refuse to participate in such war planning without prejudice to their basic appointment. (A precedent exists for those with moral objections to abortion.) Those who argue against such a step emphasize that it would be against the aims of the state, since it is a function of the NHS deemed, at present, to be of sufficient priority to warrant additional direct funding from the central Health Departments. Interestingly a third view on this has emerged. Some of the doctors charged with responsibility for this planning, who view the exercise as futile and an immoral waste of resources, arrange to use the extra funds provided for other purposes. The simplest is to use the resources to organize contingency plans for unexpected disasters such as train crashes, an activity which few would argue against but which is not covered by any special funding arrangement.

This small-scale silent rebellion – using nuclear war planning funds to serve mankind better by covering one of the many gaps in the NHS – reflects what may grow to be the most significant moral question emerging in medical discussions: the costs of the arms race. As one indication of the opportunity cost, one million children (almost double the number born each year in the UK) could be fully immunized against preventable diseases for the $5 million spent on only one Pershing II missile. Smallpox was eradicated by a major medical initiative for what seemed a vast cost of $600 million, but it is less than 0.1 per cent of annual worldwide military expenditure. These costs allow for the spending of $19,300 for each serving soldier and compare dismally with the world spending of $380 for each school-age child. When babies and young children are dying of starvation and preventable infections in developing countries, and even in the UK patients are expected to wait in endless queues for medical appointments and essential care, those with such knowledge are asking why. Despite the reservations of its Annual Representative Meeting in 1983 about entering the political arena to express public concern about nuclear defence policies, the BMA's Annual Meeting in 1984 resolved, by a large vote, to 'call for a massive and progressive reduction in world arms spending, both nuclear and conventional, with the diversion of resources thus freed to health care and welfare at home and in developing countries', thereby reflecting the growing concern of this widely representative group of doctors.

A similar statement is included in the World Health Organisation's (WHO) 1978 Alma Ata Declaration to work for the attainment of 'health for all by the year 2000'. The Declaration, to which the British Government is a signatory along with all the member nations of WHO, contains the explicit statement that:

An acceptable level of health for all the people of the world by the year 2000 can be attained through a further and better use of the world's resources, a considerable part of which is now spent on armaments and military conflicts. A genuine policy of independence, peace, detente and disarmament could and should release additional resources that could well be devoted to peaceful aims and in particular to the acceleration of social and economic development of which primary health care, as an essential part, should be allotted its proper share. (WHO, 1978)

In 1981 the Assembly of the WHO reviewed its commitment to this Declaration and to Resolution 35/58 of the UN General Assembly which states that, while peace and security are important for health, so, too, cooperation among nations on vital health issues can contribute towards peace. By 1983 the Assembly, the WHO's highest Council, comprising government representatives rather than officials, noted 'the present aggravation of the international situation and the growing danger of thermonuclear conflict'. It therefore established an international committee to study the contribution that WHO could and should make to facilitate UN resolutions on strengthening peace, détente and disarmament and preventing such conflict. This WHO Expert Committee (1984) concluded that nuclear weapons constitute 'the greatest immediate threat to the health and welfare of mankind', placing greater emphasis on the long-term risks of cancer and genetic damage than the BMA Board of Science Report. Although the 1984 WHO Assembly concluded that it was not for them to state the steps by which the threat could be removed, the European Regional Assembly (1984) in its *'Regional Targets in Support of the Regional Strategy for Health For All'* states that 'peace is not just the absence of war', and notes that 'the increasing international tension in recent years has raised this level of apprehension to a point which severely hampers the opportunities for all people in the Region to work together in harmony for a better future'. The Regional Assembly emphasizes that health professionals should take a lead in reducing international tension by promoting close, long-term collaboration on health problems across international borders.

These formal collective statements, representative of the health professions as a whole, demonstrate a determination to use their skills to the greater service of mankind. A Working Party established by the Royal College of Nursing (1984), while 'strongly endorsing the apolitical position of the nursing profession', emphasizes that it is the 'moral duty of all individuals, including nurses, to be informed about the nature, availability and effects of the nuclear weapons and of alternative defence policies so that, through peaceful and democratic means, influence can be brought to bear on decisions made on this vital issue'.

Despite many difficulties, health workers have already demonstrated that it is possible for people from differing political racial and religious backgrounds to work together. The WHO itself – with the dramatically successful smallpox eradication programme – is just one of many examples. Over recent years a new international group of doctors has emerged, concerned specifically about international misunderstandings and distrust as well as about the arms race. The prime aim of the International Physicians for the Prevention of Nuclear War (IPPNW) is to spell out to the whole world the diabolical destructive effects of nuclear weapons. They do more. At the Fifth Congress, 1,000 representatives of the 140,000 doctors from 40 countries – with the leadership being drawn jointly from prominent doctors in the USA and USSR – learned that 25 per cent of all doctors in the world had signed a global petition, 'International Physicians call for an end to the Nuclear Arms Race' (Dyer, 1985). Meeting on an annual basis, members of IPPNW continue to explore medical issues raised by the production, possession and possible use of nuclear weapons. They explore the psychological fear underlying their production, and the different fear created by their existence and possible use. They are also studying the processes required to make rational decisions in times of stress.

Members of the IPPNW demonstrate by their own initiative that an international group of professionals can work constructively together.[3] They hope to extend the growing links between the doctors themselves to involve their patients so that an interested family in the USSR may, through a local doctor, make contact with a similar family in Europe or the USA. People throughout the world could therefore maintain contact with each other even if their government are, at times, blocked by mutual distrust. IPPNW are also deeply concerned about the economic consequences for the Third World of spending on armaments. Mata (1984) describes increases in child deaths in El Salvador following major cutbacks in health spending as resources were diverted to arms production and purchase. Next door, in Costa Rica, where the army was abolished in 1949, a gradual increase in spending on social development was followed by a significant fall in mortality and morbidity, especially among children. Much more significantly, Costa Rica has been no internal fighting while El Salvador has experienced continuous armed conflict.

Conclusion

There lies before us, if we choose, continued progress in happiness, knowledge and wisdom. Shall we, indeed, choose death, because we cannot forget our quarrels? We appeal, as human beings: Remember your humanity, and forget the rest. If you can do, the way lies open to a new Paradise; if you cannot, there lies before you the risk of universal death. (Russell-Einstein Manifesto, 1955, at the start of the First Pugwash Conference on Science and World Affairs)

This book is directed at those who have eyes to see, ears to hear, and minds to think about what is happening on defence policy and planning. Some will be in positions of responsibility, making decisions which have a profound effect on others. Even though most readers will not be among the 200 or so key nuclear decision-makers in the UK, each through their life and work will contribute to decisions that affect the lives of others and will have contact with a wide network of people. Some of them may be waiting for someone else to take the initiative to help them to act. In his Bronowski lecture, Humphrey (1981) describes four major barriers to action. *Denial* is common, often accompanied by energetic immersion in 'vital' work or other activities to avoid having time to think about disturbing matters. *Helplessness* is understandable and is frequently accompanied by efforts to achieve self-reassurance that those in authority have matters well in control: 'the experts know best'. A *Dr Strangelove fascination* with the weapons – or with the intensely complex issues that surround them – may well lead to passive acceptance that the fall into the abyss is inevitable. The paralysing *social embarrassment* of daring to question those in authority is delightfully illustrated by the picture of an earnest man at a cocktail party who made the unforgivable mistake of raising the issue of nuclear weapons at a polite social gathering.

Professional groups can provide support for those who seek to contribute to psychological and physical disarmament by starting within a moral and ethical framework they understand. But no one should underestimate the profound difficulties even within a group with a common aim. Individual members of groups have found themselves subjected to what appears to be a deliberate 'put-down' policy, although this is less apparent now than when the professional groups were beginning to form. Clearly it has become less credible to imply a degree of naivety or stupidity as these organizations grow. What continues to disappoint many is the apparent gulf between those who speak their concern and those they see as key decision-makers; a gulf filled by the same misunderstandings and distrust as they identify between nations. McCormick (1983) explains how the gulf between 'the conformer' (to a certain view at a particular time and place) and 'the deviant' (who questions that view) comes to be seen as a gulf between 'good' and 'bad'. The separation is, however, utterly illogical since 'the good' (conformers) to two totally conflicting ideologies would appear to have more in common with each other than with those who question the absolutism of either or both their respective ideologies. Thus we are reminded that 'the good', by accident of birth and history, flew both Spitfires and Messerschmitts. It is 'the bad' (deviants) in both East and West who demand that their respective governments pursue more actively the cause of peace. This distinction between conformity and deviance, and its relationship to perceived 'goodness' and 'badness', may explain much of the reluctance of professional people to speak out. By background and training they are inclined to believe that moral integrity and subservience to (legitimate) authority are synonymous, but this relationship cannot be guaranteed to hold. The consequence of conformity to the goals of tolerance, friendship, humility, patience and confidence may in fact be a kind of deviance.

Appendix: professional groups involved in the UK peace movement

Architects for Peace (A4P); established 1981
c/o Secretary, 41 St James Road, Sevenoaks, Kent, TN13 3NG

Artists for Peace; established 1982
c/o 50 Kingston Avenue, Edinburgh, EH16 5SW

Book Action for Nuclear Disarmament (BAND); established 1983
c/o Flat 2, 45 Trinity Rise, London, SW2 2QP

Clergy against Nuclear Arms (CANA); established 1983
c/o 38 Main Road, Norton, Evesham, WR11 4TL

Generals for Peace and Disarmament; established 1981
c/o Centre for International Peacebuilding Studies, Southbank House. Black Prince Road, Lambeth, London SE1

Economists for Peace; established 1985
c/o Millbrook, Barcombe, Mills, Sussex, BN8 5BP

Electronics for Peace (EfP); established 1982
c/o Townsend House, Green Lane, Marshfield, Chippenham, Wiltshire, SN14 8JW

Engineers for Nuclear Disarmament (EngND); established 1982
c/o Secretary, 115 Riversdale Road, Highbury, London N5

Farmers for a Nuclear Free Future (FANFF); established 1982
c/o Lower Westcott Farm, Moretonhamstead, Devon

Lawyers against Nuclear Disarmament; established 1982
c/o Garden Court, Temple, London EC4
and
Scottish Lawyers against Nuclear Disarmament; established 1982
c/o 10 The Square, University of Glasgow, G12 8QQ

Medical Association for the Prevention of War (MAPW); established 1951
c/o 16a Prince Arthur Road, London, NW3 6AY

Medical Campaign against Nuclear Weapons (MCANW); established 1980
c/o 7 Tenison Road, Cambridge, CB1 2DG

Musicians against Nuclear Arms (MANA); established 1983
c/o 22 Munster Road, Teddington, Middlesex, TW11 9LL

Psychologists for Peace (PfP); established 1981
c/o General Secretary, Psychologists for Peace, Department of Psychology, Jenner Wing, St George's Medical School, London, SW17 0RE

Teachers for Peace; established 1981
c/o Goodwin Street, London, N4 3HQ

Scientists against Nuclear Arms (SANA); established 1981
c/o London Production Centre, Broomhill Road, Wandsworth, London, SW18

Scottish Writers against the Bomb; established 1984
c/o Springfield View, South Queensferry, EH30 9RZ

Veterinary Information Group on Nuclear Weapons and Pollution; established 1984
c/o Secretary, 11 High Street, Kinver, Stourbridge, West Midlands, DY7 6HG

13

The Churches' Role in the Nuclear Debate

William B. Johnston

The need for an informed ethical basis to the current defence and disarmament debate has been argued by other contributors to this volume. The churches clearly have a role to play in this and a large number of them have responded both to the demands of their own constituency and to the wider political process. There is, however, still much confusion surrounding the ways in which the churches have structured their response. Old questions of Church-State relationships have resurfaced, there are doubts about authority, and the very right of churches to engage in the political process is questioned. The responsibilities of the churches as institutions within society, as distinct from individual Christian responsibility, need to be established as part of the process of engaging with others in the political process.

The contrasts between the three major Church statements (from the Church of England Working Party, the US Catholic Bishops and the WCC) referred to in the Introduction (see above, pp. 10–14) are quite striking in terms of their style, structure and authority. Comparing these and other statements is a useful corrective to the point of view which sees the problem only in terms of the responsibilities of 'established' churches in traditionally 'Christian' countries committed to NATO and nuclear deterrence. The churches in eastern Europe or the Third World clearly see their responsibilities in a different light. However, the main focus of this chapter is the statements of the British churches, with special reference to the position in Scotland, which has been less widely discussed than the position of the churches in England.

Christian attitudes to war and peace

Questions of peace and war have been on the agenda of the church since earliest times. Episodes in the Gospels which involve soldiers make no comment about their profession whīch they are not at any point called on to abandon. The theological concept of peace continues the usage of the Old Testament and is set within the context of the relationship which God establishes through the death of Christ whereby the new kingdom of God's righteousness becomes manifest. Thus the particular questions about peace and war and the individual's responsibility are not put. Two principles are, however, discernible: one, that the first Christians were clear that they should not take part in any plans for the Jews to revolt against Rome, and two, that when it came to resistance in the face of persecution the proper role of the church was martyrdom and non-violence. From such evidence as there is, it appears that up to the time of Constantine the Church was largely pacifist.

The subsequent development of the Christian ethic into the Middle Ages and beyond is summarized by Ronald Bainton (1960) as follows:

Broadly speaking, three attitudes to war and peace were to appear in the Christian ethic: pacifism, the just war and the crusade. Chronologically they emerged in just this order. The early Church was pacifist to the time of Constantine. Then, partly as a result of the close association of Church and state under this emperor and partly by reason of the threat of barbarian invasions, Christians in the fourth and fifth centuries took over from the classical world the doctrine of the just war, whose object should be to vindicate justice and restore peace. The just war had to be fought under the authority of the state and must observe a code of good faith and humanity. The Christian elements added by Augustine were that the motive must be love and that monks and priests were to be exempted.

He goes on to say that this code failed to restrain the churches at the time of the Crusades: 'The crusade arose in the high Middle Ages, a holy war fought under the auspices of the Church or of some inspired religious leader, not on behalf of justice conceived in terms of life and property, but on behalf of an ideal, the Christian faith. Since the enemy was without the pale, the code tended to break down.' The idea of the crusade disappeared with the end of the Moslem threat to Europe (although the attitude of some present-day Christians towards communism has the elements of crusade) and the Church settled down to hold in tension the majority view of the just war and the minority of Christian pacifism.

The events of the First World War, its character as a 'total' war and the involvement for the first time of citizens rather than professional armies, raised many questions in fresh form. While the British churches on the whole supported the war (and indeed were sometimes to be accused of acting as moral recruiting offices), seeds of doubt began to be sown about the adequacy of the traditional ethic. For example, the pre-union Church of Scotland set up a Commission on the Spiritual Issues of the War which gave support to the war as just, but which nevertheless began a process of questioning which led in 1920 to the establishment of a permanent Committee on Church and Nation, which was continued into the post-union Church of Scotland and which has carried on a consistent monitoring of the major moral and spiritual issues of national life, and has kept the issues of peace and war constantly before the Church.

The outbreak of the Second World War again found the churches largely at one in supporting the justice of the cause. William Temple, then Archbishop of York, broadcasting in August 1939, spoke for many when he said, 'No positive good can be done by force; that is true. But evil can be checked and held back by force, and it is precisely for this that we may be called upon to use it.' However, as the war developed in intensity, some of the policies by which it was waged, such as the area bombing of cities (particularly, for example, of Dresden), aroused increasing criticism. This unease, which was basically a questioning of the adequacy of the traditional doctrine of the just war, culminated in an intense debate provoked by the use for the first time of the atom bomb.

The Church and nuclear defence policy

The early years of peace thus saw a new debate within the churches on the Christian attitude to war in general and to nuclear war in particular. The 1946 report of the British Council of Churches (BCC), *The Era of Atomic Power,* written by Dr J. H. Oldham, foreshadowed many of the themes of today's debates. Deterrence doctrines were in their infancy but the report expressed grave reservations about the desensitization of the public to the threat of mass destruction which nuclear deterrence would be likely to bring about. It took the view that 'total' war, especially if waged with nuclear weapons, could no longer be held with the restraints which have been regarded by the Christian tradition as essential to a 'just' war. In 1949 the Church of Scotland set up a Special Commission under the Rev. Dr D. H. C. Read to 'consider anew the Christian Doctrine of the Just War and its bearing upon the attitude of the Church to war in the atomic age'.

The Read Commission, while expressing some passing anxiety about the indiscriminate nature of new methods of warfare, did not see cause to depart from the traditional position and proposed (and found acceptance) that: 'The General Assembly, seeking to further the cause of peace and order among the nations, while conscious of the terrible nature and consequences of modern war, find no reason to depart from the received teaching that Christians may lawfully wage war upon just and necessary occasions' (Church of Scotland, 1950).

The attitude of the BCC was articulated in more detail in two notable documents, *Christians and Atomic War* published in 1959 and *The Valley of Decision* published in 1964. It recognized that the bomb now exists as a fact of military and political life and that therefore the Church must ask new and radical questions. It was to be accepted that there was a case for the retention of the bomb as a deterrent and also as a legitimate and effective instrument of foreign policy.

Western capacity to retaliate . . . is purely a deterrent. We do not for a moment accept it as a means of waging all-out war, but only of preventing it. (BCC, 1964, p. 36)

The fact of possession in itself ensures an influential voice in the conduct of foreign policy of the western alliance. (BCC, 1959, p. 20)

In the next two decades the main emphasis and efforts of the churches were focused on the issues of nuclear testing and the prevention of proliferation. During these years a constant pressure was maintained by the BCC on the Government, for example, to 'continue to press, as a starting point, for no more than the minimum machinery necessary to give reasonable assurance that an agreement will be observed and not to be a party to a final decision to renew tests without ensuring that the value of an agreement on atmospheric tests alone is explored' (BCC, April 1962). When in 1963 the first three nuclear powers agreed not to carry out nuclear tests in the atmosphere, the BCC then went on to press that the partial test ban should now be extended and be made total: 'A partial Test Ban Treaty has now been signed. We must seek to make this a total ban' (BCC, 1963, p. 19). The General Assembly of the Church of Scotland supported this line with appropriate deliverances in 1962, 1963 and 1964, while also adding from 1963 onwards first tentative suggestions that Britain might give up possession of an independent nuclear deterrent under some form of NATO control.

This latter proposal for a multilateral nuclear force in NATO proved to be a considerable stumbling block to progress towards a non-proliferation treaty, since the Soviet Union saw it as a device for giving access to nuclear weapons to West Germany. Nevertheless an agreement was reached in 1968, by which time the Antarctic Treaty (1959) and the Treaty of Tlatelolco (1967) had ensured the prohibition of all nuclear weapon deployment in South America and Antartica. While there was no agreement to limit the deployment of the nuclear weapons of the UK, France or China, it was possible to build on the non-proliferation treaty to begin the series of SALT talks.

During the period of détente the progress being made towards a non-proliferation and arms control agreement turned the churches' attention to what was going on in the arms trade. Both the BCC and the Church of Scotland General Assembly, for example, began to study the extent and implications of this and to become increasingly concerned at the involvement of governments. In Scotland, the Church was much taken up with the two issues of entry into the European Community, and the prospect of devolution and the setting-up of a Scottish Assembly. No major debate on defence and disarmament took place for a number of years.

In the wider world the question was now being raised of the validity of the whole concept of deterrence. In a notable lecture at Cambridge in 1962 Donald MacKinnon had questioned the accepted doctrine that it was the deterrent that was keeping the peace. Its effect, he argued, was not to stabilize but to destabilize.

Much is heard and said in these days of the 'great deterrent' . . . Those who defend this thesis appeal sometimes to something akin in certain respects to a social contract, whereby the *prima facie* contestants for global mastery agree to stalemate on the grounds that the attempt to break out from it would be mutually entirely destructive. The situation is not unlike that envisaged in the second book of Plato's *Republic* where Glaucon protrays as ideal the situation in which the 'perfectly unjust man' equipped with power akin to that conferred by Gyges' ring to make oneself invisible, re-fashions the world after his own image. Yet we well know that, unless we have such power as that ring bestows, that ideal situation is without our grasp; we live rather in a world where a rough inequality in the ability to avoid the consequences of even carefully calculated acts of rapacity holds men faithful to a conventional morality. (MacKinnon, 1963, p. 11)

This 'morality' is not derived from fundamental values.

It is the expression of no natural law, but represents something on which men have tacitly agreed as a kind of *pis-aller,* a second-best in a world where none are endowed with power akin to that bestowed by Gyges' ring. The grounds of men's faithful observance of the dictates of this conventional morality are to be sought in a principle of utility, received as counselling restraint rather than encouraging hope for enlarged possibilities of achievement, conservative rather than radical in its undertones . . . We are committed to the continued search for anti-rings, and it may indeed seem to some that this state of affairs introduces an element of radical instability into the system. (MacKinnon, 1963, p.12)[1]

Views of this kind became stronger as the churches moved through the decade of the 1970s when it became ever clearer that nuclear weapons were proliferating both in quantity and in destructiveness. Thus in 1979 the BCC recorded that:

the number of states possessing nuclear weapons has increased from one at the time of the first [BCC] report to six or seven at the present time; the number of nuclear warheads has increased from ten or a dozen in 1946 to around 40,000; and the destructive power of nuclear weapons has grown from the kiloton bombs of 1945 to weapons one thousand times as powerful. (BCC, 1979)

This kind of escalation increasingly undermined the argument of those who held that the deterrent was only being retained as a step towards abolition and seemed to confirm MacKinnon's view that the continual search for newer and better anti-rings was indeed a recipe for instability. In the face of these developments the churches turned to a re-examination of the traditional just war doctrine. The General Assembly of 1972 received a major report on 'The Christian Doctrine of the Just War' which was sent down to presbyteries and Kirk Sessions for study. In addition to its questioning of the deterrent theory this report also raised the important question whether there is a qualitative difference between nuclear war and warfare waged by conventional means. Is there really any difference, other than in scale, between the carnage battles of conventional war, such as the Somme or Stalingrad, and the explosions over Hiroshima and Nagasaki, or has the fact that nuclear weapons are indiscriminate in their effects and uncontrolled in their consequences introduced a new and different element into the moral question? In other words, can a distinction be drawn between the morality of conventional warfare, on however large a scale, and nuclear warfare? Can an individual approve the use of conventional arms and reject the use of nuclear arms without moral contradiction?

Most Church opinion seemed to agree that this distinction was valid and that it was therefore possible for many who would support the retention and use of conventional weapons under the old just war conditions to move towards a rejection of nuclear weapons in some form and to some extent, and the ground of debate now shifted to the questions, in what form and to what extent? The scene for the now familiar argument between unilateralism and multilateralism was now set.

This was the debate that was to characterize the discussions within the churches as the 1970s moved into the 1980s. Although to date none of the mainstream churches, with the notable exception of the Society of Friends, has reached a unilateralist position officially, the support for that view has noticeably increased and the multilateralist position has been modified by a number of circumstances. There is much support for unilateral steps among many who would reject one-sided disarmament policies. All the discussions have been affected by the growing influence of the peace movements such as

CND and the spreading concern for peace issues within the churches and beyond. On an even wider scale the comparison between the money spent on nuclear arms and the amount given in aid to Third World developing countries has seemed to many to bring western governments to a point of near hypocrisy. Thus the General Assembly of 1980, for example, resolved that in its view 'the increasing gap between the "haves" and the "have-nots" is the greatest threat to world peace', and on that ground condemned the British Government's proposal to spend (at that time) £6½ billion on the replacement of Polaris by Trident. The failure of successive administrations to recognize this outrage to conscience has led many towards a unilateralist position as the only alternative.

The raising of the question of the cost of the Trident programme together with doubts about deterrence has led in the churches to very serious questioning about either the need or the advisability of this further escalation. Thus the Assembly of 1981 declared its position in three stages. It invited Church members to support the World Disarmament Campaign, declared that 'we must support the maintenance of a British nuclear force in order to fulfil our commitments to NATO', but at the same time resolved to 'urge Her Majesty's Government not to proceed with the costly Trident programme'. Two years earlier the BCC Assembly had come to the same conclusion as follows: 'The Assembly believes that the non-replacement by the UK of its present nuclear strategic deterrent (the Polaris missile system) would strengthen moves for nuclear non-proliferation and urges Her Majesty's Government to take a decision to this effect; [and] invites other Governments to take comparable confidence-building measures of restraint or renunciation' (BCC, 1979).

The debate sharpens

The Trident programme was not, and has still not been, abandoned, and the position of the churches as the stockpile of the nuclear powers grew higher and more devastating became ever more critical. For a number of reasons the year 1982–3 was critical. In June 1982 the UN Special Session on Disarmament so failed to make any progress that the attending non-governmental observers stated that 'the obvious failure of the Session has caused us such deep concern that it has been difficult to find words properly to express our sense of outrage.' In the US the Session focused the attention of church peace groups which engaged in the largest and most comprehensive march for peace ever seen in New York, and for the churches also the failure of the Session was deeply disappointing. The immediate results were the strengthening of the peace movements (both the Presbyterian Assemblies meeting immediately after the Session passed motions of strong support) and the publication of the Roman Catholic Bishops' Declaration. In Europe the WCC issued the report of its 1981 Amsterdam Hearing entitled *Before It's Too Late* (Abrecht and Koshy, 1983). The WCC Central Committee recommended that the churches should take clear positions: rejecting deterrence as morally unacceptable; welcoming unilateral as well as multilateral initiatives for disarmament; and urging Christians and others to refuse to cooperate with or accept employment in any projects relating to nuclear weapons and nuclear warfare.

In the UK statements on the moral inadmissibility of both the use and the possession of nuclear weapons became stronger. In 1980 the Roman Catholic Pastoral Congress (a lay gathering) resolved that 'the great majority agreed that it is very difficult to justify any war on moral grounds and completely impossible to justify nuclear war. It was the opinion of the majority that both the possession and use [of nuclear weapons] must be condemned.' In 1982 both the BCC Assembly and the Church of Scotland General Assembly passed resolutions recording their view that use and possession of nuclear weapons is morally repugnant and theologically indefensible. The Church of Scotland decision (on a vote of 255 to 153, in a poorly attended session) was: 'The General Assembly call[s] upon the Church of Scotland . . . to oppose the use of nuclear power for warlike purposes . . . and to press for the immediate cessation of the further manufacture of such armaments.' It was strenuously argued in succeeding months whether such a declaration was or was not unilateralist. The following year (1983) the position was restated unequivocally that the Assembly 'affirm[s] their conviction that nuclear arms, including readiness to use them, are by their nature morally and theologically wrong.' This statement was taken further by a call to Her Majesty's Government to 'negotiate . . . with energy to achieve an immediate freeze on further research, development and deployment of such weapons.'

This same year (1982) saw the publication of the major report by the Church of England Board for Social Responsibility entitled *The Church and the Bomb* for debate in that Church's General Synod. This examination in depth over a three-year period included among its recommendations the renunciation by the UK of the independent nuclear deterrent and the immediate cancellation of the Trident programme to be followed by the phasing-out of Polaris missiles and submarines. The debate on the report took place on 10 February

1983, under conditions of intense publicity, including the televising of the entire proceedings. Much of the debate was made difficult by two factors; one, inherent in the report, being the proposal for British unilateral renunciation of the independent nuclear deterrent while affirming at the same time Britain's membership of NATO and therefore an acceptance of the American nuclear umbrella. The other difficulty was the fact that the chairman of the Board of Social Responsibility which sponsored the report (the Bishop of London) was himself opposed to its recommendations.

The difficulty of the inherent contradiction of renunciation while remaining within NATO found an apparent solution in the proposal of the Bishop of Birmingham that the Synod should adopt a position of 'no first use'. He argued that deterrence, including nuclear deterrence, is a 'positive duty of the State' in its proper role of protecting its citizens from aggression, but the deterrent should at the same time be seen as a form of defence and never of attack; hence it would be proper and realistic for the Church to require that it be used only in reply to a nuclear attack and never as a weapon either of first strike or of reply to non-nuclear aggression. This seemed to provide a way of lessening the nuclear risk without undermining NATO and the Synod voted for this position by 275 votes to 222.

The Bishop of Salisbury who championed the report maintained, however, that certain basic questions had still not been answered.

1 Are there some weapons so dreadful that it can never be right to use them?
2 Can it ever be right to threaten what it would be wrong to do?
3 Do we have different standards for judging our enemies and ourselves?
4 Why is it right for us to have nuclear weapons but wrong for others, for example Israel or Brazil, to have them?
5 Can the values we believe in ever be defended by nuclear weapons?

These questions remain.

The report of the Church of England was followed quickly in time by the pastoral letter of the Roman Catholic Bishops in the US, issued on 8 May 1983. This document summed up its message in a quotation from Pope John Paul II: 'In current conditions "deterrence" based on balance, certainly not an end in itself, but as a step on the way towards a progressive disarmament, may still be judged morally acceptable. Nonetheless, in order to ensure peace, it is indispensable not to be satisfied with this minimum which is always susceptible to the real danger of explosion.' The Bishops commented that this teaching implied no use of nuclear weapons which would violate the principles of discrimination and proportionality, and agreed with the Church of England position that non-nuclear attacks must be resisted only by non-nuclear means.

These attitudes were soon to receive even sharper challenge, however, by the decision of NATO governments to accept the deployment of Cruise and Pershing missiles in western Europe and opposition rose to a new intensity. Peace marches were held in the main cities of Europe, the level of obstruction tactics as, for example, at the Women's Peace Camp at Greenham Common was sharply increased, and a Gallup Poll in November 1983 showed strong majorities against such deployment in West Germany and Italy and a marginal majority (48 per cent as against 41 per cent) in the UK. An unofficial but influential group, representing all the main Scottish churches, took the unusual step of presenting a letter to the Queen expressing their deep concern at the defence policies of her government, and requests by the churches for the opportunity to discuss these matters with the Secretary of State for Defence were met only after much pressure and under considerable limitations.

As the debate moved on and the criticism by the churches became sharper (and the gulf between them and Government widened with the collapse of consensus), other dissentient voices in the churches emerged publicly. A group of academics based at King's College, London, combined to discuss 'What hope in an armed world?' The major theological contribution to this symposium by Richard Harries is in defence of the deterrent. Harries has been much influenced by Niebuhr's distinction between the ethics of the individual and that of the group and particularly the ethics of the State (1960). It is, in fact, one of the main criticisms of the Anglican report on *The Church and the Bomb* that the lesson taught to a previous generation has been forgotten or ignored by this one. On this basis Harries goes on to apply the doctrine of the just war to the nuclear age to reach the conclusion (through a labyrinthine and tortuous argument) that nuclear deterrence is necessary, has a good chance of succeeding and must be made to succeed. Whether that is a counsel of hope or one of despair is not made clear.

A somewhat different group, though based on the same appeal to the work of Niebuhr, also emerged under the name of 'Shalom'. Shalom's contention was that the criticisms by the churches of western defence and deterrent policies had not been sufficiently theologically grounded and that, because most of the arguments deployed had been pragmatic or prudential, they had therefore had a divisive effect within the churches. What was needed was to find a common ground which would go beyond the polarization of the unilateralist-multilateralist divide and the need for the churches was therefore to engage in a process of theological enquiry and education. What effect these and other initiatives have had is difficult to say. So far there has been little indication that the debate has altered in any fundamental way.

What is clear is that, having entered into the debate on defence policy, the churches have become shapers of opinion as well as commentators on policy. There are signs that some churches are willing to accept a campaigning role. For example, the Scottish churches have become closely identified with the growing movement for a nuclear freeze.[2] The Church of Scotland General Assembly of May 1985 took the step of commending the nuclear freeze campaign to the general membership of the church and a petition urging the government to take a lead in initiating a freeze was made available in all churches for signing in a 'Freeze Endorsement Week'. More than 150,000 signatures were collected, including those of leaders of the main Christian denominations. This is perhaps only the beginning of the churches' effort to work out the practical implications in institutional terms of their moral condemnation of nuclear weapons and deterrence.

Authority and credibility

It is now many years since Paul Ramsey published his polemical work entitled *Who Speaks for the Church?* (1969), in which he examined carefully the statements of the World Council's 1966 Geneva Conference on Church and Society. The main question that he poses is this: when conferences of churchmen adopt resolutions addressing themselves to governments on matters of social or political ethics, what can they usefully and justifiably say? The difficulty is that either they have to be content with pious platitudes which, if they harm no one, certainly benefit no one ('they are against sin'!) or else they have to make particular judgements of a political or economic or even a military kind which they have no competence to make.

The way out of this dilemma for Ramsey is to recognize that

the purpose of the address of the church to the world . . . ought to be the broadening and deepening of public debate on urgent questions; it ought not to be to stop or narrow down this debate or polarise the debate that is going on by a finding in favour of a specific policy behind which we are seeking merely to mobilise opinion. (Ramsey, 1969, p. 119)

On this basis Ramsey proposes what he calls 'provisional models for specific political pronouncements', which turn out to be statements which provide for a specific attitude on the part of Christian opinion if government takes a certain line of action; that is, if something were the case, then there would be a *measure of support* from Christian opinion.

Ramsey's models, despite his forceful argumentation, have not found much acceptance, mainly because they are far too imprecise and academic. Church statements on socio-political issues are almost always *ad hoc* and are meant to focus the minds of those who hear them on a particular situation and therefore they require to be much more realistic than the 'ifs' and 'buts' of the Ramsey models. It may well be, in fact, that Ramsey's strong objection to any form of situation ethics has led him to the opposite extreme of vagueness.

A second, more recent, grapple with this dilemma is that of John Habgood (1983). For Habgood the main thrust of any church statement must be in its theological credibility. Indeed, he writes:

The prime Christian contribution to social ethics is in the indicative rather than in the imperative mood. In terms of the principles by which people should live and societies order themselves, Christians have little to say that could not be said by any reasonable person of goodwill. It is Christian belief about the kind of place the world is, about the depth of human sinfulness and the possibilities of divine grace, about judgement and hope, incarnation and salvation, God's concern for all and his care for each . . . it is beliefs such as these which make the difference and provide the context. (Habgood, 1983, p. 168)

While this emphasis on theology is to be welcomed and is indeed fundamental, the assumption seems to be that theology is a 'given' from outside the situation; and when it is applied it somehow changes the situation or at least the parameters. This exteriorizing is in some ways like the Ramsey models which in the event fail to tackle the real frontier between the Church and the world. It is only in the interplay of the Christian faith as it is lived out in the events of the world that the word of God is really heard; prophecy is always particularized, which is both its virtue and its scandal. It is when the insight of the Christian has to be 'cashed' that the ethical decision is made. Habgood's own simplistic view of the rights and wrongs of civil disobedience which follows the passage cited above is a clear illustration of the inherent weakness of his position; that the individual has the right to disobey the state for conscience' sake, and must be prepared to suffer the consequences, but 'I cannot endorse the view that there is any Christian obligation to support them.' (!)

Given, therefore, the claim (and often the expectation) that the Church must have something to say, the role of the churches remains uncertain in three main areas.

In the area of authority

With what authority do churches speak? Hierarchical churches answer this question by the use of pronouncements varying from Papal Bulls to pastoral letters. The view that the Bishops are the guardians of doctrine is extended to include the assumption that they are also the guardians of morals and that, as they claim a special inspiration in the one sphere, this extends to the other. Churches like the Church of Scotland cannot fall back on this argument and, since it never claims infallibility even for its General Assembly, the nature of the authority of its various statements is left vague. On matters of doctrine there is provision for decision-making by the whole Church through a lengthy discussion process between Assembly and presbyteries, but this is not so on the moral and social declarations of the Church and Nation Committee and the Board of Social Responsibility. Thus it is possible to revise the Church's position on abortion by a single debate with a single vote in a particular Assembly by a majority of 40 votes out of a total of 800 (Church of Scotland, 1985).

Incidents like this raise two further questions. One is about the extent of participation that is proper for a particular view to be credible when claimed as being that of the whole church. And this applies to many of the major issues on which the churches are deeply divided within themselves because they thus mirror the deep divisions within the community, for example on abortion, on nuclear weapons and on civil disobedience. Even in Roman Catholic circles the authority of the Pope in isssuing encyclicals such as *Humanae Vitae* is greatly undermined by its being ignored in practice.

The other question has to do with the expectation of obedience on the part of the faithful and the role of dissidence. Since it is the role of dissident groups to challenge the 'establishment' at vulnerable points, there must be a means whereby such dissidents can be heard and their witness assessed; we must 'try the spirits'. But how far can dissidence be tolerated without a surrender of authority? Even in churches which claim to be broad-based, toleration must stop somewhere if identity is to be retained; but the limits of toleration are themselves a matter of major dispute.

In the area of the doctrine of the Church

Wherein lies the Church's claim to enter the socio-political field?

For Habgood – as indeed for most Christians – the fundamental claim would be a theological one, that we have a particular world view which comes from an understanding of the work of God as Creator and Christ as Saviour, not only of individual souls but of the whole cosmos, and of the Holy Spirit as the agent of renewal. We are therefore the representatives of the transcendent in the ongoing events of the world; we are there to remind the decision-makers of their ultimate responsibility to God and to urge them to act in the consciousness of their stewardship.

That is all right so far as it goes but, having said that, we are open to the reminder from decision-makers, both politicians and civil servants, that the questions with which they are most occupied are second and not first order questions. That is to say, there is broad agreement about general principles; we are all for justice and against war. The debate is about how these principles are to be expressed and realized; therefore it is about political (or military) means and structures. At this point the discussion has to be particularized into the technicalities at the very point where the churches are in the habit of saying, 'We have no expertise in these matters.'

At this stage three possible dangers emerge. One is that the Church withdraws from the field altogether, taking up a position similar to that of Ramsey in which, having pronounced some rather vague general principles, it then hands over to the politicians as so-called 'experts' and/or to the true experts, administrative or military, whose decisions are necessarily technical and a-theistic. Thus the Church denies the true nature of the 'polis' and exteriorizes its own understanding of the Faith.

The second danger is that of personalization whereby, daunted by the complexities of the second order decision, the Church takes refuge in a simplistic individualism which believes that 'if you change the individual you will then change the world.' To escape along this route is in effect to deny the reality of community; it is not only evil people who have to be changed but evil structures that have to be reformed. The Church's call for renewal must therefore be to society as well as to the individual, and to social practices and institutions (including the Church itself) as well as to persons. This is, in fact, the old realist-nominalist argument in a modern form.

The third danger is that the Church becomes a pressure group. There are many both within and outside the Church who would see the role of the Church in this way, as a campaign base and organization to promote a particular policy. It may, of course, be that there are times when it is possible to say that one particular policy is right and all the others are wrong, but many of the choices are not of that kind. This is where Ramsey's fears of a wrong kind of involvement are relevant, for it is not usually the Church's job to support a particular party, but in his phrase 'to broaden and deepen' the public debate and often to try to distinguish the real issues at stake through the smokescreen which the political hustings so often throws up.

In order to avoid these dangers, the Church's role is to go further than simply the formulation of primary principles on a 'take it or leave it' basis and the next step is to enter into the realm of second order questions with a view to determining certain secondary or more specialized principles which may apply the primary principles, at least in a provisional way, to the field of action where guidance is needed. This leads to the formulation of what have been called 'middle axioms'; that is, provisional statements which 'are not such as to be appropriate to every time and place and situation, but . . . are offered as legitimate and necessary applications of the Christian rule of faith and life to the special circumstances in which we now stand' (Baillie, 1944). It was this search for appropriate middle axioms which was the foundation of the work of Baillie, Temple (1942), and others in the years of the Second World War, looking forward to the kind of world for which the post-war years would call.

In the area of Church and society

Such a search implies a meeting of theologians with the specialists on the field where appropriate guidance is needed, and this provides the arena in which the grapple of Church and world must take place. Hence the importance of such bodies as the Council on Christian Approaches to Defence and Disarmament, or the work of Edinburgh University's Centre for Theology and Public Issues, or the Foundation for the Study of Christianity and Society. Churches (through their Social Responsibility Boards or Church and Nation Committees) must learn to use these and other think-tanks as necessary resources for their ongoing work. The authority of Church statements must ultimately depend on their inherent credibility which in turn is conditioned by the accuracy of the research that lies behind them. There is evidence that, where this grappling is honestly and faithfully done, the churches are taken seriously; where it fails the churches bring themselves into disrepute.

The development of the nuclear debate is a good example of the way in which over the years the cooperation of church people and the strategists and politicians has progressively increased. Theologians have realized that they must enter into political and military conversations and that an abstract theology, divorced from a knowledge of the technicalities of nuclear weapons and their possession and use, cannot illuminate the witness of the Church; while at the same time those most close to the development and deployment of these weapons have become more and more conscious of their need for an element of the transcendent to help them understand their task of control and ultimately of disarmament.

For the Church this process has led to an increasing concern about the structures within which the secular decision-makers have to operate, even though it is still difficult to make Church assemblies and synods understand that their moral pronouncements must be rooted in realism. This was perhaps one of the points where the Church of England Synod debate on the Church and the bomb was especially weak, but the churches are learning. It is in the nature of such a learning process to raise even more radical questions; such as, for example, whether middle axioms are sufficient or whether the utterances of the Church must not be even more specific.

This process has also led to a heightened awareness by the Church of the need that the decision-makers have for sensitive pastoral care. It is not enough for the Church just to tell them to go away from church on Sunday and work out their Christian witness in their daily work; those who make decisions of this gravity and magnitude need much more constant and informed support than is often realized. The relationship that existed in the US between Roosevelt and Reinhold Niebuhr is a case in point, probably an almost unique one; but churches must be aware of this need when, and possibly before, they issue their critical anathemas. Such criticisms have to be kept in proportion. The ultimate calling for the Church is a constructive one, to be a sign of peace and justice for all, and that is a venture of faith, hope and love.

14

Power and Powerlessness

Elizabeth Templeton

Not through human institutions can man achieve that insight into his actual situation which must inevitably preface any intimate amelioration. For the institutions in which he trusts are in a measure the reflection of his estimation of himself, and if that estimation be perverted, the whole social frame of itself is necessarily distorted.

There is no indictment of the virtue of justice in itself, only an explicit rejection of the assumption that existing human institutions, built on a false estimate of human dignity, can be a genuine mechanism of social and individual fulfilment. They too are under judgement, the judgement of the Cross. (MacKinnon, 1940)

To stand and take side with his people, Moses had to leave Pharaoh's palace and become fugitive. He had to wander for forty years together with his father-in-law. It was not possible for Moses to stand as an Egyptian authority who fought for his people's destiny. (J. Widyatmadja, Christian Conference of Asia, Singapore, 1977)

What is possible and what is impossible belong rather to the sphere of people's commitment in the world than to the bare description of it. If we are right to resist determinism in the political sphere, what can be done is, at least to some extent, a function of the will to try doing it. Yet it is not simply a function of the will to try. There appear to be layers, or levels of powerlessness, which confront those who would transform the world. Some of the impotences are explored in other parts of this book: the intellectual difficulty of offering a convincing alternative to the liberal humanist tradition, the frustrations of engaged professionals meeting the inertia of their peers, the risk that theology becomes the prisoner of cultural pressure, the apparent impenetrability of networks of military and strategic planning.

At one end of the spectrum between hope and despair, there are people, among them children and young people, who take it for granted that nuclear holocaust will occur in their lifetime. Mothers in a children's playgroup I attended in Edinburgh had serious conversations on at least one occasion about whether and how they might pre-emptively kill their children painlessly in the event of an impending nuclear strike. Others believe, conversely, that the very existence and deployment of the weapons guarantee their *non*-use. Peter Calvocoressi in the 1983 Martin Wight memorial lecture concedes the impossibility of reversing the nuclear 'Fall', but suggests that it may have its own virtues: 'We cannot get out of the nuclear age, because what makes it nuclear is inescapable: namely knowledge. But there are ways of living with this knowledge and with these weapons. Indeed, nuclear weapons, once invented, become needful, for in a nuclear world, only nuclear weapons can deter a major war.' (1984, p. 101) Implicitly or explicitly, both these positions imply that the dismantling of the nuclear weaponry is impossible, and that all our human life must now be lived more or less securely in its shadow.

At the other extreme, Helen Zealley reminds us of the wording of the Russell-Einstein Manifesto: 'Remember your humanity and forget the rest. If you can do, the way lies open to a new Paradise.' Many in the peace movements hope that a nuclear-free Europe, and ultimately a nuclear-free world, are real political objectives, albeit hugely difficult ones.

Other contributors to this volume have issued caveats against the twin theological and political failures of pessimistic fatalism and romantic utopianism. But whose assessment of possibility and impotence is the touchstone of reality? Supposing we have in some measure documented the dense warp of political, historical and ideological data into which our energies all weave, from what cosmic vantage point does one read the pattern of the emerging fabric?

To many, the difficulties involved in that question, at once theoretical and practical, make it seem almost wanton to pursue it. Can commitment wait for the outcome of enquiries about probabilities; about the details of weapons systems and their parameters of use; about the likely impact of one nation's policy decisions on another; about the real motives of governments, and so on? Such complex and often sophisticated material is accessible to a small minority of those who care about the surrounding nuclear crisis. Even to read most of the chapters of this book, one would have to be as unrepresentative a member of the public as the typical *Guardian* reader: able to cope with fairly sophisticated prose, sustained argument, detailed and technically demanding facts and the absence of a manifesto. To be engaged by this way of presenting the issues, a reader would have to be relatively well-educated, interested both in theoretical and practical questions, and able to distance him- or herself from the polarized rhetoric of the government versus CND debate, disclaiming either alignment.

That minority of citizens in such a position is, from some political perspectives, an elite, from others a relic. If you are neither equipped by education, cultural context nor pressures of everyday living to read and appraise the sources of your political judgement, you may be envious of those who can, who have access to a kind of power which eludes the illiterate. On the other hand, there are others, both articulate and passionate about defence and deterrence, who are sure that the time for reading is past, and that in the face of the urgency of averting disaster further study of issues is evasion. To be agnostic enough still to be asking whether unilateralists or multilateralists have the stronger case: to be unsure whether these exhaust or obscure the possibilities of constructive movement: to be seeking more information about Soviet intentions or NATO's role in European security: above all to be scrutinizing the rationality of their own beliefs, and asking how much it matters that they have some transmoral basis; all this fills some peace activists with consternation, as the most evident failure to be aligned where it counts.

This issue is about where the power lies to change things, and what sort of power it is. Is the restricted constituency to whom this book might address itself simply the predicted audience of a group of people whose habitat is the British professional middle class? Certainly, with whatever twinges and critical misgivings, all the authors are professionally embedded in the institutional structures of university, Church, health service, and so on. Was it simply another impotence, the restriction of our professional idiom, from which the elect potential readership of this book emerged, or is it still true that some significant power to affect our social and political life lies in the hands and voices of this group?

Helen Zealley's chapter on 'Professional Voices' most directly articulates the sense that, as our society works, it is worth doggedly trying to modify the understanding and concern of those with professional status, where the values of European humane liberal tradition still have some stronghold, however currently beleaguered. Teachers, doctors, lawyers, economists, journalists, priests and scientists have important opportunities to extend the communication of informed judgements outwards to pupil, patient, client and reader. They may also represent informed and humane concern 'upwards' in the hierarchy of relative political power. If one can catch the ear of representative professionals of goodwill, they may in time have access to the ear of local authorities, national politicians, programme-planners, bishops or international agencies. If the people with such access begin to discuss more flexibly and intelligently, resisting dogma and rhetoric, perhaps with luck, will, grace and time, the ripples of such discussion may lap on the shores of statesmen, ministers, military planners and others whose pressures and commitments nudge them away from open-ended and open-minded vistas.

The question asked by some outside the professional structures is whether it is now an illusory hope that change can come from such influences. It is not malice or envy which inspires the doubt, for often it comes from those who experienced the alleged power of educated professional status. Nor is it the naiveté of a romantic utopianism which flounces away from political engagement as soon as dreams refuse to materialize. There are in British society at the moment men and women who feel that, for all their apparent resources as citizens in a democracy, they are in fact powerless, at least in terms of standard democratic procedures.

This sense is voiced by Steven Mackie in his theological essay on civil disobedience (1983). He identifies the position in Christian terms, but secular variants certainly exist. He speaks for those who 'see the Government, though elected by a democratic process, as maintaining a defence policy based on the readiness to act in a way which, as Christians, they regard as wholly immoral and indeed blasphemous . . . They have discovered that normal constitutional methods and legal methods of protest . . . show no signs of changing government policy' (Mackie, 1983, p. 11). This is one critical instance of felt impotence, even among those qualified, so to speak, as capable citizens. Analogous frustrations might be documented in other spheres, among teachers who find their educational goals distorted by demands for quantifiable success; among doctors who find that the real priorities of human wellbeing are unrealizable under present conditions of working: and, conspicuously, in recent times among civil servants, where regularly voiced critical dissent could not be tolerated by 'the system'.

Even within the professional worlds, with their associations of stability and security, some questions nudge their way into consciousness. Are we all, in fact, prisoners by education, financial dependence, social expectation, of a self-perpetuating world in which the basic tendency must be conservative, lest those with relative power at present have to lose it, or share it? In the earlier context of the 1960s and early 1970s, the suggestion was almost commonplace, an outcome of the dialogue between Marxist theory and the young academic world. Helmut Gollwitzer, for instance, interpreting the student revolution, describes the strength and seductiveness of trying to operate within the legitimated structures, and its collapse as a convincing mode.

For a long time, they too tried the way of resolutions. All at once, they perceived that by doing so they played the game of a society which keeps the rules of the game because by doing so it secures itself against unwelcome changes. Then they broke these rules of the game. Then they became bad citizens and disagreeable. A new mentality spread among them, a new freedom. They set on one side the bourgeois respectability which toes the line and waits, and produces petitions. They are the children who openly say that, in spite of his new clothes, the emperor is naked. A so-called new Eastern policy, a so-called university reform, a so-called protection of democracy for the time of crisis. Their laughter tears away the mask. Suddenly, the hollowness of the serious-minded, the mediocrity of the politicians, the hypocrisy of liberals, the corruption of prominent people can no longer be overlooked. (1970, pp. 91–2)

It is interesting that Gollwitzer identifies the action of radically dissident students as the demystifying voice to which Duncan Forrester summons the theological community. One need not assume, of course, that all those who play the game of established society do so out of wilful and self-conscious desire to perpetuate their own interests. Subjectively they may be well-intentioned, sincere, concerned for the underdog, and so on. Nevertheless, they may have been pulled into a web of complicity which they are themselves now incapable of recognizing until a fresh challenge is presented. Then they face the crisis of now active connivance, or of changing ground and refusing to participate.

That 'either/or' may face people in many spheres if, as Mackie suggests, Britain shows signs of becoming a much more authoritarian society than it has been under most recent governments. Specifically it is voiced with reference to issues of defence and deterrence by the peace movement, particularly by such actions as the establishment of peace camps, and the practice of 'direct action'. It need not, of course, be felt by particular people as an either/or, between using all legitimated channels of influence and also being involved in actions which are formally illegal. But there is an issue, both political and theological, about where you have to be standing in order to see straight.

Certainly the question put to our sober investigations from the vantage point of Greenham Common is a specification of that question. As members of a study group, we have done scholarly research. We have met people of different national, social and political backgrounds. We have even drunk NATO's wine and eaten its salad in an extended effort to scrutinize the case for our current defence policies. But have we put ourselves at risk in the sort of way we would be at risk in the wilderness of deprivation inhabited by those at the bottom of the social hierarchy? Is our humane concern capable of representing the pain, outrage and alienation of those who cannot even hope that things will change for them: the perpetual poor trapped in Britain's poverty spiral, the ethnic minorities of English cities: the macrocosmic counterparts of those who die in the Third World's famines and epidemics?

As individuals, of course, many of the Greenham women are not in that position either. They are educated, articulate, politically vocal, and have at their disposal the physical and emotional resources of their own middle-class backgrounds. Nevertheless, the camp as a corporate enterprise is an 'outsider' situation, physically precarious, under constant pressure from the local authority, the police, Newbury residents and the media. It cannot take its existence for granted, but must live with the constant risk of its non-existence. That is what gives it existential kinship with those who analyse the world as marginals, outwith the mainstream life of the dominant community.

Central to the structure of life at Greenham is a critique of society's normal perception and distribution of power, and the struggle to maintain an alternative one. Many participants in the Peace Camp have documented the terror and exhilaration which come from exploring this quite different style of coexistence, of political statement. As they do so, their questions to our national, in-stitutionalized political life become more radical, as do questions about education, the media and the system of law and order.

As the debate has developed between Greenham Common and the Government, each has denounced the other as abusing power. The empirical conclusion to the saga remains to be seen. But clearly the engagement is about power. Michael Heseltine taunts the Peace Camp supporters with words like 'naive', 'politically unrealistic', and derides their vagueness about actual defence strategies: what would they actually do to defend Britain or western Europe? How would they operate a ministry committed to defend British interests against aggression, or do they believe that we have no enemies with aggressive designs on our territory or our ideological integrity as a democracy? The Greenham women are disillusioned with and distrustful of the actual workings of Parliamentary democracy. The language of this uncommunicating dialogue takes us back to the in-sistence of all the contributors to this volume that any worthwhile dialectic must engage with sociological and military power, avoiding both extremes of fatalistic pessimism and romantic utopianism.

Certainly the Greenham activists intend to be engaging with power, since they aim to identify and counter the roots of its abuse which lies in the will to dominate. On their own scale, they explore alternative ways of taking decisions. In *Greenham Common: Women at the Wire*, the editors comment:

We are starting from scratch, developing attitudes and methods that make domination and opting out unnecessary. We try to give every woman a role

– as in meetings where every woman speaks in turn around the circle – and this makes us listen to each other. We are teaching each other in an intense way. And this means that women who have been identified by the press as spokeswomen have no more impact on decision-making than the women who may have arrived the day before. (Harford and Hopkins, 1984, p. 3)

While the domination-subjection models of power seem to some of the Greenham women to be exclusively or characteristically male, others see them as an incipient risk, whether by innate 'sinfulness' or cultural contagion within the camp itself.

There was the almost inevitable impatience on the part of one or two to do things without discussion, and so they became leaders, and lots of the others had a tendency to fall in behind them. So we had, outside the base fence, a set-up like the one inside, and like the one that had set up the base. (Harford and Hopkins, 1984)

Clearly questions must be asked, even by those who love and marvel at the courage and persistence of the Greenham protest, about how this microcosm relates to the 'real world'. It cannot be a working scale model. One cannot translate decision-making by consensus after equal participation on to a political scale larger than a few dozen nor can there be a referendum on every major political issue. Greenham may be a long way from having political answers in terms of practical recommendations for the large-scale restructuring of our community, yet the spread of radical self-questioning is probably the necessary precondition of any creative new development in our democratic self-understanding. Being sure what you *don't* want to be and do may focus the energy on concretely possible alternatives.

Certainly the Greenham presence is both prophetic and evangelical in its own self-understanding. The women wish to denounce the false standards of power, mastery, superiority and security which they find placarded as political goals. They will do whatever they can to destroy those, or challenge them, except do violence to other people. But they want also to celebrate an alternative which is actually being wrestled out, where 'power' is still a relevant category, but it is the power of common and mutual trust, of real and costly community and shared, supportive energy. This too, they want to affirm, is *Realpolitik*, capable of winning actual political battles, like the reversal of Government nuclear policy on Cruise and Trident. It may take longer, be clumsier in some ways than playing the games of hierarchical power politics, but it maintains the integrity of free community which is the supposed goal of our defence policies in any case.

Of course, as antagonists are quick to point out, compared to some other places in the world, dissidents get off lightly. There are countries where the lorries and trucks would drive on into protesters, countries where they would 'disappear' and be rendered incapable of further demonstration. While not quite treated with the courtesy of Her Majesty's Opposition – 14 days in Holloway is no joke – they suffer at present discomfort and political antagonism rather than the more searching threats of long-term incarceration or even death. Nevertheless, with whatever accuracy of self-knowledge, many of them say that when the pro- and anti-nuclear defence argument is pushed to its limits, when they are asked whether they would not press the button if Soviet invasion were the clear alternative, they still say no. They would rather be the victims of attack, even nuclear attack, than inflict it on any human being, and so renounce their humanity.

There is no specifically Christian engagement at Greenham, though some of the camp members are there out of Christian conviction. The base lines of shared commitment are expressed, however, in secular terms – though with analogues to religious language – as being about the openness and vulnerability of human community as opposed to its protection by hierarchies of self-perpetuating power and threats to exclude other human beings.

As Greenham puts a question to accepted social norms of well-being and security, so it seems to address directly any group with Christian involvement in the present confrontation about peace. To ignore the movement of which that camp is a symbol and a signal is 'bad faith' in the existentialist sense, like the woman in Sartre's *Being and Nothingness* (1956a) who neither repulses nor responds to the fondling of her hand by the man sitting beside her, but sits as if it were not happening. We are theologically challenged by Greenham, I believe. Either we must say that it is a late, secular expression of the Manichean/Calvinist ambivalence about engagement with power, a protest gesture which, albeit brave and imaginative, is basically irrelevant to the real world of political decision-making, or we must say that the insights into how human society works and the choices are a vehicle of genuine prophecy, and reproclaim the Gospel's dialectic about power and powerlessness.

That dialectic is being most conspicuously explored today in the liberation theologies of the Third World, which again repeat the impossibility of being neutral. Not only does your existence work for or against the freedom and fulfilment of your neighbour, but your theory, your vision, your 'doctrine' is conditioned by your existence. The Beatitudes are addressed to those who are really poor, who cannot defend themselves, whose vulnerability and impotence are manifest in the various Golgothas of our earth. They cannot be appreciated by those who have their own power of safeguarding their existence. The creativity of God is promised to those who cannot organize their own destiny, and will surprise both them and their oppressors.

This is not the renunciation of political involvement, the common western division between physical-social and spiritual, which delights those who want to keep their socio-political standing intact; nor is it the passivity of resignation in the hope that a *deus ex machina* will swoop down and magic everything right. The passion of liberation theology is that of people whose existence depends on the transformation of the world, whose energy is dedicated to it, and yet who live at risk in that commitment, because it generates crisis for those with investments in the old order. If it simply seeks to reverse the old order, and create a new pattern of power and impotence with the actors changing roles, it is no longer liberation theology.

From the place where the British government and NATO stand, the wellbeing of most western peoples can only be safeguarded by an immensely costly defence strategy which presupposes the constant antagonism of the superpowers. What is being defended is allegedly freedom and democracy, but from where the world's poor sit it is the ability also of relatively few people to dictate and determine the quality of life of many others. That is a perspective which could only be a Via Dolorosa for the politician, because the promotion of peace would then involve the real cost of relinquishing this power. We may not make scapegoats of military and political leaders whose stances are merely enlarged and grotesque projections of our will to keep what we have.

As Bill Johnston well documents in the previous chapter, the churches in Britain have engaged in debate or discussion about nuclear issues for decades, and have at the level of Council and Assembly recognized that there is a need to be alert and alarmed about developments in the political and strategic life of the nation. These are doubtless meant sincerely, as are the donations to the world's poor and hungry, but the cry of the poor is not for some of our surplus wealth, it is for a reappraisal of our corporate structures of existence.

At the Hearing on Nuclear Disarmament organised by the WCC, Burgess Carr of Liberia spoke for many when he said:

One major theological concern relates to the nature and functions of the state, especially the 'national security' state: The question for us is, what is the role of the state in God's plan of creation? Is it to be an instrument for mediating his justice on behalf of the helpless, the defenceless and the poor? Or is it the end in itself, endowed with a permanent status that must be defended at any and all cost – even if that means liquidating the entire population? What is the role of government? Is it primarily to defend the state, and to maintain the stability required to attract foreign capital investment? What is the function of political leaders? Are they to serve the people, or are they no more than a local elite dependent on external support for their personal survival? (Abrecht and Koshy, 1983, p. 75)

This has strong echoes of the questions about our political structures which Greenham poses; and I doubt whether it begins to be more than peripheral as an issue to the mainstream body of church life in Britain. It is true that the boat has been occasionally rocked in recent years – at the time of the Falklands War, the coal dispute and the inner-city riots – but the rocking is conspicuous because the British churches are, on the whole, sailing happily on the waters of our not-yet-disintegrated economic and political system. What MacKinnon means in the quotation which opened this chapter, about the crisis for institutional complacency presented by the Cross, is not at all the nerve centre of life in the British churches (though it may be in El Salvador or Czechoslovakia).

The demand for realistic, politically convincing, manageable solutions to the problems of national defence is as tempting to the Church as to the secular world, not least because it wishes to be esteemed as both wise and capable. It would be terrifying to face the abyss of *not* knowing what must be done beyond the commitment to dismantle our present structures of injustice, an intolerable, irresponsible risk to wait for the creativity of the new relationships which might or might not then emerge. Too many states in Africa and elsewhere testify to the repossession of exorcised houses by more demons than were driven out.

Further, even if the churches were anything like committed to risking their institutional life for the painful creativity of God, and His invitation to vulnerable human-ness, what would that have to do with the surrounding secular world? What rationale could urge such risky commitment as a trans-moral claim, binding across cultural and ideological divides?

Such questions return us to the opening section of the book, with its exploration of how the Kingdom of God may relate to secular ethics and political structures. Has the Kingdom of God the power to be actualized in our historical, communal existence? Will it always be at some eschatological distance, putting our relative managements of human affairs in crisis? Can directions of improvement be identified, institutionalized, stabilized? Can there be convergence between the vision of *shalom* in Biblical imagery and the prudent self-interest of nations?

We, of course, have not answered them, though we have warned against suspect answers which idealize or demonize human beings and their political options, and charted some of the ways of interpreting the relations between Church, world and Kingdom. My plea is that we do not fail to hear the address of those who risk the wilderness of political impotence and alienation. It may not be possible to better the lot of the Hebrew slaves while we live, even on the edges of Pharaoh's palace establishment, with our basic accreditation coming from there. What that means is not something we have much explored, but it needs exploring. It will take us beyond the reach of theory to where the test is our alignment or non-alignment with those who suffer most from present policies.

15

Postscript

Howard Davis

It has not been the primary purpose of this book to prescribe an alternative defence policy. Although the need for change is accepted by all the contributors, the priority has been to demystify present arguments. For the members of the SRT study group, nothing illustrated the need to do this more clearly than conversations with political and military spokesmen at NATO and the military headquarters at SHAPE. Having some awareness of offical policy we worked hard to find out if we were missing something in the moral, political or military arguments for current strategies. It appeared that we were not and that further discussion would be of limited value. Progress would require a language and morality less corrupted by the 'realism' which defines what is possible in terms of what is; and a willingness to reject the paradoxical 'security' which depends on ever-increasing preparedness for war. Then, as now, it is rare to find the goals of defence policy being spelled out, let alone expressed in value terms. The military and political ends which have been sought by the governments of the NATO Alliance have been stated clearly enough – in the NATO Treaty, for example – as being to promote peace and stability in international relationships. But the years which have passed since the formation of the western Alliance have seen many changes in the political system, strategy, forces and weapons which seem to threaten these stated goals. We have tried to reveal something of the hidden agenda which explains this divergence between means and ends.

Another purpose has been to probe into the underlying problems which have prevented the churches from speaking unequivocally on nuclear weapons. The Church has features of a social institution and a popular movement as well as a spiritual body so it is not surprising to find that considered debate exists alongside popular protest and the quest for a new spirituality. Looked to as interpreters of morality even within the wider, post-Christian society, the churches have been faced with a major reassessment of their theological and ethical assumptions, their role as moral guardians and educators, and their position as institutional partners in the political process. The process will continue in each of these areas. We hope that it will proceed with the understanding that theological and ethical theory has to engage with the language and imagery of politics, with economic power, with patriotism and pride, with professional commitment and personal life-style; and not go round in the ever-decreasing circles which have been the fate of many previous discussions of morality and deterrence.

The absolute priority for collective human responsibility for the future is to ensure that there will be a future and to combat those tendencies which threaten not just 'ways of life', be they liberal, capitalist or socialist, but the continuity of life itself. While human action has always had and always will have hazards, the horror of our present situation is that human existence itself has become part of the calculus of risk. Recognition of this fact, when it does not lead to despair, can be a powerful driving force behind the search for an alternative to the *status quo*. It is the first step towards transcending the ideological and political divides of our time. The conviction of all the contributors to this book is that the present, with all its fears, uncertainties and prophecies of doom, is a time of opportunity to think imaginatively about the future. Such thinking is imperative because of the high risks involved in standing still, and the even higher risks of allowing present trends to continue. It is a basis for a method of discovery which must lead back to ethical principles that can meet the challenge of coming events.

Contributors

Dr Tony Carty Lecturer, Department of Public International Law, University of Glasgow

Dr Howard Davis Director of Society, Religion and Technology Project at the Church of Scotland 1983–5; Lecturer in the Faculty of Social Sciences, University of Kent.

Professor John Eldridge Department of Sociology, University of Glasgow; Member of Glasgow University Media Group.

The Rev. Professor Duncan Forrester Department of Christian Ethics and Practical Theology, New College, University of Edinburgh.

Dr David Holloway Center for International Security and Arms Control, Stanford University, and Department of Politics, University of Edinburgh.

The Very Rev. William B. Johnston Colinton Parish Church, Edinburgh. Moderator of Church of Scotland General Assembly, 1980.

Fr Columba Ryan Member of the Dominican Order, Glasgow Blackfriars.

Elizabeth Templeton Theologian, Edinburgh.

Dr Ian Thompson Moral philosopher, Senior Educationalist in the Education and Training Division of the NHS (Scottish Health Education Group).

Dr Helen Zealley Community Medicine Specialist, Lothian Health Board, Edinburgh.

Notes

Chapter 1 Introduction: thinking the unthinkable

1 This has always been widely admitted. Strobe Talbott (1985, p. 33) quotes an article published in 1982 by President Carter's National Security Adviser, Zbigniew Brzezinski, as follows:

> I was personally never persuaded that we needed [the new weapons] for military reasons. I was persuaded reluctantly that we needed [them] to obtain European support for SALT. This was largely because Chancellor Schmidt made such a big deal out of the so-called Euro-strategic imbalance that was being generated by the Soviet deployment of the SS-20. To keep him in line we felt that some response in Europe on the intermediate level would be necessary.

2 For a stimulating discussion of the New Right and the churches see 'The New Right and Christian Values' Occasional Paper No.5 from the Centre for Theology and Public Issues, New College, The Mound, Edinburgh.
3 Cf. the activities of the Scottish Churches Peace Team, the British Council of Churches Peace Forum, etc.

Chapter 3 Moral theory and the nuclear debate

1 Such arguments abound in, for example, Prins, 1983; Alternative Defence Commission, 1983; Chivian, 1982; and many chapters of other books cited.
2 On the link of 'containment theory' with Niebuhr's distinction between morals and politics, see the excellent analysis by Barrie Paskins in Harries, 1982, p. 117.
3 On this basis, Hughes goes on to argue that we cannot speak of actions in themselves being wrong, but only types of action being so, which leaves it to be decided whether an action is of such-and-such a type; the moralist is confined to general propositions about types of action and has to leave it to others, historians and so on, to decide whether an action belongs to this or that type.

4 One of the cardinal issues in the nuclear debate is whether, even though one may regard the *use* of nuclear weapons as immoral, the *intention to use* them implied in deterrence policy must also be immoral; but in discussions of this issue it is more often than not taken for granted that the concept of intention is quite clear.

Chapter 6 The origins of the doctrine of deterrence and the legal status of nuclear weapons

1 Spaight, Principal Assistant Secretary at the Air Ministry, refers to a Foreign Office formulation dated 10 May 1940 in which they 'now publicly proclaim that they reserve to themselves the right to take any action which they consider appropriate in the event of bombing of the enemy civilian population' (Spaight, 1947, p. 266).
2 Middlebrook states that area bombing was a form of warfare to which the RAF devoted 46 per cent of its wartime effort and which may have taken the lives of 500,000 German civilians at the cost of 20,000 RAF casualties (Middlebrook, 1984, p. 338). Meyrowitz quotes an estimated figure of 410,000 (Meyrowitz, 1981, p. 3). This is not as remarkable as the discrepancy which the same writer notes for Japanese civilian casualties; that is, 900,000 by American estimates and 300,000 by Japanese estimates (p. 3).

Chapter 7 Legality and nuclear weapons: doctrines of nuclear warfighting

1 Weston points to the striving of the non-formal members of the international community as evidence of a growing conviction that use of nuclear weapons would be illegal. Votes of the majority of the members of the UN, naturally the majority most concerned, point in the same direction. Latest figures are 121 in favour, 19 against, 6 abstentions (Weston, 1983, pp. 568–73). The difficulty is that the general customary law basis of obligation in international law does not allow for voting by majority. One sense of such an approach is that the absence of an internationally organized sanctions system means that there is no come-back against the policies of the nuclear powers.

Chapter 8 Nuclear weapons in Europe: political and moral considerations

I would like to express my thanks to Philip Farley and Matthew Evangelista, as well as to my colleagues in the Edinburgh group, for their very helpful comments on an earlier draft of this paper.

1 The first position is reflected in the essays in Stein et al., 1981; the latter in Ramsey, 1968.
2 See the discussion in Thomas Risse-Kappen, 1984, pp. 186–213. I have found this a helpful discussion of the issues. Those who reject deterrence unconditionally and those who give it conditional acceptance may be united in the aim of abolishing nuclear weapons and eliminating reliance on them for national defence. But they differ in one important respect: an unconditional rejection of deterrence ought to lead to a policy of unilateral nuclear disarmament, irrespective of whether the other side reciprocates or not. A conditional acceptance of deterrence, on the other hand, implies that, under certain conditions, we may retain nuclear weapons until such time as both (or all) governments rid themselves of nuclear weapons.
3 There is a very large literature on nuclear weapons in Europe. See, for example, Freedman, 1981; Kaldor and Smith, 1982; Schwartz,1983. A word on terminology: I have used the traditional term 'tactical nuclear weapons', which refers to weapons for use on the battlefield against enemy forces. These are now often referred to as 'short-range theatre nuclear forces'.
4 The West German Catholic Bishops cast their three criteria more broadly: 'existing or planned military means must make war neither more feasible (fuehrbarer) nor more probable'; 'only such means and so many means may be deployed as are necessary for the purpose of deterrence aimed at preventing war'; 'all military means must be compatible with effective arms limitation, arms reduction and disarmament' (Die Deutschen Bischoefe, 1983, pp. 53–5). Risse-Kappen (1984) suggests that these criteria may be generalized as follows: the first is the importance of preventing war, and especially nuclear war; the second is that of interdependent security: we should not, and indeed cannot, enhance our own security by diminishing that of the other side; third, a policy of peace must seek to move away from primary reliance upon force or the threat of force for security, and seek the true basis of peace in a more just world order.
5 The West German Catholic bishops reflect this fear in their pastoral letter on peace, for they do not join their American counterparts in advocating a policy of no first use.

Chapter 9   The new Cold War

1 Arms Control and Disarmament Unit, Foreign and Commonwealth Office. Pamphlet on Defence and Disarmament Issues No.1. (London: FCO). The phrasing is almost identical to the *Statement on the Defence Estimates 1983*, Cmnd 8951, vol. I (London, HMSO).
2 For a well-informed assessment of the Soviet ABM programme see the contribution by John Pike in Thompson, 1985.

3 'If the nuclear destruction of Russia is foreordained, in some premillenial schemes, might not a fundamentalist politician or general regard his finger on the button as an instrument of God's eternal purpose?', asks William Martin (*Atlantic,* June 1982).

Chapter 11   Media, public opinion and disarmament

This chapter draws upon the experience of two international conferences which the author attended in 1983. The first was the UNESCO international symposium on the media and disarmament held in Nairobi in April 1983. The second was a UK–USSR seminar on the role of public opinion and the media in the movement towards peaceful relations between the Soviet Union and the West. The was jointly organized by Quaker Peace and Service and the USSR–GB Society and was held in Sochi (USSR) in December 1983. It also refers to research work by the Glasgow University Media Group on television coverage of defence and disarmament issues.

Chapter 12   Professional voices

1 More than a dozen such groups came into being in the early 1980s. Typically, their membership numbers several hundreds and they play a supportive but independent role in relation to the mass membership peace organizations. For further details and contact addresses see the Appendix to chapter 12.
2 Ford was given eye-witness accounts of incompetence including a report that President Reagan, unlike his predecessor Jimmy Carter, had failed to assimilate the complex information in his 75-page briefing manual. In a simulation 'war game' he was heard to say, 'What do I do now?' and 'Do I push this button?' When instructed to push the button he did so without seeking any further information.
3 On 10 December 1985, IPPNW was awarded the Nobel Peace Prize for its work in raising public awareness, in both East and West, of the issues raised by nuclear weapons. In view of the observations by John Eldridge it was interesting to observe the careful campaign to belittle this achievement, involving a Parliamentary statement in the House of Lords and hostile radio, television and newspaper reports. Subsequently only a tiny proportion of the correspondence sent to newspapers from doctors and others in the UK was published. Similar campaigns to denigrate the work of IPPNW were observed in the USA and West Germany.

Chapter 13   The Churches' role in the nuclear debate

1 MacKinnon has updated and supplemented these views in his Boutwood Lectures for 1981; see MacKinnon, 1982.

2 In a Marplan poll carried out for the British Freeze organization, 24–28 October, 1985, 72 per cent of respondents said they would support a freeze. Only 19 per cent were opposed.

Bibliography

Abrecht, P. and Koshy, N. (eds.) 1983: *Before it's Too Late: the challenge of nuclear disarmament.* Geneva: World Council of Churches.

Acton, Lord 1907: *Historical Essays and Studies,* appendix (ed. J. Figgis and R. Laurence). London: Arno.

Aldridge, R. C. 1983: *First Strike! The Pentagon's Strategy for Nuclear War.* London: Pluto Press.

Alternative Defence Commission 1983: *Defence Without The Bomb.* London: Taylor & Francis.

Anderson, D. (ed.) 1984: *The Kindness that Kills.* London: SPCK.

Anscombe, G. E. 1981: *Collected Philosophical Papers, Vol. III.* Oxford: Basil Blackwell.

Arendt, H. 1968: *Totalitarianism.* New York: Harcourt Brace Jovanovich.

Aristotle 1972: *Nicomachean Ethics,* Book vi, 5. (Trans. and introduced by Sir David Ross.) London: World Classics.

Aubrey, C. (ed.) 1982: *Nukespeak: the media and the bomb.* London: Comedia.

Augustine 1945: *The City of God.* (Trans. by J. Healey.) London: Dent.

Ayer, A. J. 1955: *Language, Truth and Logic.* London: Victor Gollancz.

Bacon, F. 1950: Of Heresies, *Essays: Religious Meditations.* English Experience Series No. 17. London: Walter J. Johnson.

Baillie, J. 1944: *The Interpretation of God's Will in the Present Crisis.* Reports to the General Assembly of the Church of Scotland. Edinburgh: Church of Scotland.

Bainton, R. 1960: *Christian Attitudes to War and Peace.* Nashville, Tenn.: Abingdon Press.

Ball, D. 1981: *Can Nuclear War Be Controlled?* Adelphi Paper No. 161. London: Institute for Strategic Studies.

Ball, D. 1983: *Targeting for Strategic Deterrence.* Adelphi Paper No. 185. London: Institute for Strategic Studies.

Beauchamp, T. and Childress, J. 1979: *Principles of Biomedical Ethics.* Oxford: Oxford University Press.

Becker, J. 1983: Methodological Problems of Dealing with Disarmament in the Press. *Current Research on Press and Violence,* 1, pp. 29–51.

Bernstein, B. and Matusow, A. 1966: *The Truman Administration, A Documentary History.* New York: Harper & Row.

Best, G. 1983: *Humanity in Warfare: the modern history of the international law of armed conflicts.* London: Weidenfeld & Nicolson.

Black Report 1980: Report of a Working Group on *Inequalities in Health*. Edited for wider publication by P.Townsend and N. Davidson, 1982: Harmondsworth. Penguin.

Blix, H. 1978: Area Bombardment: Rules and Reasons. *British Year Book of International Law*, 49.

Bridger, F. (ed.) 1983: *The Cross and the Bomb*. London: Mowbray.

British Council of Churches (BCC) 1959: *Christians and Atomic War*. London: BCC.

BCC 1962: *Assembly Report* (April). London: BCC.

BCC 1963: *The British Nuclear Deterrent: report of a working group of the British Council of Churches*. London: SCM

BCC 1964: *The Valley of Decision: the Christian dilemma in the nuclear age*. London: BCC.

BCC 1979: *Assembly Report*. London: BCC.

British Medical Association 1983: *The Medical Effects of Nuclear War*. Report of the Board of Science and Education. Chichester: Wiley.

Brownlie, I. (ed.) 1983: *System of the Law of Nations. State Responsibility Part I*. Oxford: Oxford University Press.

Butler, S. F. J. 1982: Scientific Advice in Home Defence. In *The Nuclear Arms Race; Control or Catastrophe*. London: Frances Pinter.

Calder, A. 1971: *The People's War, Britain 1939–45*. London: Panther.

Caldicott, H. 1978: *Nuclear Madness*. Brookline, Mass.: Autumn Press.

Calvocoressi, P. 1984: Nuclear Weapons in the Service of Man (1983 Martin Wight Memorial Lecture). *Review of International Studies*, 10, pp. 89–101.

Campbell, A. 1972: *Moral Dilemmas in Medicine*. Edinburgh: Churchill Livingstone.

Campbell, D. 1982: *War Plan UK: The Truth About Civil Defence in Britain*. London: Burnett.

Camus, A. 1954: *The Rebel*. New York: Random House.

Carlton, D. and Shaerf, C. (eds) 1975: *The Dynamics of the Arms Race*. London: Croom Helm.

Chivian, E. (ed.) 1982: *Last Aid*. Freeman.

Chomsky, N., Steele, J., and Gittings, J. 1984: *Superpowers in Collision: The New Cold War of the 1980s*. Harmondsworth: Penguin.

Church of England Working Party of the Board for Social Responsibility 1982: *The Church and the Bomb*. London: Hodder & Stoughton.

Church of Scotland: *Reports to the General Assembly*. 1944; 1949; 1950; 1962; 1963; 1964; 1967; 1972; 1980; 1981; 1982; 1983; 1985. Edinburgh: Church of Scotland.

Clifford, C. M. 1984: NATO: A Landmark of the Truman Presidency. *NATO Review*, 32 (2), pp. 25–30.

Conan-Doyle, Sir A. 1974: The Valley of Fear, Study in Scarlet. In *Complete Adventures and Memoirs of Sherlock Holmes*. London: J. Murray & Cape.

Cowen, D. 1961: *The Foundations of Freedom*. Oxford: Oxford University Press.

Craven, W. F. and Cate, J. L. 1953: *The Army Air Forces in World War II*. Kingsport, Tenn.: University of Chicago Press.

Die Deutschen Bischoefe 1983: *Gerechtigkeit Schafft Frieden.* Bonn: Sekretariat der Deutschen Bischofskonferenz, April.

Diem, H. 1959: *Kierkegaard's Dialectic of Existence.* London: Oliver & Boyd.

Dimbleby, J. 1982: The media and defence in past and future. In M. Clarke and M. Mowlam (eds), *Debate on Disarmament.* London: Routledge & Kegan Paul.

Downie, R. S. 1971: *Roles and Values.* London: Methuen.

Duncan, A. S., Dunstan, G. R. and Welbourn, R. B. (eds) 1981: *Dictionary of Medical Ethics.* London: Darton, Longman & Todd.

Durkheim, E. 1957: *Professional Ethics and Civic Morals.* London: Routledge & Kegan Paul.

Dyer, J. 1985: Co-operation Not Confrontation: The Imperative of a Nuclear Age. *British Medical Journal,* 291, pp. 191–3.

Emmet, D. 1966: *Rules, Roles and Relations.* London: Macmillan.

European Security Report 1983: *Strengthening Conventional Deterrence in Europe.* London: Macmillan.

Faculty of Community Medicine 1984: *Health Care Planning in Relation to Nuclear War.* London: Faculty of Community Medicine.

Falk, R. 1965: The Shimoda Case: A Legal Appraisal of the Atomic Attacks upon Hiroshima and Nagasaki. *American Journal of International Law,* 159, pp. 759–93.

Fallows, J. 1981: *National Defense.* New York: Random House.

Fanon, F. 1970: *The Wretched of the Earth.* (Trans. C. Farrington.) Harmondsworth: Penguin.

Feis, H. 1961: *Japan Subdued, the Atomic Bomb and the End of the War in the Pacific.* Princeton, New Jersey: Princeton University Press.

Fiddick, P. 1984: In the *Guardian,* 28 May.

Ford, D. 1985: A Reporter at Large (US Command and Control). *New Yorker,* 1 and 8 April.

Ford, J. C. 1970: The Morality of Obliteration Bombing. In R. A. Wasserstrom, (ed.), *War and Morality.* Belmont, California: Wadsworth.

Freedman, L. 1981: *Britain and Nuclear Weapons.* London: Macmillan.

Fulbright, W. 1970: *The Arrogance of Power.* Harmondsworth: Penguin.

Fuller, J. F. G. 1972: *The Conduct of War 1798–1961.* London: Methuen.

Galbraith, J. K. 1984: The Military Power. In G. Prins (ed.), *The Choice, Nuclear Weapons Versus Security.* London: Chatto & Windus.

Gallie, W. B. 1984: The Military and Political Background of the Nuclear Age. In G. Prins (ed.), *The Choice, Nuclear Weapons Versus Security.* London: Chatto & Windus.

Galtung, J. 1984: *There Are Alternatives! Four Roads to Peace and Security.* Nottingham: Spokesman.

Garrison, J. 1980: *From Hiroshima To Harrisburg.* London: SCM Press.

Garrison, J. 1982: *The Darkness of God: Theology After Hiroshima.* London: SCM Press.

Generals for Peace and Disarmament 1983: *Ten Questions Answered.* Published in association with Just Defence, 21, Union Street, Woodstock, Oxford, OX7 1JF.

Genet, J. 1966: *The Balcony.* (Trans. B. Frechtmann.) London: Faber.

Genet, J. 1973: *The Thief's Journal.* (Trans. B. Frechtmann). London: Faber.

Gerth, H. H. and Wright Mills, C. 1948: *Max Weber: Essays in Sociology*. London: Routledge & Kegan Paul.

Gill, R. 1984: *The Cross Against the Bomb*. London: Epworth.

Gillon, R. 1985a: Medical Oaths, Declarations and Codes. *British Medical Journal*, 290, pp. 1194–5.

Gillon, R. 1985b: Philosophical Medical Ethics. *British Medical Journal*, 290 and 291. Weekly series from 13 April to 27 July.

Gladwin, J. (ed.) 1985: *Dropping the Bomb: The Church and the Bomb debate*. London: Hodder & Stoughton.

Glasgow University Media Group 1985: *War and Peace News*. Milton Keynes: Open University Press.

Gollwitzer, H. 1970: *The Rich Christians and Poor Lazarus*. Edinburgh: Saint Andrew Press.

Goodwin, G. (ed.) 1982: *Ethics and Nuclear Deterrence*. London: Croom Helm.

Gould, L. N. 1969: *The ENDC and the Press*, Stockholm Papers No. 3. Stockholm: Stockholm International Peace Research Institute.

Gowing, M. 1964: *Independence and Deterrence, Britain and Atomic Energy 1945–1952*. (2 vols) London: Macmillan.

Greenwood, T. 1975: *Making the MIRV: A study of defense decision-making*. Cambridge, Mass.: Ballinger.

Gruchy, J. de and Villa-Vicencio, C. (eds) 1983: *Apartheid is a Heresy*. Guildford: Lutterworth.

Habgood, J. 1983: *Church and Nation in a Secular Age*. London: Darton, Longman & Todd.

Halliday, F. 1983: *The Making of the Second Cold War*. London: Verso.

Harford, B. and Hopkins, S. (eds) 1984: *Greenham Common: Women at the Wire*. London: Women's Press.

Harries, R. (ed.) 1982: *What Hope in an Armed World?* Basingstoke: Pickering & Inglis.

Harris, R. 1983: *Gotcha! The Media, the Government and the Falklands Crisis*. London: Faber.

Hartigan, R. S. 1982: *The Forgotten Victim, A History of the Civilian*. Chicago: Precedent.

Holloway, D. 1983: *The Soviet Union and the Arms Race*. New Haven, Conn.: Yale University Press.

Holm, H.-H. and Petersen, N. (eds.) 1983: *The European Missile Crisis*. London: Frances Pinter.

Home Office and Central Office of Information 1980: *Protect and Survive*. London: HMSO.

Home Office 1983: Letter to all Regional Scientific Advisers: *BMA's Report of their Inquiry into the Medical Effects of Nuclear War*, 8 April.

Howard, M. 1981: *War and the Liberal Conscience*. Oxford: Oxford University Press.

Howard, M. 1983: *The Causes of Wars*. London: Counterpoint.

Howe, Sir G. 1985: Defence and Security in the Nuclear Age. *Arms Control and Disarmament Newsletter*, Jan.–March, pp. 4–21.

Humphrey, N. 1981: *Four Minutes to Midnight*. London: Menard Press.

International Committee of the Red Cross 1984: Info/Dif Nr. 1/7 20 June.

John Paul II 1982: *Message of His Holiness Pope John Paul II to the United Nations General Assembly Second Special Session on Disarmament, 11 June 1982.* London: Catholic Truth Society.

Johnson, P. 1983: Christians, Awake! *The Times,* 29 January.

Jungk, R. 1960: *Brighter than 1000 Suns.* Harmondsworth: Penguin.

Kaiser, K. et al. 1982: Nuclear Weapons and the Preservation of Peace. *Foreign Affairs,* Summer, pp. 1157–70.

Kaldor, M. 1982: *The Baroque Arsenal.* London: Deutsch.

Kaldor, M. and Smith, D. (eds) 1982: *Disarming Europe.* London: Merlin Press.

Kant, I. 1949a: *Critique of Practical Reason and Other Writings on Moral Philosophy.* (Trans. and ed. by Lewis White Beck.) Includes 'On Perpetual Peace' and 'What is Enlightenment?'. Chicago: University of Chicago Press.

Kant, I. 1949b: Groundwork to the Metaphysic of Morals. In *Critique of Practical Reason and Other Writings in Moral Philosophy.* (Trans. and ed. by Lewis White Beck.) Chicago: University of Chicago Press.

Keeney, S. and Panofsky, W. 1981/2: Mad Versus Nuts. *Foreign Affairs,* Winter. pp. 287–304.

Kennan, G. F. 1958: *Russia, the Atom and the West.* London: OUP.

Kenny, A. 1985: *The Logic of Deterrence.* Firethorn Press.

Kierkegaard, S. 1941a: *Concluding Unscientific Postscript.* (Trans. by David Swenson and Walter Lowrie.) Princeton, New Jersey: Princeton University Press.

Kissinger, H. A. 1979: NATO: The Next Thirty Years. *Survival,* November/December.

Knightley, P. 1982: *The First Casualty. The War Correspondent as Hero, Propagandist and Myth Maker.* London: Quartet.

Krakau, K. 1967: *Missionsbewusstsein und Voelkerrechtsdoktrin in den Vereinigten Staaten von Amerika.* Frankfurt am Main: Alfred Metzner.

Lauterpacht, H. 1952: The Problem of the Revision of the Laws of War. *British Year Book of International Law,* 29. pp. 360–82.

Les Grandes Textes 1983: *Documentation Catholique,* No. 46. Paris.

Lippmann, W. (Cited in N. Angell) 1922: *The Press and the Organisation of Society.* London: Labour Publishing.

McCormick, J. 1983: Living Together. *The Lancet,* 30 August. p. 448.

McDonald, J. I. H. 1986: Towards a Theology of Peace. In D. Forrester (ed.), *Theology and Practice.* Ormskirk and Northridge: Hesketh.

McDoughal, M. and Feliciano, F. 1961: *Law and Minimum World Public Order.* New Haven, Conn.: Yale University Press.

McGeorge Bundy, F. 1979: The Future of Strategic Deterrence. *Survival,* November/December.

McGeorge Bundy, F. 1983: *New York Review of Books,* 16 June. pp. 3–8.

McGeorge Bundy, F., Kennan, G. F., McNamara R.S., and Smith, G. 1982: Nuclear Weapons and the Atlantic Alliance. *Foreign Affairs,* Spring, pp. 753–68.

MacIntyre, A. 1981: *After Virtue.* London: Duckworth.

Mackenzie, D. 1984: Nuclear War Planning and Strategies of Nuclear Coercion. *New Left Review*, Nov.–Dec., pp. 31–56.

Mackie, J. L. 1977: *Ethics – Inventing Right and Wrong*. Harmondsworth: Penguin.

Mackie, S. 1983: *Civil Disobedience as Christian Obedience*. London: BCC/International Fellowship of Reconciliation.

MacKinnon, D. M. 1940: *God, the Living and the True*. London: Dacre Press.

MacKinnon, D. M. (ed.) 1963: *God, Sex and War*. London: Fontana.

MacKinnon, D. M. 1982: *Creon and Antigone: Ethical Problems of Nuclear Warfare*. (Boutwood Lectures for 1981.) London: Menard Press.

McNamara, R. 1983: The Military Role of Nuclear Weapons. *Foreign Affairs*, 62.

Maritain, J. 1964: *Moral Philosophy*. London: Geoffrey Bles.

Maritain, J. 1972: *Three Reformers: Luther, Descartes, and Rousseau*. New York/London: P. Kennikat.

Maritain, J. 1974: *Integral Humanism*. Notre Dame, Ill.: University of Notre Dame Press.

Martin, L. 1981: Reith Lecture. In *The Listener*, 19 November.

Martin, D. and Mullen, P. (eds) 1983: *Unholy Warfare*. Oxford: Basil Blackwell.

Mata, L. 1984: Reported in R. Smith, IPPNW Conference Report, Nuclear War: Preventable or Inevitable?. *British Medical Journal*, 288. pp. 1901–4.

Medvedev, R. and Medvedev, Z. 1982: The USSR and the Arms Race. In E. P. Thompson (ed.), *Exterminism and Cold War*. London: New Left Books/Verso.

Meszaros, I. 1970: *Marx's Theory of Alienation*. London: Merlin Press.

Meyer, S. M. 1984a: *Soviet Theatre Nuclear Forces, Part I, Development of Doctrines and Objectives*. Adelphi Paper No. 187. London: Institute for Strategic Studies.

Meyer, S. M. 1984b: *Soviet Theatre Nuclear Forces, Part II, Capabilities and Implications*. Adelphi Paper No. 187. London: Institute for Strategic Studies.

Meyrowitz, H. 1979: La Stratégie Nucléaire et le Protocole Additional aux Conventions de Génève de 1949. *Revenue Generale de Droit International Publique*, 83. pp. 905–61.

Meyrowitz, H. 1981: Le bombardment stratégique d'après le Protocol additional aux Conventions de Génève. *Zeitschrift für ausländisches oeffentliches Recht and Völkerrecht*, 41. pp. 1–67.

Meyrowitz, H. 1983: Le statut des armes nucléaires en droit international – 2e partie. *German Yearbook of International Law*, 26.

Middlebrook, M. 1984: *The Battle of Hamburg*. Harmondsworth: Penguin.

Ministry of Defence 1980: *The Future United Kingdom Strategic Nuclear Deterrent Force*. London: Ministry of Defence, Open Government Document 80/23. July.

Morgan P. M. 1983: *Deterrence: a conceptual analysis*. London: Sage.

Murnion, P. J. (ed.) 1983: *Catholics and Nuclear War: A Commentary on the Challenge of Peace*. London: Geoffrey Chapman.

Myrdal, A. 1980: *The Game of Disarmament. How the United States and Russia Run the Arms Race.* Nottingham: Spokesman.

Nathan, O. and Norden, H. (eds.) 1960: *Einstein on Peace.* New York: Schocken Books.

Naval War College 1966: *Studies in the Law of Naval Warfare.* Newport, Rhode Island: International Law Studies.

Niebuhr, R. 1940: *Why the Christian Chruch is not Pacifist.* London: SCM Press.

Niebuhr, R. 1960: *Moral Man and Immoral Society* (first published 1932). New York: Scribner's.

Nietzsche, F. 1909: *The Will to Power.* (Two vols, Trans. by Ludovici.) Edinburgh/London: T. Forbis.

Nietzsche, F. 1955: *Beyond Good and Evil.* Chicago: Gateway Edition, Henry Regnery.

Nietzsche, F. 1967: *The Birth of Tragedy and Contra Wagner.* (Trans. by Walter Kaufmann.) New York/London: Random House.

Nincic, M. 1982: *The Arms Race: the Political Economy of Military Growth.* New York: Praeger.

Nisbet, R. 1976: *Twilight of Authority.* London: Heinemann.

Norman. E. R. 1979: *Christianity and the World Order.* Oxford: Oxford University Press.

NATO 1983: *NATO Handbook.* North Atlantic Treaty: Preamble. Brussels: NATO Information Services.

O'Brien, W. 1982: *The Conduct of Just and Limited War.* New York: Praeger.

Okin S. M. 1984: Taking the Bishops Seriously. *World Politics,* July, pp. 529–30.

Oldham, J. H. 1946: *The Era of Atomic Power:* Report of a Commission Appointed by the British Council of Churchs. London: SCM Press.

Openshaw, S. and Steadman, P. 1982: *On the Geography of the Bomb.* Presentation to Conference of the Institute of British Geographers, Edinburgh, January.

Palme, O. (ed.) 1982: *Common Security: A Programme for Disarmament.* London: Pan.

Pascal, B. 1966: *Pensées.* (Trans. A. J. Kraisheimer.) Harmondsworth: Penguin.

Paskins, B. and Dockrill, M. 1979: *Ethics of War.* London: Duckworth.

Paul VI 1968: *Encyclical Letter: Humanae Vitae.* London: Catholic Truth Society DO 411.

Pavlic, B. 1983: *UNESCO Mass Media Declaration and Disarmament.* Paper presented to UNESCO international symposium on the media and disarmament, Nairobi, April.

Payne, K. and Grey, C. 1984: The Defensive Transition. *Foreign Affairs,* 62, Spring. pp. 820–42.

Pieper, J. 1952: *Leisure, the Basis of Culture.* (Introduced by T. S. Eliot.) London: Faber.

Plato 1960: *The Gorgias* (Trans. and Introduced by W. Hamilton). Harmondsworth Penguin.

Ponting, C. 1985: *The Right to Know.* London: Sphere.

Popper, K. 1957: *The Open Society and Its Enemies.* (two vols). London: Routledge & Kegan Paul.

Popper, K. 1977: *The Poverty of Historicism.* New York: Harcourt Brace Jovanovich.

Powers, T. 1982: Choosing a Strategy for World War III. *The Atlantic Monthly,* November, pp. 82–110.

Prins, G. (ed.) 1983: *Defended to Death: A Study of the Nuclear Arms Race.* Harmondsworth: Penguin.

Prins, G. (ed.) 1984: *The Choice: Nuclear Weapons Versus Security.* Chatto & Windus.

Pursell, C. W. Jr (ed.) 1972: *The Military-Industrial Complex.* New York: Harper & Row.

Pym, F. 1980: Commons Speech on 24 January 1980. In *Parliamentary Debates* (Hansard), 24 January 1980, col. 674.

Quinlan, M. 1985: Can the possession of Nuclear Weapons be Morally Justifiable? *The Modern Churchman,* New Series, 27(2). pp. 22–7.

Ramsey, A. M. 1960: *From Gore to Temple.* London: Longman.

Ramsey, P. 1969: *Who Speaks for the Church?* Edinburgh: St. Andrew Press.

Ramsey, P. 1968: *The Just War: Force and Political Responsibility.* New York: Scribner's.

Rauch, E. 1980: L'Emploi d'Armes Nucléaires et La Réaffirmation et Le Développement du Droit International Humanitaire Applicable dans Les Conflits Armés. *Revue Hellenique de Droit International,* pp. 53–95.

Richter, H.-E. 1983: The Threat of Nuclear War and the Responsibility of the Doctor. *The Human Cost of Nuclear War.* MCANW and MAPW.

Risse-Kappen, T. 1984: The Double Face of Deterrence. Politico-Scientific Observations on the Ecclesiastical Controversies surrounding Nuclear Deterrence and the Conduct of War. In F. Boeckle, and G. Krell (eds), *Politik und Ethik der Abschreckung. Theologische und sozial-wissenschaftliche Beitraege zur Herausforderung der Nuklearwaffen.* Matthias-Grünewald Verlag, Mainz and Chr. Kaiser Verlag Munich.

Ritschl, A. 1900: *The Christian doctrine of Justification and Reconciliation.* (Trans. by H. R. Macintosh and A. B. Macaulay.) Edinburgh: T. & T. Clarke.

Rogers, B. W. 1984: Follow-on Forces Attack (FOFA): Myths and Reality. *NATO Review* 32, (6), December, pp. 1–9.

Roman Catholic Pastoral Congress Resolution 1980.

Rosen, S. (ed.) 1973: *Testing the Theory of the Military-Industrial Complex.* Lexington Mass.: Lexington Books.

Roth, G. 1984: Max Weber's Ethics and the Peace Movement Today. *Theory and Society,* 13, pp. 491–511.

Royal College of Nursing 1984: *Nuclear War: Civil Defence Planning: The Implications for Nurses.* Report of a Working Party. London: Royal College of Nursing.

Ruston, R. 1981: *Nuclear Deterrence – Right or Wrong?* London: Catholic Information Services, 7 Gallows Hill Lane, Abbots Langley, Herts.

Sankar, C. 1983: Loud on War, Soft on Peace. Mimeo for UNESCO Conference on the Media and Disarmament Nairobi 1983.

Sartre, J.-P. 1946: *Two Plays.* London: H. Hamilton.

Sartre, J.-P. 1956: *Being and Nothingness.* (Trans. Hazel Barnes.) London: Methuen.

Schell, J. 1982: *The Fate of the Earth*. London: Picador.

Schwartz. D. 1983: *NATO's Nuclear Dilemmas*. Washington, DC: Brookings.

Schwarzenberger, G. 1968: *International Law, The Law of Armed Conflict*. London: Sweet & Maxwell.

Smith, J. and Smith, R. 1981: Medicine and the Bomb. *British Medical Journal*, 283. pp. 771–4; 844–6; 907–8; 963–5.

Solms. F. and Reuver, M. 1985: *Churches as Peacemakers?* Rome: IDOC International.

Spaight, J. M. 1947: *The Law of Air Warfare* (3rd edn). London: Longmans & Green.

Steadman, P. 1981: The Bomb: Worse than Governments Admit. *New Scientist*, 90. pp. 769–71.

Stein, W. (ed.). 1981: *Nuclear Weapons and Christian Conscience*. London: Merlin Press.

Stimson, H. and McGeorge Bundy, F. 1948: *On Active Service in Peace and War*. New York: Harper Brothers.

Stockholm International Peace Research Institute (SIPRI) 1983: *World Armaments and Disarmament*. SIPRI Yearbook. London: Taylor & Francis.

SIPRI 1984: Shorter Yearbook. *The Arms Race and Arms Control*. London: Taylor & Francis.

Talmon, J. L. 1952: *The Origins of Totalitarian Democracy*. Introduction and Part I, iii. London: Mercury.

Tammen, R. 1973: *MIRV and the Arms Race: An Interpretation of Defense Strategy*. New York: Praeger.

Taylor, R. and Pritchard, C. 1980: *The Protest Makers: The British Disarmament of 1958–65 Twenty Years On*. Oxford: Pergamon.

Temple, W. 1942: *Christianity and Social Order*. Harmondsworth: Penguin.

Thompson, E. P. (ed.) 1982: *Exterminism and Cold War*. London: New Left Books/Verso.

Thompson, E. P. (ed.) 1985: *Star Wars*. Harmondsworth: Penguin.

Thompson, H. 1985: 'There Will Always Be Another Moonrise', Computer Technology and Nuclear Weapons. *Computing and Social Responsibility Newsletter*, March, pp. 1–7.

Tillich, P. 1951: *Systematic Theology* (three vols). London: Nisbet.

Tillich, P. 1954: *Love, Power and Justice*. New York and Oxford: Oxford University Press.

Tillich, P. 1963: *Morality and Beyond*. London: Routledge & Kegan Paul.

Tillich, P. 1968: *History of Christian Thought* (ed. Carl Braaten). London: SCM Press.

UN 1978: Final document of the Special Session of the United Nations General Assembly Devoted to Disarmament.

UNESCO 1980: *Many Voices, One World*. Report of the International Commission for the Study of Communication Problems (The MacBride Report.) London: Kogan Page.

US Catholic Bishops 1983: The Challenge of Peace: God's Promise and Our Response. A Pastoral Letter on War and Peace. *Origins*, 13(1), 19 May. Also published in 1983 in book form by CTS/SPCK.

US Department of Health, Education and Welfare 1978: *The Belmont Report: Ethical Principles and Guidelines for the Protection of Human Subjects of Research*. Washington, DC: US Department of Health, Education and Welfare.

US Office of Technology Assessment, Congress of the United States 1980: *The Effects of Nuclear War*. London: Croom Helm.

United States Strategic Bombing Survey (USSBS) 1945: *Overall Report, European War*. Washington, DC: Government Printing Office (GPO).

USSBS 1946a: *Japan's Struggle to End the War*. Washington, DC: GPO.

USSBS 1946b: *The Effects of Strategic Bombing on Japan's War Economy*. Washington, DC: GPO.

USSBS 1947: *The Effects of Strategic Bombing on German Morale*, Vol. I. Washington, DC: GPO.

Vaerno, G. 1983: A Public Opinion Strategy. *NATO Review*, 3 and 4. pp. 26–31.

Vaihinger, H. 1961: *The Philosophy of 'As If'*. London: Routledge & Kegan Paul.

Veatch, R. 1981: *A Theory of Medical Ethics*, Part III. New York: Basic Books.

Versfeld, M. 1972: *Persons*. Cape Town: Buren Uitgewers.

Walzer, M. 1974: World War II, Why was this war any different? In M. Cohen, T. Nagel and T. Scanlon (eds), *War and Moral Responsibility*. Princeton, New Jersey: Princeton University Press.

Warnock Inquiry 1985: *Inquiry Into Human Fertilisation And Embryology*. London: HMSO.

Watt, D. W. 1979: Restraints on War in the Air Before 1945. In M. Howard (ed.), *Restraints on War*. Oxford: Oxford University Press.

Weber, M. 1948: Politics as a Vocation. In H. H. Gerth and C. Wright Mills (eds), *From Max Weber*, London: Routledge & Kegan Paul.

Webster, C. and Frankland, N. 1961: *The Strategic Air Offensive Against Germany 1939–45*, Vols I–IV. London: HMSO.

Weston, B. 1983: Nuclear Weapons versus International Law. *McGill Law Journal*, 28. pp. 542–90.

Wieck, H.-G., 1984: The Soviet Union and the Future of East-West Relations. *NATO Review*, 32(2) April. pp. 19–24.

Wilson, A. 1983: *The Disarmer's Handbook of Military Technology and Organisation*. Harmondsworth: Penguin.

Wittgenstein, L. 1958: *Philosophical Investigations*. Oxford: Basil Blackwell.

World Council of Churches (WCC) 1968: *The Uppsala 68 Report: Official Report of the Fifth Assembly of the WCC, Uppsala 1968*, ed. Norman Goodall. Geneva: WCC.

WCC 1983: *Gathered for Life: Official Report of the Sixth Assembly of the WCC, Vancouver 1983*, ed. David Gill. Geneva: WCC and Eerdmans: Grand Rapids.

World Health Organisation (WHO) 1978: *Primary Health Care*. Report of the International Conference, Alma Ata, USSR. Geneva: WHO.

WHO European Regional Assembly 1984: *Regional Targets in Support of the Regional Strategy for Health for All*. Copenhagen: WHO, European Office.

WHO Expert Committee 1984: *Effects of Nuclear War on Health and Health services*. Geneva: WHO.

Wortley, B. A. 1983: Observations on the Revision of the 1949 Geneva Convention. *British Year Book of International Law*, 54. pp. 143–66.

Wright Mills, C. 1956: *White Collar*. Oxford: Oxford University Press.

Wright Mills, C. 1959: *The Power Elite*. New York: Oxford University Press.

Wright Mills, C. 1960: *The Causes of World War III* (2nd edn). Oxford: Oxford University Press.

Zuckerman, S. 1985: Deterrent Strategies. In J. Sterba, *The Ethics of War and Nuclear Deterrence*. Belmont, California: Wadsworth.

Index